Dr Naomi Fisher is a clinical psychologist who specialises in autism, trauma and alternative approaches to education. She is the mother of two teenagers and the author of several books on psychology, education and mental health. She has over eighteen years of clinical experience, both inside and out of the NHS, and supervises and trains other therapists. Naomi is a regular keynote speaker at conferences for professionals and parents. She runs highly successful webinars for parents, advising them on how to help with their children's mental health. Together, Naomi and Eliza created *The Art of Low-Demand Parenting* webinar series, which has to date reached thousands of parents. She can be found at www.naomifisher.co.uk

Eliza Fricker is an author and illustrator who has written and illustrated two books of her own (*The Family Experience of PDA* and *The Sunday Times* bestseller *Can't Not Won't*) as well has having illustrated several others. She runs a successful illustrated blog about her experiences with her daughter's school attendance struggles (missingthemark.co.uk) and created the Missing the Mark podcast, an exploration of what happens when a child isn't happy at school. She has spoken at the Rethinking Education conference and gives talks to local authorities on what it's like for families when a child can't attend school.

When the Naughty Step Makes Things Worse

Dr Naomi Fisher & Eliza Fricker

ROBINSON

ROBINSON

First published in Great Britain in 2024 by Robinson

3 5 7 9 10 8 6 4 2

Copyright © Naomi Fisher and Eliza Fricker, 2024

The moral right of the authors has been asserted.

Important Note
This book is not intended as a substitute for medical advice or treatment.
Any person with a condition requiring medical attention should consult a qualified medical practitioner or suitable therapist.

A CIP catalogue record for this book is available from the British Library

ISBN: 978-1-47214-868-1

Typeset in Times by Initial Typesetting Services, Edinburgh
Printed and bound in Great Britain by Clays Ltd, Elcograf S.p.A.

Papers used by Robinson are from well-managed forests and other responsible sources

MIX
Paper | Supporting
responsible forestry
FSC
www.fsc.org
FSC® C104740

Robinson
An imprint of
Little, Brown Book Group
Carmelite House
50 Victoria Embankment
London EC4Y 0DZ

An Hachette UK Company
www.hachette.co.uk

www.littlebrown.co.uk

To the parents who know that it isn't working,
and the children who show us another way.

Contents

Introduction

NAOMI: Hello, and welcome to this book. I'm Naomi Fisher and I'm a clinical psychologist. I specialise in trauma, autism and alternative education.

ELIZA: And I'm Eliza Fricker, also known as Missing the Mark. I'm an illustrator and author of several books.

NAOMI: And this is our book about parenting, for families who need something different. This book is the culmination of a couple of years of developing the ideas and running webinars together – but we started working together before that. In fact, I can't remember how we met – you got in touch with me Eliza, but I don't know how you found me.

ELIZA: This is what I love about these communities we create. The first time I heard about your book was actually a consultation I was doing with a family, and they mentioned your book *Changing Our Minds*, and I hadn't even heard of it.

NAOMI: Then you got my book, and discovered that I lived twenty minutes down the road?

ELIZA: Yes!

NAOMI: This was during the pandemic. We met up sitting outside, several metres apart from each other, shivering outside a cold café. Then we started talking and we realised that we had come to similar places in our parenting but in different ways.

ELIZA: I think that's the thing when you go down this alternative approach to parenting. There are different ways that people go, but then, at the same time, there are lots of elements that are very similar.

NAOMI: It's really validating to find that other people have found similar ways to make it work and that it's not just you.

We were both working with parents as well. I remember when I was working with parents, they would be saying, 'What is this approach called? Is there a book I could read?' I would think to myself, I'm not quite sure.

When you and I talked about it, it felt like we needed to pull these ideas together and write them down.

ELIZA: There was nothing out there for people to access as a parent that chimed in any way with my experience.

We started out by pulling out some of the key triggering things, things like behaviour, screen time, sleep, food. Things we got asked about all the time.

NAOMI: We wanted to produce something that explained what life is actually like in lots of families. How it actually looks; an honest insight into parenting.

People were asking me all the time, 'Is it okay for our family to look really different to other people? Is it okay if they don't do this, or only eat that?'

I felt that I was in this privileged position. I worked with lots of families and I heard stories of how things really were. I had an insight into many families beyond my own. I realised most people didn't have that. It all happened behind closed doors.

ELIZA: In this book and in our work, we tell it like it really is. People do comment sometimes; once someone said that it was a bit depressing. But we said, 'No, we sometimes go low, but we come back up.'

NAOMI: It's true that we often start by going down when we talk about something. We don't gloss over things.

ELIZA: That's something I always felt was a problem with the parent-oriented things I was sent. They really glossed over reality. We don't do that.

NAOMI: Lots of parenting courses and books never talk about how hard it can be. Then you're left thinking, Is it really like that for these people? Because it's not like that for us.

ELIZA: I think it's not often that we feel safe enough to say it's really hard.

NAOMI: In this book, we wanted to tell the truth about how hard things can be – but also be hopeful that things can get better and that parents can make a difference. It can be really difficult to hold onto hope, particularly if you don't know anybody else going through the same experience and you're worried that your family life will be very difficult forever.

ELIZA: It can be very difficult to share stuff because a lot of people *aren't* going through the same things you are.

NAOMI: In a way, you're always just testing a little bit to see whether someone can take it or whether they're going to go, 'Oh, what are you on about?'

ELIZA: Yes, and usually it is met with a generic and unhelpful suggestion. What was the one I always remember? It was always about food, about blending in the vegetables in a sauce to hide them.

NAOMI: Oh, hidden vegetables.

ELIZA: I thought, There's no way my child will not sift through and find it.

NAOMI: Of course. Any self-respecting child is going to pick out the vegetables. I used to line them around my plate. Or they're just going to say, 'No sauces. If you're going to hide vegetables in sauce, then I won't have the sauce.'

ELIZA: 'I'm going back to cheese and pasta.'

NAOMI: Exactly. 'Plain pasta, please.' No way that you can hide anything then. Although I do remember buying some pasta that actually had the vegetable hidden in the pasta.

ELIZA: No way.

NAOMI: Of course it didn't work. They just said, 'This is weird; we're not eating it.' I was thinking, Of course it's weird, it's got spinach in it.

So we've established that this book is not about how to hide the vegetables.

ELIZA: It's for families for whom mainstream parenting makes things worse and whose children react very badly to things that everyone tells you to do. The point is to create a more harmonious family life for all families.

In this approach, I think there's a lot less of 'They should be doing this' or 'They should be able to do that.' Instead, families become more able to just meet the child where they're at. Wherever that is.

That brings back their connection with their child and that is so important.

What many of us discover when we're following mainstream parenting and going against what our child actually needs is that we create a real disconnect. It's very disheartening as a parent to not have that connection with your child.

NAOMI: In the book, we call that the Reality Gap. It's when you're yearning after this idea of the life you thought you'd have, and that you think everyone else is having. You're thinking, This is what we should have had, this is the life we should have had, and it means you can't make the most of the life that you're really having. You are constantly tense.

This book is about how to embrace the reality you have, the child you have, and live a life which is happier for all of you.

ELIZA: It is not really a book that tells you what you should be doing. It is not going to say 'You should be doing this.' It is more like the reassuring friend. It's the reassuring voice saying. . .

NAOMI: 'You're doing okay.' You are all doing okay, and it's okay to listen to your child and to feel good about that.

In each chapter there will be lots of illustrations by Eliza, examples and anecdotes and some theory, and there will also always be a bit like this, where Eliza and I chat about the ideas in the chapter. At the end of each chapter there will be a summary and some suggestions of other books to read if you want to. Those books aren't always totally aligned with the approach we're talking about here, but they all have interesting ideas. Take what works for you.

We have designed this book so that you can dip in and out of it as you like, and so that even when reading it feels like too much, you can just look at the illustrations. But if you skip straight to the chapter on screens, for example, you won't get as much out of it as you would starting at the beginning – it will make more sense if you read at least some of the earlier chapters. We hope you enjoy it.

1

My Child Hasn't Read
the Parenting Books

'Right,' said Yulia to her son Peter. 'That behaviour is unaccept-able. You can't kick your sister. You need to go to sit on the Naughty Step.'

Peter snapped his head around. 'Nope.'

Yulia made her voice firmer. 'Peter, right now. I said *now*. Or I'll take you there.'

Peter sat down and held tight to the chair beneath him. 'No. I'm not going and you can't make me. If you do, I'll kick you harder and punch Tania until her head bleeds.'

Yulia spoke with authority, 'Peter, if you don't move right now, I'm going to call your father and stop your pocket money. I'll count to three. One. . . two. . . two and a half. . .'

Peter was unmoved. 'You can have all my pocket money and tell Daddy. I don't care.'

Yulia weighed up her options. She could carry Peter with the chair attached over to the step while he fought her. She could leave the room with his sister but then he would almost certainly follow her. She could start pleading with him but she knew that wouldn't end well. She could try bribery but the idea of giving him sweets to go to the Naughty Step didn't sit well. And then once he was there she'd have to keep him there for at least a few minutes. The books said a minute for every year of his age, and he was six. . . It was meant to be 'time to reflect' but Peter didn't look like he was in a thoughtful mood.

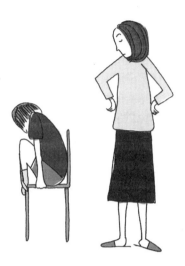

Tania started to cry. Yulia felt like joining in herself. 'Please, Petey. . .' she said. Her tone wasn't firm anymore.

'No,' he replied. 'You can't force me.'

Yulia wondered what she was getting wrong. Everything she read said that being loving but firm was the way to be a good parent. Her mother told her that Peter's behaviour showed he was desperate for boundaries and that they would help him feel safe.

Yet whenever she tried to be firm with Peter, it went wrong. Peter utterly refused to do what she asked. The firmer she tried to be, the less it seemed to work. He would turn right around and start telling her to go into Time Out herself. It didn't seem like the boundaries made him feel safe. He seemed to be constantly angry.

She had read all the books about showing children that she was the leader and about how to use consequences in a firm but loving way. She understood the theory. She tried to be consistent and calm but Peter's behaviour was equally consistent and he had no qualms at all about sitting there for hours rather than complying with her requests. He simply wouldn't do anything that he was asked to do, and the more she tried to persuade him, the less likely he was to change his mind.

Yulia was inundated with advice. The health visitor had told her he just needed to learn who was in control and that she was the parent. His teacher said he could sense that she was afraid of him and she needed to be more authoritative. People in the Facebook groups she had joined said that if Peter was securely attached, he'd want to please her and would be cooperative. The lady at the library had asked her if he saw violence at home and what she thought the source of his anger was. Her friends said apparently 'helpful' things like 'Where has he learned that this behaviour is acceptable?' Yulia would seethe at the implication that her home was an environment in which hitting other people was acceptable.

The GP suggested books and parenting courses that made Yulia laugh. It was like the authors and course leaders had never met a child like Peter. In the books, children were motivated by rewards and would stay in Time Out. They could be sent to their bedrooms without their parents having to physically put them there and hold the door shut while they battered it from the other side. Parents laid down the law and, for the most part, the children complied. There were books where the suggestions started with 'Have your child. . .' and she would think, How??! Why does everyone assume that you can just decide your child will do something?

Then there was the concern, which drove her crazy. Whenever she was honest about Peter's needs – about the way that she couldn't leave him alone with his sister because he would push her off the sofa, how he never played independently and how he still needed hours of a parent lying with him at night in order to fall asleep, then people would say things like, 'Oh, it would really worry me if my child did that.' Or worse, 'I wouldn't let a child of mine get away with that.'

How exactly am I letting him 'get away' with this? thought Yulia. What am I getting wrong that everyone else seems to get right? It felt like there was a secret code handed out in the maternity ward which she'd missed, and she was still struggling in the dark, unable to unlock the parenting magic. Other children just didn't react like Peter. She'd seen it for herself. Some parents could control their children's behaviour with a raised eyebrow, while others did the counting-to-three trick and their children scurried into place at two and three-quarters. She thought of the long years stretching ahead of her – the other thing people said when they saw her trying to persuade Peter to leave the playground as he lay on the floor and refused to budge was 'Just wait until he's a teenager!' Or even, 'If you don't get him under control now, you'll have an awful time when he's older.'

It was enough to make her want to go to bed and stay there. Things were hard now, and it seemed like all she had to look forward to were things getting worse and worse. This wasn't what she had imagined when she had dreamt about having a family.

What's going on?

I meet a lot of parents like Yulia and they tell me about their children. Children who don't play by the rules. Children who refuse to be persuaded, and whose behaviour sometimes frightens their parents with its intensity. Children with whom family life can quickly become a series of conflicts, even as their parents tell themselves that they'll 'pick their battles'. A battle over getting dressed, over coming downstairs, over having breakfast, over putting shoes on, over leaving the house. As one parent said to me, 'I have decided to pick my battles, but my daughter hasn't got the memo. She picks every battle available. Even ones I never imagined could be battles.'

Many of these parents are deeply worried. They're concerned that there is something wrong with their children, and also that they are getting it wrong. They are worried that their children's behaviour means that they have failed as parents, and there is no shortage of other people telling them how this is the case.

It's not your fault. There's nothing wrong with you or your child. The problem is that what you've been told to do doesn't work for your child.

You need something different.

Code breakers

When you have a child who responds differently to other children, it can be very confusing. You rarely get the responses that you expect – and that others tell you to expect – and so it can feel like you are constantly on unstable ground, unsure of the right thing to do.

When I meet a child or a family, my first priority is to try to make sense of what is happening for them. This is a fundamental part of being a psychologist. Making sense of a situation involves looking at all the different aspects of what is going on, and taking some guesses as to how they all connect. There are things that we can see or hear – behaviour, and what people say – and then there are things that go on under the surface – emotions, the nervous system and thoughts. Psychologists try to work out how they all connect. Then, based on that, we generate some ideas about what might help. We try something out, see if it makes any difference, and if it doesn't, we stop doing that and try something else.

In this book, I'm going to help you make sense of what is going on in your family. I'll show you some of the ways in which I help families make sense of their children's experiences, so that you can do this for yourself.

I'm going to start by explaining a simple way to think about children's behaviour and wellbeing. It involves using a flow chart to identify the different parts of what is going on. I call this flow chart the code breaker. That's because the point of it is to help you crack the code of your child's confusing reactions. This code breaker involves three main parts: what happens before; the child's reaction to that (internal and external); and what happens next.

The code breaker helps you to identify clues about what might be going wrong – and to get some ideas about what could be changed. It doesn't tell you the answers, but it might help you make some good guesses.

The code breaker starts with the context. This includes what you are doing, what is going on in the immediate surroundings, but also what might have happened in the past. It's what happens before any given situation.

Next, we have the child's reaction. This can be broken into two parts. Firstly, the child will be reacting to what is happening in their body and brain – but these reactions are invisible. They happen inside the child. Because they are invisible, adults sometimes assume that they aren't there at all.

The second part of the child's reaction is more visible. This is when the child does show us how they feel – often through their behaviour, but sometimes through telling us.

And then finally, we have what happens afterwards, often as a result of those visible reactions. If the visible reaction is behaviour such as shouting or hurting someone else, then what happens next might be an angry parent telling the child off.

This code breaker has the acronym BIVA to help you remember the order:

Before. Invisible reaction. Visible reaction. After.

Google tells me that Biva is a Bengali girl's name meaning sunlight, shine or light, which is just about perfect since the point of this code breaker is to shine some light on what is going on.

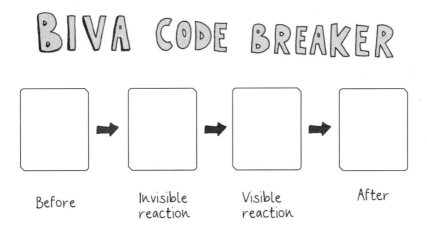

BIVA CODE BREAKER

Before — Invisible reaction — Visible reaction — After

The BIVA code breaker can be applied to lots of situations. It's a way to help us make sense of what is happening – and to generate some hypotheses. It doesn't make any assumptions about how a child should respond or should feel in reaction to something, it's just a way of observing the patterns – and generating ideas as to what to do. Children will have different reactions to their environment and what is happening to them, due to the different ways in which they experience the world.

When we've filled in the boxes in the code breaker, we can then draw additional arrows going between the different boxes to identify the connections. Let's apply this code breaker to Peter and Yulia.

What about Peter?

Some children are very sensitive to what is going on in their environment, particularly to pressure or expectations on the part of their parents. They react with anxiety and fear (invisible reactions). When children feel anxious, their visible reaction can be a range of things, but their motivation is usually to get away from the anxious feelings. Peter is like this. For some children, this means that they refuse to do a lot of what they are asked to do. Instead they may shout, they become disruptive or they withdraw and stop talking. Or they may try to distract their parents in a range of ways.

What happens then is that their parents often react with anger and more pressure – and this then increases the child's fear and anxiety – which means that they are even less likely to do what they were told.

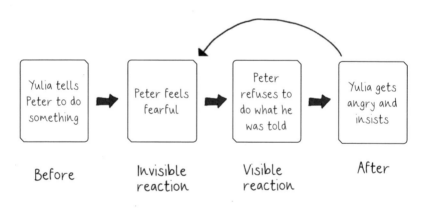

| Before | Invisible reaction | Visible reaction | After |

This is what is happening between Yulia and Peter. Yulia's expectations are making Peter feel fearful. His way of expressing that is anger and resistance. The more pressure Yulia puts on him, the more fearful he becomes – and the way that he deals with his fear is to say 'No.' Yulia and Peter are stuck, because the way that Yulia is reacting makes Peter less able to do what she wants him to do. Things are going downhill fast.

Feedback loops

That arrow going from Yulia's behaviour back to Peter's invisible reactions is really important. It creates a loop. The angrier Yulia becomes, the more fearful Peter becomes – and the more he refuses. These loops are why so many parents get stuck. They react to what they see – behaviour – and they try to make the child change their behaviour. But in doing so, they inadvertently increase the invisible reaction. In this case, that's fear and anxiety. And the invisible reaction is what drives the visible reaction. Yulia's efforts to change that visible reaction are in fact making it worse.

The code breaker means we can make some sense of a confusing situation. It helps us to see what is happening more clearly. And it helps us see things we might otherwise miss.

Most parents come asking for help with their children's visible behaviour. They ask questions like 'How do I get them to be more cooperative?' As you can see from the code breaker, this risks missing out a vital step – the invisible thoughts and feelings that drive the behaviour. Children often can't tell us about those invisible reactions but that doesn't mean they aren't there.

This book looks beyond visible behaviour to ask why something is happening, and how you as a parent could change so that things improve for you and your child. It will help you see your child's behaviour in context, and will give you some ideas as to how you could change what you are doing, to help your children and you come unstuck.

Pressure sensitivity

So, what about those invisible reactions – and why is Peter reacting the way he is? Invisible reactions are the way that our bodies and brains react to the world around them. There are certain predictable patterns – most people will feel angry if something is stolen from them, for example – but there's also a large degree of individual variation. People experience the world differently. Just think of roller coasters. I hate roller coasters. They make me feel sick, sometimes before I have even got on. I try to avoid them as much as I can. Other people love them so much that they travel for hours and pay lots of money to go to theme parks full of them. One person's fun can be another person's misery.

The realisation that different people can experience the same thing in different ways seems trivial, but when it comes to children it sometimes seems that most adults don't get it. There is often an assumption that all children will enjoy the same things. People say things like 'children love parties', ignoring the fact that a significant number of children really dislike large groups and organised games with prizes, which form the core of many children's parties. Many children's activities are set up with assumptions about what all children like. This means that if your child doesn't enjoy the things that 'all children' enjoy, you're left wondering what's wrong.

Appreciating diversity of experience is a fundamental part of this book. The starting point is that different children experience the world differently. In some ways, you have to become a detective, observing your child's visible reactions and making informed guesses about their invisible reactions. You have to be ready to try things out and then change tack if they go wrong.

One way in which children vary is that some are very sensitive to pressure. For them, things that do not cause other children anxiety can cause them to feel like they are under threat. And when humans feel under threat, we act to protect ourselves. By fighting or running away or freezing. By trying to avoid the threat.

Parenting techniques such as telling off, taking away privileges or using Time Outs do not work well with these children. They make them feel under more threat, and the way that the child reacts is to try to push away the threat by refusing or protesting. This creates a loop – just like with Yulia and Peter.

I call these children pressure sensitive. You may have also heard them called 'demand avoidant'. There are many other ways that these children are described. Badly behaved, difficult, oppositional, naughty, resistant, defiant, badly brought up – these have all been used to describe children who don't respond to standard parenting. I tend to use 'pressure sensitive' because I think it helps us think beyond the child to what is going on in their environment. It also has the benefit of not being related to any specific diagnosis.

Some pressure-sensitive children have a neurodevelopmental or psychiatric diagnosis and these diagnoses can vary. Some will be autistic, some will have a diagnosis of oppositional defiant disorder, others will have diagnoses of ADHD or high anxiety. Many will have been described (or identified by their parents) as having pathological demand avoidance (PDA). Some might have diagnoses of post-traumatic stress disorder. Some will have no diagnosis. For the purposes of this book, diagnosis doesn't matter. Pressure sensitivity is transdiagnostic, meaning that it is shared by people who have different diagnoses as well as those who have none at all.

Pressure-sensitive children feel pressured by things that don't feel pressuring to other people. Those could be day-to-day things like getting dressed, or eating at the table. They can feel pressured by expectations from others like saying please and thank you. They can feel pressure inside themselves to do something well, meaning that they never get started with things. I sometimes refer to them as clear-sighted, because they are exceptionally good at detecting hidden control and expectations others have missed.

This sensitivity to pressure causes anxiety. Children react to that anxiety in a range of ways, including refusal, being disruptive, meltdowns and trying to control other people. This often appears to resemble 'bad behaviour' to the adults around them, and so the adults react in ways which make things worse.

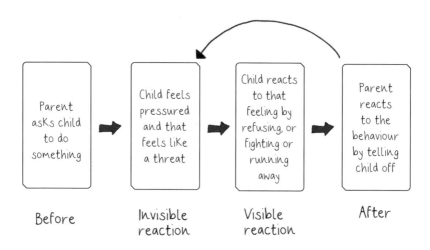

| Before | Invisible reaction | Visible reaction | After |

When adults respond to a child's behaviour in a way that increases their anxiety, they create a feedback loop. Anxiety drives the child's behaviour – and so the thing that the parent is doing to try to improve their child's behaviour actually makes it worse. Parents can also get stuck in a loop when they keep insisting on the thing that causes the child to feel under pressure. Maybe the child finds it very hard to do homework. It leads to high levels of anxiety (invisible reaction) and so they loudly refuse (visible reaction). Every time they start to calm down, their parent reminds them of their homework – and off the loop goes again.

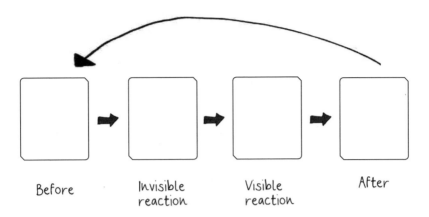

Before   Invisible reaction   Visible reaction   After

This code breaker chart shows the loops that many parents and children get stuck in. Once you're stuck in a loop, it doesn't matter how much energy you put into trying to solve the situation. All your effort just makes the loop go round faster. You burn through your resources very fast, while getting nowhere. Everyone starts to feel under more and more pressure. It's like you and your child are stuck on a hamster wheel.

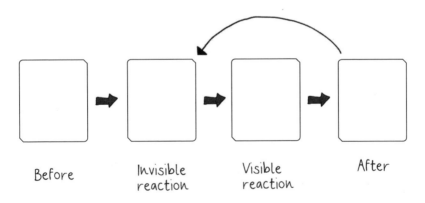

Before   Invisible reaction   Visible reaction   After

Who are pressure-sensitive children?

It seems very likely to me that there have always been children whose behaviour confuses their families and friends. This isn't a new thing. Names like 'demand avoidance' are new, however, and so our way of understanding these children has changed.

In the process of writing this book I've spoken to adoptive families, families of autistic/PDA children, families of children with other forms of neurodivergence, families of children who have experienced trauma, families of children on the foetal alcohol spectrum, families of children with complex medical conditions and many other families whose children are very sensitive to pressure for no apparent reason. They all tell me that the descriptions resonate with them. Pressure sensitivity is not exclusive to any group.

Pressure sensitivity changes as children grow. For some it seems to be a developmental phase, while for others it's more of a character trait. Some children are extremely pressure sensitive as young children and then as teenagers are quite different, while for others it goes the other way. As a psychologist, when I meet a child I can't tell what they will be like when they grow up. No one can tell you that for sure. I can make some guesses, but I can't be certain.

One of the reasons that I can't tell you what your child will be like is because child development is a very complex process. There are many different factors, all of which can affect how a child develops. The environment that they grow up in will make a big difference, as will their genes – and those two things will interact. Both those things will affect how they learn to think and feel about themselves. They will affect how they relate to other people. I cannot tell you what your child will be able to do when they grow up – all we can do is focus on helping them thrive right now.

How does pressure sensitivity show up?

How do you know if your child is pressure sensitive? What are the visible reactions that you might see? Here are a few of the things parents have told me about their children.

They respond very badly to techniques such as Time Out or the Naughty Step.

They are impossible to persuade and have a very strong will.

They refuse to do things that other children do with no problem.

Offering them rewards and bribes gets you nowhere.

They have explosive meltdowns that are hard to predict.

They do not seem to understand hierarchies and do not respect authority.

They use parenting techniques back at you, for example counting to three or telling you that your behaviour is unacceptable.

They are very sensitive to tone of voice.

They can behave in completely different ways with different people – with some they are relaxed and happy; with others they will not come out from under the table.

Getting firmer makes them less cooperative, not more.

They don't seem to care what other people think.

They sometimes appear to be fine and then suddenly they aren't.

Things escalate very quickly from a small starting point.

They really dislike instructions like 'Stay quiet in the library' or 'Don't walk on the grass' and sometimes do the opposite.

They are unpredictable – something that worked one week doesn't work the next.

You feel like you are walking on eggshells around them.

They can be controlling of other people.

Sometimes they really want something but then when it arrives they can't do it.

They respond differently to your other children.

They find children their own age difficult to manage unless they can control them.

They can get very focused on one thing to the exclusion of everything else.

They ask very direct questions that can be embarrassing but which other people are too nervous to ask.

They see through a hidden agenda and refuse to have anything to do with it.

They find it hard to change what they are doing or move from activity to activity.

When you ask them to do something calmly, they respond as if you have yelled at them.

They are extremely strong-willed and you know that you will lose any battle with them.

You find yourself in battles over things that seem extremely trivial to you.

Routines and structures are very hard to stick to.

They may wake very easily and have nightmares or night terrors.

They can be devastatingly honest and direct.

When they are doing something they want to do, the whole experience is completely different for everyone compared to when they are doing something that they feel made to do.

Looking at that table above, you might be wondering if it fits your child. Maybe you recognise some of it, but not others. Maybe you're not sure how extreme your child's behaviour is and whether they're really very different to other children.

Here's the thing. It doesn't matter how your child compares to others. Pressure sensitivity isn't something one group of children have and others don't. It's something we can all experience at different times and it's a common part of the human condition. For some, it is much more extreme and lasts a lifetime, while for others it might come and go. If it's part of you and your child's experience right now, then this book is for you.

Is it wired into their brain?

Why is your child like this? You might have heard people say that it's all down to their brains, that they are differently wired, and that explains it. Their neurology is the cause.

I don't often talk about differently wired brains. That's for a couple of reasons. The main one is that in my experience when people hear 'differently wired' they tend to think that this means 'set in stone'. It brings up connotations of an electrical circuit, wired in by an electrician and unchangeable. People hear 'differently wired' and they understand 'that's how their brain works and always will be.'

Electrical circuitry is a good metaphor for the brain in lots of ways. Our brains do work by forming connections between brain cells, which then form neural networks.

Despite that, there's one very important difference between the electrical circuitry in your house and your brain. If you want to change the wiring in your house, you need to do some major invasive work. You'll be digging holes in the walls and you'll need experts to do it if you don't want to risk electrocuting yourself.

Brains, on the other hand, change their wiring all the time with no need for an electrician. Since you started reading this book, the connections in your brain have changed because of what you've read.

Your brain isn't so much 'wired' as 'constantly rewiring' – a process called *neuroplasticity*. This is particularly true for children and adolescents. Their brains are going through intense periods of restructuring and growth. The experiences that they have will make a big difference to how that happens.

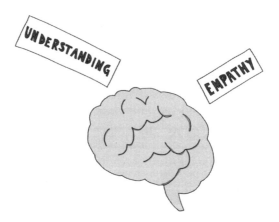

There is another reason why I don't use 'differently wired'. It seems intuitively true to many people that if there are differences between people's brains, then those neurological differences must be the *cause* of differences in behaviour. It seems obvious that brains cause behaviour. This is too simplistic, and here's why.

Human brains are amazingly good at adapting to the environment. In fact, this is one of the things that make humans different to other animals. My family went on a trip to Morocco recently where we encountered lots of cats. Those cats behaved very much like the cats that we have at home. Despite growing up in a very different environment, most of their behaviours were clearly shared by cats everywhere. Cats will adapt to their environments a bit, but if you bring a Moroccan cat to England, they'll soon be indistinguishable from the cats there. In other words, domestic cat behaviour isn't that varied, no matter where they live. I'll bet that ancient Egyptian cats behaved very similarly to my two cats, despite living in a very different time and place.

Humans, on the other hand, develop very different behaviour depending on the environment that they live in. You can see those differences in their brains. Brains wire differently depending on life experience.

Imagine this. . .

A group of alien researchers comes to Earth, and they notice people behaving very differently to each other. They notice that some people speak different languages and can't understand one another. They want to know why this is the case, so they take a group of Japanese speakers and a group of people who don't speak any Japanese, and they scan their brains while playing audio in Japanese to them.

On the scans, they'll see distinct differences in how those brains respond to the Japanese language. The Japanese speakers' brains will process the Japanese as meaningful information, while the non-Japanese speakers will just process it as sounds. Their brains will show different connectivity when they hear Japanese.

'A-ha!' say the aliens. 'We've cracked it! It's their brains. They have differently wired brains, and that's why they speak different languages. Now we know why they behave differently.'

At one level, they aren't wrong. The brains of Japanese speakers and non-Japanese speakers are differently wired. They react differently to the world in a way which can be seen on a brain scan.

But I hope it's obvious to you (if not to the aliens) that the different brains of those who speak Japanese have not *caused* them to speak Japanese (although it is their brains that make it possible for them to speak Japanese). The brain differences are a result of the interaction between a brain that could acquire language and an environment that made learning Japanese possible. That environment isn't visible on a brain scan.

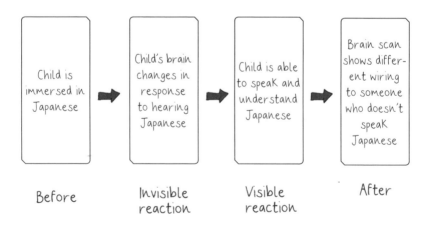

Child is immersed in Japanese → Child's brain changes in response to hearing Japanese → Child is able to speak and understand Japanese → Brain scan shows different wiring to someone who doesn't speak Japanese

Before   Invisible reaction   Visible reaction   After

When researchers look at brains in action, they find differences everywhere. One study found that when London taxi drivers learn 'The Knowledge' – memorising the streets of inner London – there are visible differences in their brains compared to those who have not learned it. Researchers can actually see the difference that learning has made to their brains.

If you think about it, where else is that learning going to be? Of course our brains are going to reflect our experiences and the environment around us. Our neurobiology reflects our experiences, just like the biology of our bodies reflects how we live our lives.

Do we need a diagnosis?

Okay, you're probably thinking, Why's she going on about brain wiring when I just want to know how to help my child and stop all the fighting? It's because this is how we try to explain what is going on and how we think about difference.

One particular way that we think about unusual children in the twenty-first century is through the lens of a neurodevelopmental diagnosis. Neurodevelopmental diagnoses are based on the medical model, which sees differences such as autism and ADHD as 'disorders' or even 'diseases'. The purpose of a diagnosis is to identify who might need treatment or intervention, and so the symptom lists are focused on deficits and perceived impairments. They are essentially lists of things that the children in question do less well than other children their age.

I've worked in neurodevelopmental clinics diagnosing children with autism and ADHD. There are lists of symptoms in big, standardised manuals, mostly written by committees of psychiatrists (who are medical doctors with specialist training in mental health). When we diagnose, we conduct detailed interviews with the aim of matching a child's behaviour to these symptom lists. We ask parents and teachers and we conduct tests with the children to see if we think they fit the criteria. We sometimes give each symptom a severity score and we add the scores up. If the child gets a high enough score, then they get the diagnosis. They don't have to meet all the criteria, and two people who get the same diagnosis may not have much in common at all. If a child doesn't cooperate, it may not be possible to give a diagnosis.

Some people score just high enough for a diagnosis, while others just miss it. There's no clear distinction. There are no behaviours that are exclusive to those who get a neurodevelopmental diagnosis. It is always a matter of degree. When someone like me gives a neurodevelopmental diagnosis, we are drawing a line that isn't there in nature. Someone who doesn't receive a diagnosis might in fact be very similar to someone who does, because they sit just the other side of that line. The location of the line changes over time, and even between countries and professionals. Every so often, the diagnostic manuals are updated and reissued and the lines change. Most recently that happened in 2013, when the way that autism was diagnosed changed significantly and people who previously would have received a diagnosis of 'Asperger's syndrome' or 'Pervasive Developmental Disorder – Not Otherwise Specified (PDD-NOS)' were brought together under the 'Autism Spectrum Disorder' category.

If you have a pressure-sensitive child you may have tried to get a diagnosis of pathological demand avoidance (PDA) and been told that it's not a diagnosis. That's because it is not in the manuals and therefore is not an official diagnosis. It was described by Elizabeth Newson and colleagues in the UK in 2003. It hasn't been standardised in the way that the other diagnoses have, meaning that it's far less clear how it should be diagnosed and what that diagnosis might mean in the long term. Some professionals will give it anyway, while others won't. I find the concept of a demand-avoidant profile helpful as a way of thinking about some children at some times, whether or not it is used as a diagnosis.

Unlike physical health diagnoses, there are no biological tests for neurodevelopmental diagnoses. Getting a diagnosis of autism is not like getting a diagnosis of COVID. With COVID, a diagnosis means the virus that causes the symptoms has been identified. With a neuro-developmental diagnosis such as autism or ADHD, all we have done is given a name to the group of symptoms. It's a description.

When someone receives a diagnosis, people often get the impression that they are part of a separate group with others who have received the same diagnosis. Some people believe that their specific type of brain has been identified and that they share this with others. The biological research does not back this up.

Geneticists and neuroscientists have not been able to find biological differences between different psychiatric diagnostic categories, despite decades of trying to do just that. Sometimes a study shows a difference, and then the next study finds something different. That's probably because diagnostic categories don't reflect clear groups. Differences between people are dimensional. They usually fall into what is called a 'normal distribution'. This just means that most people cluster around the average, and there are fewer and fewer people as we go towards the extremes.

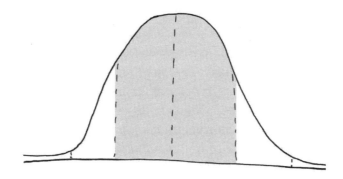

Large-scale genetic studies have found that those who receive a neurodevelopmental or mental health diagnosis don't have different genes to other people; they have combinations of the same genetic differences that everyone shares. As behavioural geneticist Robert Plomin puts it, 'the abnormal is normal.' He means that the genetic research shows us that what gets diagnosed as a 'disorder' (like autism) is one end of the normal distribution. The behaviours that get someone an autism diagnosis are there across the whole population – they are not unique to autism. Getting the diagnosis is about the quantity of behaviours and how extreme those behaviours are. Scientists have not identified behaviours that only exist in autistic people (and the same applies for most psychiatric diagnoses).

If you're interested to know more about genetics and how they apply to behaviour and neurodevelopment, Robert Plomin's popular science book is interesting and easy to read. It's called *Blueprint: How DNA Makes Us Who We Are*.

What about brains? Researchers in Canada have looked at the brains of children with diagnoses of autism, ADHD and OCD. They found that they could not predict what diagnosis a child had by looking at their brain scan. Children who had the same diagnosis did not share the same neurobiological differences. If you want to know more about this, look up the Province of Ontario Neurodevelopmental Network (POND). One of the neuroscientists there, Evdokia Anagnostou, has given some talks for parents explaining their research, which are now available on YouTube.

These findings fit well with the idea of neurodiversity. Neuro-diversity is the idea that differences between people are a natural part of human variation, and don't have to be seen as a 'disorder'.

Think of it like height. People are very different heights. There is a gradual change from tall to short and there's pretty well every height in between. Most people are in the middle (which is the average) and there are fewer very tall people or very short people. Scientists call this the 'normal distribution'. The further you get from the average, the fewer people there are. It's a distribution that shows up in humans again and again, for many different characteristics.

Clothing sizes divide people up on the basis of height. Women's clothing is sometimes divided into 'Tall', 'Regular' and 'Short'. I'm on the cusp of 'Regular' and 'Short'. Sometimes I buy one, sometimes the other. If I go to another country where most women are shorter than me, I might suddenly become 'Tall'. I'd have to adjust my buying habits.

In a furniture shop, I can buy tables, sofas and bookcases. Those categories don't blend into each other. I don't go into the furniture shop thinking that I'm looking for something on the cusp of being a sofa or a bookcase and could go either way. Those categories are distinctly different to each other. Clothing sizes, on the other hand, are an artificial way to divide up people who have real differences. Someone has chosen a height and decided that people to one side of it are 'Regular' while those on the other side are 'Short'. They could have chosen a different height (and different shops do in fact choose different heights). There are real differences between people, and you'll see this if you compare a group of tall people with a group of short people, but the groups – 'Tall', 'Regular' and 'Short' – blend into each other.

Neurodevelopmental diagnoses are like clothing sizes. They reflect real differences between people, but whether you get a diagnosis or not (and which diagnosis you get) comes down to where someone decides to draw the line. There are training programmes for professionals to help them decide where to draw the line, because it isn't at all easy to get it right. I've been on some of them. They last several days. Deciding who gets a diagnosis and who doesn't is often not at all obvious.

Diagnoses can be really useful: they can be key to obtaining support in the school system, and can help people get reasonable adjustments in the workplace. But the drawback to diagnoses, from a psychological perspective, is that sometimes they can stop people thinking more deeply about what might be going on, because diagnoses aren't much help as an explanation. They don't really tell us *why*.

Say a child is having trouble concentrating and sitting still at school, and they're sent for an assessment. The professionals will ask lots of questions, some of which are to do with how that child concentrates and sits still at school. They might then give the child the diagnosis. Now, people will say, we know why they can't concentrate! They have ADHD!

But the diagnosis doesn't add new explanatory information. We still don't really know why that child can't concentrate. Maybe it's because they find the schoolwork boring. Maybe they are right, and it *is* really boring. Maybe it's because the school is expecting them to sit at a desk when they are still of an age where they would prefer to be running around outside. Maybe the teacher isn't managing to engage the child's interest or maybe the teacher talks in a way that makes the child feel anxious. Or it might be because there are things going on at home or school that make it impossible for them to stay calm. The diagnosis doesn't tell us why they can't concentrate – we just have a name for the fact that they can't.

This wouldn't matter except that sometimes the diagnosis stops people really asking why. I have met children who have been told that they can't be treated for anxiety, because they are autistic, and the autism is the cause of their anxiety. There are many reasons why a child might be anxious, and saying that it's caused by their autism doesn't really explain anything. Instead it seems to stop people from thinking further.

When I see a child and their family, a diagnosis isn't enough to help me work out what might help them. I have to understand the child as an individual and ask questions about what is going on around them. I have to make sense of what is happening in their life before we can begin. A diagnosis gives me descriptive information, but isn't an explanation.

Okay, enough about diagnoses and what they are and aren't. Suffice to say, your child doesn't need a diagnosis for you to find this book useful, but having a diagnosis doesn't rule you out either. This book is for parents of all pressure-sensitive children.

What does the science say?

All brains are wired differently and are constantly rewiring in response to the environment.

Behavioural traits like pressure sensitivity or demand avoidance are not confined to one group of children and are present to some degree across the whole population.

The genetic and neurobiological research shows that brains (and people) are not clearly divided into different types by their diagnosis. Categories blend into each other. Differences are real, but the categories we put people into can and do change over time.

Most genetic, neurobiological and behavioural differences between people are a matter of degree.

Why does it matter?

It's important that we don't fall into the trap of thinking that a child's potential or future is fixed, particularly when it comes to children and young people and what we tell them about their brains.

Not all young people want to be told that they are different – and the reality is that we are all the same in some ways and different in others.

It's important that we look for real explanations, because that is the way that we can actually help young people thrive.

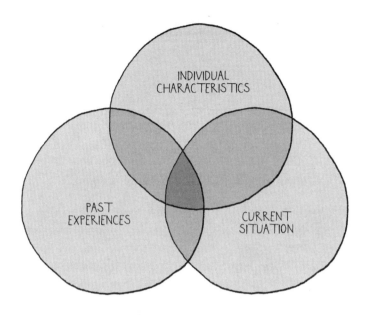

Talking to children about difference

I meet many children who have been told that their brains are differently wired. They are told this by well-meaning adults who want them to feel good about their differences and not to blame themselves. Just like adults, kids tend to interpret this in a particular way. They think this means that their brain will always be like this and they will always be different in the way that they are now.

For some kids, this helps them to accept themselves. For others, it isn't such a positive experience. Some children think it means that life will never get easier for them. It makes them feel despondent about the future. Particularly for those who are having a terrible time at school, it can remove their hope that things will get better. They think it will be this terrible for life.

This is particularly true for adolescents. Adolescence is a developmental stage when peer acceptance becomes really important. Many adolescents don't want to be told that they are different to others and always will be. Some adolescents I know have sought to get their childhood diagnoses removed because they feel that it does not reflect them and their identity. They discover that it's almost impossible to get a neurodevelopmental diagnosis removed from your medical record. It's there for life, whether or not the young person themselves wants it there.

When I talk to young people about their differences, I talk about similarities too. I talk about how everyone has things that they find harder and easier, and just because they find something hard now doesn't mean that it will be like that forever – nor that the people who find things easier now will continue to do so forever. They can usually think of something that they used to find hard but now find easy, like riding a scooter or swimming or even learning to walk.

I tell them that brains are changing and developing all the time. I tell them that just because they are finding this time in their life hard doesn't mean that it will always be that way. Different people find different times in life hard – those who find being a child hard sometimes really prefer being an adult with more control over their life, while those who enjoyed childhood sometimes find becoming a teenager or adult much harder.

I also tell them that a diagnosis is one way to think about themselves and their differences, but it's not the only way. They are the ones who can choose how to think about themselves. I find this is particularly important for pressure-sensitive kids, who can sometimes feel that everyone around them expects them to adopt a positive neurodivergent identity, making them feel under pressure to do so, which means that they can't. Their identity is something that they need to work out for themselves.

I look for connections with family members who share character-istics with them – often there will be aunts and uncles who, as children, were a lot like them (or may still be a lot like them). They are the same as others, as well as uniquely different to others. Just like all of us.

Cracking the code

I know I've just said a lot about the inadequacies of diagnosis and brain wiring as a way to explain differences. You might well be think-ing, Well, all right then, but why is my child like this if it isn't caused by their autism, their PDA or their brain wiring? Are there no explan-ations at all? Are we just stuck being confused?

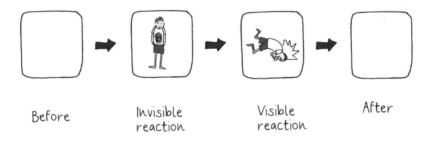

Before   Invisible   Visible   After
              reaction   reaction

I'm a psychologist, and that means that the way I look for explan-ations is through looking closely at different situations and generating hypotheses as to what is going on. That's where the code breaking comes in. The more you can develop the ability to do this for your-self, the better equipped you'll be to solve problems as they arise. A useful code breaker will generate some ideas as to what you could do differently.

Remember the BIVA code breaker I introduced earlier on? In the next sections I'm going to go more deeply into why some children react in the way that they do, particularly thinking about their invisible and visible reactions to the environment.

What is really going on?

This morning, my cats started my day by jumping on my face to wake me up. They wanted feeding. In order to do that, I had to climb up to get a new box of cat food, which then caused several other boxes to fall down, which I had to clear up before the cats ripped open the pouches I had got down. Then my son came down and it turned out that we had no food that he wanted to eat for breakfast, so I gave him some money and he went to the shop. When he came back, he'd forgotten to get milk so I went out this time so I could make my cup of coffee. Then, finally, I was able to sit down and drink some coffee – just in time for the cats to knock a glass of water all over the floor.

My morning was full of little challenges to my emotional equilibrium. Each time a new thing happened, I had to work out how to deal with the new problem, while not losing my cool.

This happens to everyone, all the time. We are always managing new challenges and obstacles. Our ability to do this without becoming overwhelmed is part of what makes life harder or easier for us. Some people are easily frustrated. They might have become angry about the forgotten milk or fallen cat food boxes. Others might have felt that this was all too much before breakfast and given up or drunk the coffee black.

Of course, your capacity to cope also varies according to the other things going on in your life at a particular time. If I'd been up all night with a crying child or if I hadn't eaten for a couple of days, it would have been much harder for me to maintain my emotional balance. When you're under a lot of stress, a spilled glass of water can feel like the last straw and you lose the capacity to hold it together.

We move between different emotional states all the time. Being able to do so is an essential part of managing our emotional balance. We get frustrated or angry and then we return to feeling okay. We feel low or unhappy, and then we return to feeling okay again. When we experience lots of challenges in a row, it gets harder to keep returning to our state of calm.

For young children, maintaining their emotional balance is hard. They get frustrated by many things, and they find it hard to find their way back. For them, the wrong colour cup or a broken fish finger can be enough to send them over the edge and they show us loudly and dramatically. They need a lot of help from their parents to bring themselves back. A lot of what children are learning as they grow is how to tolerate and regulate their emotions. They become able to manage disappointments without it feeling so extreme.

The window of tolerance

One way to think about our capacity to keep ourselves balanced is the 'window of tolerance' (a term coined by psychiatrist Daniel Siegel). Our window of tolerance is the emotional zone within which we can keep ourselves calm and manage the stresses of everyday life. When we're in that zone we can manage to navigate life's challenges without losing our cool. When we go out of that zone, we start struggling to manage, and if we are a long way out of our window of tolerance, then the tiniest thing can push us over the edge. The window of tolerance is not just about our brain. It's about the way our whole nervous system reacts.

When the Naughty Step Makes Things Worse

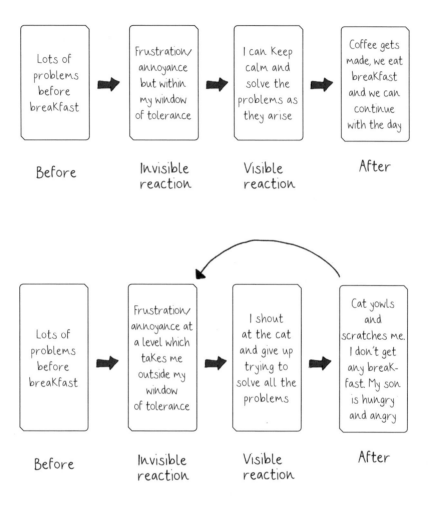

Here's a code breaker of my frustrating morning – and two possible scenarios. Up to a certain point, I could keep myself in my window of tolerance and solve each problem as it came up. But as the frustrations accumulate, at some point I will go over the edge and stop being able to manage. That's the point when I might start to express anger and frustration to others or myself. They will then react to me – and that's when my day could go in two very different directions, depending on whether I manage to stay in my window of tolerance or not. We could get stuck in a loop where everything that happens pushes me further out of my window of tolerance.

Exercise: Cracking your own code

Cracking codes is hard, particularly when you have to guess your child's invisible reactions because they can't tell you. To practise, it's helpful to start with yourself. The advantage of starting with yourself is that your invisible reactions might be easier for you to detect than your child's.

Start with a recent situation when you have had to manage something that was a bit challenging. Don't pick your worst and most embarrassing moment. Choose something you can think about calmly now.

Now think about those four boxes. What happened before, what were your invisible reactions, your visible reactions – and what happened after? Were there any loops formed? Did you get stuck?

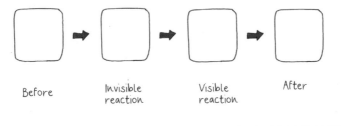

Before   Invisible reaction   Visible reaction   After

A narrow window of tolerance

The size of a person's window of tolerance depends on many things. Age, for example. Young children tend to have a narrow window of tolerance. They are easily unbalanced. As they get older, this expands but at different rates. Genetics and individual personality play a part, but so do the experiences that a child has had, both in the past and on that day.

Some children are pushed out of their window of tolerance easily. Everyday expectations or requests feel like threats to them, and they react accordingly to try to get away from the threat. They refuse, they shout, or they kick and punch. They use more subtle types of avoidance such as distraction. These children are pressure sensitive.

SUPERMARKET

If a child has experienced a lot of trauma and adversity, their window of tolerance will narrow and they may not be able to cope with very much at all before they get very distressed. At a more immediate level, if a child is hungry or tired, that will narrow their window of tolerance.

SCHOOL

Some children seem to be born with a narrow window of tolerance and that's clear from early on. Some babies find it particularly difficult to adjust to being in the world. They want to be close to their mother at all times, can't stay asleep alone and are rarely relaxed and calm. They need lots of active soothing, all the time. They are sometimes called 'high needs' or 'sensitive' babies. They often respond very badly to routine-driven parenting approaches.

PARK

Others have experiences that narrow their window of tolerance, and these can accumulate. These can occur very early in life; a difficult birth or early medical problems could feel very frightening to a baby who has no way to make sense of what is

HOME

happening. Lots of experiences of feeling under threat will tune your nervous system so that you develop super-sensitive threat detectors. It's a survival response, designed to keep us alive.

Children with a narrow window of tolerance are more likely to experience the world in a threatening way, which means that their already narrow window can get even smaller due to repeated experiences of feeling under threat. Mainstream parenting practices like leaving a baby to cry themselves to sleep, putting a child alone in Time Out or on the Naughty Step, telling a child off or punishing them feel unpleasant to all children – this is, after all, how they work. The idea is that the child will want those unpleasant feelings to stop, and so they will change their behaviour.

For some children, those unpleasant feelings will be intolerable. They will feel like a threat, with the result that their window of tolerance will narrow, and they will struggle more to keep their emotional balance.

This means that mainstream parenting techniques can make some children's behaviour (and emotional wellbeing) worse. They create loops, because the more their parents try, the smaller the child's window of tolerance gets.

The good news

The good news is that this is avoidable. For if mainstream parenting techniques can make a child feel under threat, and therefore make their behaviour worse, low demand parenting strategies can help a child feel safe – and (in the long term) hopefully mean that their window of tolerance can expand rather than shrink.

This has really significant implications. Because if a child spends most of their time outside their window of tolerance, they can't learn effectively. They are spending their time struggling for survival. All of their energy goes into keeping afloat. In contrast, when they are in their window of tolerance, they can learn and develop new skills. They can spend their energy doing this, instead of spending all their time in survival mode.

Remember what I said about brains and wiring? Our brains are rewiring all the time. They rewire in response to the environment and that means that there is an opportunity for parents. If we can create an environment that feels safe enough to the child, while also providing opportunities for them to experience new things and stretch their comfort zone, then their brains will gradually rewire to be less reactive. Their window of tolerance will expand and they will learn how to manage their reactions for themselves. That isn't something you can tell them to do or make them do. You can't just tell them that they are safe, even if you think they are. It's their perception that matters. What parents can do is to identify what is going on, and then create an environment that breaks the loops.

At the heart of everything in this book is this premise. We want to parent our children so that over time their capacity to manage the pressures of the world can expand rather than shrink. We want to change the environment and the way that we react so that they aren't always in survival mode. We want to break the loops that are keeping them (and you) stuck. This is the aim of low demand parenting.

Eliza and Naomi:
These books just don't apply

NAOMI: What do parents tell you that they notice when they first realise that their family is not going to work in a conventional way?

ELIZA: I think it's usually when they're getting advice about things. People telling them to do things and they know that it's not going to work.

NAOMI: It's things like, 'Have you tried the Naughty Step?' Then they know. . .

ELIZA: 'Have you tried lavender oil?'

NAOMI: 'Have you got a bedtime routine?'

ELIZA: 'Have you got a whiteboard?'

NAOMI: 'A nice bath before they go to bed'. . . and you just know every step of the way along here is going to be a struggle. I remember thinking about the Naughty Step and Time Out and I couldn't even visualise these children for whom these strategies worked.

I mean, think of what has to happen in order to use the Naughty Step. First, you've got to tell them that they're meant to be there. Then they've got to agree enough to comply and go there. Then they've got to stay there. Then they're meant to calm down. Then there was something I was told about how they're meant to stay there for the number of minutes they are old.

ELIZA: I remember seeing in a friend's house, they had a list up of things that the child had to achieve that week, and then they'd get a prize at the end of the week for doing it.

They would tick off things like laying the table. Part of me was thinking, I should be doing this, but then there was also a sense of *No way would that work*. There's a reason why we haven't tried that approach.

NAOMI: There's also guilt. A feeling of maybe that is how it's meant to be done. Maybe parenting is meant to be like that. I would read books about parenting, and they would say, 'Have the child do. . .' I'd be like, 'How do you do that? How does one *have* a child do something?'

It was like they thought you could simply say to the child, 'Do this', and the child would do it. What if the child says no?

ELIZA: I remember trying to get my baby to sleep early on, and it was like she refused. She would do anything to stop falling asleep. But then as soon as she came in the bed with me, she was like, 'I can sleep.'

NAOMI: I used to comfort myself at times like that by saying that my baby would have been the survivor if we'd been cave people. Those placid babies that apparently you can put down 'drowsy but awake' and they go to sleep, they would have been easy prey for any predatory animal.

What self-respecting baby is going to allow themselves to be put down? They can't run. They can't do anything to protect themselves. If you put them down and they stay asleep, any lion that walks past is going to be like, 'Tasty.'

ELIZA: When I was on holiday recently, I still see it. I'm sixteen years down the line and I still see things that make me go 'How?' I saw a baby on holiday completely asleep. They must have been four months old on the sun lounger.

NAOMI: I used to carry my son everywhere in a sling because that was the only place he would fall asleep. I had to be upright and walking as well. If I had to stand on the train or the bus or something, I would just have to rock the whole time because the moment I stopped, he would wake up.

ELIZA: I used to walk around and think, I wonder if I could just lie down on that bench and go to sleep. Because I knew if we tried to get home, they'd wake up.

NAOMI: You just cannot do that transition. I remember that feeling, *I've got to keep moving now because they're sleeping. The moment I stop moving, that will be over*, yet I was being told I should be putting them down. You get this sense that none of the things you're being told actually works.

ELIZA: There isn't anyone to tell you that. No one says, 'That doesn't work and you need something different.'

Too much to read, too little time?

1. Some children respond very badly to conventional parenting approaches. When parents try to be firm or strict, their child's behaviour gets worse.
2. These children can be thought of as pressure sensitive or demand avoidant.
3. Pressure sensitivity is an individual characteristic but (as with most behaviours) it is the result of an interaction between the person's genes, their environment and their past experience.
4. One way to think about pressure-sensitive children is as having a narrow window of tolerance. Maintaining an emotional balance is hard for them and they are easily pushed out of the zone in which they can keep themselves calm.
5. Many mainstream parenting techniques such as the Naughty Step or Time Out work by making children feel bad. This can result in children's windows of tolerance becoming even narrower, making everything worse.

More to read if you are interested

The Family Experience of PDA – Eliza Fricker

The Whole-Brain Child – Daniel Siegel and Tina Payne Bryson

Behavioural genetics:

Blueprint: How DNA Makes Us Who We Are – Robert Plomin

The Genetic Lottery: Why DNA Matters for Social Equality – Kathryn Paige Harden

Neurobiology:

POND study (https://pond-network.ca)

2

Parenting

In Chapter 1, I talked about children whose behaviour confuses their parents. Children who haven't read the parenting books, and for whom many of the strategies their parents use seem to make things worse. I introduced the idea of pressure sensitivity to explain these children's behaviour and introduced some code breakers to help understand what is going on. I showed how parents and children often get stuck in loops when what parents think they should be doing makes the situation worse.

In this chapter, I'm going to take a sideways step to look at parenting. What does 'parenting' really mean, and where did it come from? I'm going to talk about parenting as a cultural practice we are all immersed in, and about the social taboos that push us towards conforming – and why it feels so bad when we don't follow the rules.

Let's start by thinking about you. Why do you parent the way that you do? How do you know what to do when your child is angry, upset or unable to sleep? Do you do what your parents did with you, or did you learn it from a book or TV? How do you know if you're doing it right or wrong? Did you go on a course or join the membership of a parenting guru?

Parenting is a multi-million-pound industry (which this book is of course a part of). There are books to tell you how to get it right and how not to get it wrong. Books that claim that it's all about behaviour and books that suggest it's all about connection. There are books that are all about techniques and routines, and there are books that suggest you need to acquire a higher level of spiritual consciousness in order to be an effective parent. Some books talk about parenting as a means of self-development. All of this can put the bar very high. A good parent must be engaged, attentive, self-aware, emotionally literate – and loving every 'precious moment'. And then of course there are books on how to be the imperfect parent, how to be good enough. . . it goes on and on.

Parenting culture is so all-encompassing that it's sometimes hard to remember that 'parenting' itself is a relatively new way of thinking about the relationship between parents and children – and also that there is no worldwide consensus on what the best way to parent is. Parenting is different across cultures and across social class. And it is certainly different across time.

Parenting in the past

The world of parenting advice is a relatively new one. Before the sixteenth century, parents would probably have looked to the people around them for advice on how to care for their children. When manuals for parents started to appear, they were focused on practicalities: nutrition, hygiene and how to make sure that children developed the correct moral behaviours. As time went on, the focus shifted towards the 'scientific', with the books usually written by doctors. They advised on breast feeding and told mothers to give their children cold baths.

Early parenting books were written by men and were mostly aimed at mothers. These authors took a clearly expert position; they instructed women on the 'correct' way to bring up their children. To the modern ear, some of the advice is clearly impossible to follow – one book from 1894 tells parents to schedule their children's bowel movements and to allow two a day. I imagine the nineteenth-century mothers worrying over the long-term consequences when their child stubbornly insisted on pooing only once or three times a day.

By the early twentieth century, notions of parenting had expanded beyond children's physical wellbeing. Books started to prescribe how parents should respond to their children's behaviour and emotions. Mostly, it seems, the answer was *not* to respond – several authors recommended ignoring your child's crying, not hugging or kissing them or letting them sit on your lap.

Modern parenting culture

Up to the 1950s, most parenting advice was simply whatever the author of the book thought or perhaps had learned through having their own children. There had been very little research. This changed with the publication of psychologist Diana Baumrind's research on middle-class American families, in which she defined parenting as varying in two important ways, which she called *responsiveness* and *demandingness*.

Demandingness, as Baumrind defined it, is a measure of the amount of control that a parent has over what their child says and does. Responsiveness is about how willing a parent is to meet their child's needs and be emotionally warm with them.

Baumrind divided parenting into styles. If you do a quick internet search for 'parenting styles' you'll still find variations of her original categories everywhere. Popular magazines, medical information sites and parenting hubs all describe the same basic categories – and they'll all tell you how to be the best parent. For Baumrind didn't just describe parenting. She ranked the different styles according to how good they were for children. These are the styles Baumrind described:

Authoritarian (or strict) parenting involves high demandingness and low responsiveness. Parents who fall into this category are rigid in their approach. They may describe themselves as having 'high standards' or 'holding children accountable'. They use punishment when their children don't comply.

Permissive parenting involves low demandingness and high responsiveness. Baumrind saw these parents as overly responsive and lacking in consistent rules. Children are allowed to do what they want.

Authoritative parenting involves high demandingness and high responsiveness. This is clearly what Baumrind favours and what her research showed had the best outcomes for children. These parents are firm but not rigid and are responsive to the child's needs but still hold their boundaries.

Later researchers have added **Neglectful** parenting to the list, to reflect parents demonstrating the combination of low demandingness and low responsiveness.

Baumrind's research found that authoritative parenting had the best outcomes for young people (by which she meant things like school achievement, conforming to social norms and behaviour). She thought that the best parents had high levels of control over their children but were also warm and loving. Her values are very much of their time. She thought that spanking children wasn't detrimental if used 'correctly'.

Being a good parent

Why am I going on about an American psychologist from the 1950s? It's because her research still influences parenting culture today and almost certainly will have influenced you and the parents around you.

Baumrind's ideas saturate parenting culture in the anglophone world, reaching many people who have never heard her name. The association of good parenting with 'being in control' comes from her work. It's what most parenting experts (and parenting programmes) have suggested ever since. It's what many parents have internalised, without even realising it.

When I see a family, I sometimes ask parents what they think a good parent does. Their answers are usually very similar. They start with boundaries, meals at the table, regular bed times, not giving in to tantrums and not allowing children to 'get away' with bad behaviour. In other words, being in control. When you see someone on a Facebook group worrying that they might be a permissive parent because their screen-time boundaries aren't strict enough – that comes from Baumrind's theories.

You've probably worked out already that I'm not a great fan of Baumrind's way of thinking about parenting. She defined controlling children as an essential part of good parenting, and saw parenting as something that active parents did to their passive children. But the most problematic part of her legacy, for me, is the idea that good parents control their children, and if a child isn't 'under control' then that's because their parents aren't doing it right.

The control paradigm of parenting

Baumrind defined controlling a child as a good thing, no matter what behaviour was being controlled. She didn't discriminate between small things like controlling where a child sits or what they wear and big things like stopping them from running in front of a car or hitting other people. All of them come under 'being under control'. You can see the echoes of this today in the way that some schools control children's behaviour. They focus on the small things – black ankle socks or how you sit in your chair – in the belief that if a child gets used to these details being controlled it will make it easier to control the big things. In this paradigm, control is good for children. The challenge of parenting is simply how best to ensure that control while still remaining warm and loving. End of story.

Science has moved on since the 1950s, and we now know a lot more about the long-term effects of being controlled. A large number of psychology studies have found that removing choices and autonomy from children has long-term effects on the quality of their motivation and learning (if you're interested in knowing more, *Drive* by Daniel Pink is a good place to start).

Another way in which science has moved on is that we now know a lot more about child development. Baumrind saw parenting as something parents 'do' to children. Children were the product, while parenting was the process. The children didn't have much influence in how that happened. They were essentially the raw materials, to be trained and moulded. This doesn't actually fit with more recent scientific discoveries – of which more later.

Baumrind's research doesn't account for the child who does not comply with authoritative parenting. In fact, there isn't really a role for the child at all, except as a passive recipient of the parenting. If a child isn't complying, all that Baumrind's theory offers is to try harder with the same strategies. Firmer and even more consistent. More control.

The long term impact of this is that many parents are ashamed when they find that mainstream parenting strategies aren't working for them and their children. They feel that this must be a failure on their part, particularly when their children don't conform to the sorts of outcomes that other parents look for. Compliant, 'well-behaved', easy-going, high-achieving. . . all of these characteristics in a child are likely to gain praise for parents. And the opposite – well, you can guess. Or maybe you know already from experience.

I'll use the shorthand Good Parenting™ throughout this book to refer to the culturally accepted norms around parenting we all pick up, and which you will become very quickly aware of when you break them. I'll do this to hopefully make it clear that I do not think this is really 'good parenting', but it's the sort of performative parenting that gets approval from others. Setting strict boundaries, telling your child off, insisting on sharing, reading to your child every night, controlling what they eat and their use of screens are just some of the ways in which Good Parenting™ shows up.

Good Parenting™ is the type of parenting most people do without even questioning. It's what was done to them and they have never thought too deeply about it. It's the type of parenting it's assumed we all agree is right. Even in the supermarket queue when a child is having a meltdown.

Social norms and transgressions

Cultural practices like parenting are based on social norms. Things that 'we all do' (even if we don't really). Things that we learn from the world around us. Good Parenting™ means conforming to the social norms of whatever culture you are in. In the UK and the USA (and much of the anglophone world), this means controlling children.

Culture is maintained through social pressure. A lot of that is silent. It's there in the way we dress, the way we are in public, the way we talk to other people. Some things are socially acceptable, others are not. Culture is invisible to those who are immersed in it. It's just 'the way that things are'. It becomes visible when you go to another country and discover that they do things differently. Suddenly you are wearing the wrong clothes, talking and eating in the wrong way.

When we moved to France, one parenting difference I noticed immediately was mealtimes. English families generally feed their children early, at around 5 or 6 p.m. In France no one eats their evening meal before 7 and the parents of my children's friends looked askance when I asked them if they wanted me to feed their eight-year-old before they were picked up at 6.30. They have a 'goûter' (snack) when they come back from school and then they wait until later. I soon learned to stop asking and to fend off my own children's hunger until after they had gone. The French cultural practice of eating late is embedded in their society – restaurants typically don't open until 7 or later. If you want to eat early, you'll have to do it at home.

Social pressure to conform is generally invisible until you (or your child) break the rules. Then the tutting starts. In parenting culture, it is socially acceptable to tell another person to comply with the Good Parenting™ rules, but not to ask that they don't. This leads to the situation where it is socially acceptable for someone to tell a parent to be more controlling (as in 'Get your child under control') – but much less so to tell another parent to be less controlling.

How does this play out? When a child comes round for a playdate, it's not uncommon for their parents to state some rules the hosting parent is obliged to follow – perhaps only thirty minutes of screen time, or no sugary snacks. That is not socially transgressive. In contrast, I'm yet to meet a parent brave enough to say 'I'd appreciate it if you don't expect them to say please or thank you and by the way they only eat pudding' even when they know that the child will find the playdate hard and that those things might help. That would be socially taboo, and the parent of the other child would react accordingly. That child probably wouldn't get invited round again and their parent might be whispered about in the playground.

When everyone around you is doing Good Parenting™ it's hard to do something different. It feels transgressive. You are breaking social taboos. You can expect funny looks and raised eyebrows. Just try not telling your toddler off in the playground when they next push someone else off the swings for a practical demonstration of this. Telling off is (in many cultures) one of the ways we recognise a Good Parent™, even if the telling off has no effect whatsoever and in fact makes everything worse as the toddler reacts by having a meltdown and pushing several more children off the slide before you can catch them. Good Parenting™ is about doing what other people and the culture around you think you should be doing.

Exercise: The rules of Good Parenting™

What do Good Parents™ do in your culture? How is it expected that parents will behave?

Spend some time thinking about the ways in which others expect you to parent, and the things people feel able to say about parenting. You could think specifically about the following areas (and feel free to add your own). The aim of this exercise is to spend some time making the invisible visible. Think about the rules 'everyone knows'.

Food
How are parents expected to behave around food? What is the 'ideal child' when it comes to food?

Sleep
What are the expectations around sleep? When is a child meant to sleep alone and how should this be achieved?

Behaviour
What do Good Parents™ in your culture do when their child isn't behaving well? How do the children of Good Parents™ behave?

Relationships
How are children meant to react to other people? How are Good Parents™ meant to facilitate that? What is considered rude for a child? Is it possible for adults to be rude to children?

Education
How do Good Parents™ relate to their child's school? How do the children of Good Parents™ perform at school?

A common part of parenting culture is the idea that a parent can be judged by their child's behaviour – by how well they are 'under control' in fact. If your child is behaving 'badly', you will be quickly judged for it, particularly if you are their mother. Even in adulthood, if an adult does something terrible, questions are often asked about what their upbringing was like, and their mothers are assumed to be to blame.

Of course the relationship between parents and children is crucially important in child development. Of course what parents do matters and of course a difficult upbringing can have long-term effects. Having a stable loving home is really important for children. There is, however, something missing in the way that we understand Good Parenting™.

That something is the child. Parenting is talked about as if it is a process of moulding children, rather as if they were empty vessels or lumps of clay. Good Parents™ have 'good' (read: compliant, high achieving and calm) children. Get the parenting right, and you'll get the best possible outcome. Just get them under control (while also showing them that you love them) and all will be well.

Children create the world they live in

Did you know that how much TV your child (or you) watches is influenced by their genes?

One of the most intriguing scientific findings in recent years is that our environment is genetically influenced. Things like whether a person gets married, or how many video games they play, are influenced by their genes. You might be thinking that sounds impossible – but it's only impossible if you see a person as a passive recipient of their environment.

Imagine if you have two children, both with free access to a television. One of them loves to watch documentaries and spends hours every day absorbed. The other is far more interested in outside play, and while they occasionally glance at the TV, they would rather go to the adventure playground than sit and watch a show. They spend hours bouncing on a trampoline. The difference between those children will be at least partially genetic. They interact with the world around them in different ways because of their genetic make-up. More than that, their development and learning will now be affected by the environment they have created for themselves – one learns all about whales and wildlife, while the other learns how to do the monkey bars and turn somersaults.

Recent behavioural genetic research indicates that children bring much more to the table than was previously thought. They are not blank slates in any sense of the word. Studies have consistently found that many more things have a genetic influence than we realise. Individual differences between people matter, and each unique child will interact with their environment in a different way. People create their environments.

You can probably think of some ways in which your child has created an environment for themselves. It happens right from early childhood. Children change the environment around them to suit their interests and preferences. One child is interested in diggers, and they manage to persuade the adults around them to take them to visit diggers and to read books and sing them songs about diggers. Their environment is full of diggers and this influences their experience of life. Another child might find diggers totally boring, and instead want to spend all their time with cats – and responsive adults will help them do that. They learn a lot about animal care while the other child is learning about machinery. Environmental differences come about in response to individual differences in children – and those environmental differences then change how the child develops and what they learn. Children are active participants in changing the behaviour of those around them, and changing their environment. This is called 'bidirectionality' in psychology.

Parenting is something else that children influence. Children interact with their parents, and this affects the parenting they receive.

Just think of the difference between a baby who suffers from colic for the first three months of life and cries constantly, compared to a calm and placid baby who sleeps easily and rarely cries. Their parents will have a very different experience of early parenthood. They will feel very differently about their parenting ability – and they are likely to have very different quantities of sleep, which will affect how they are with the baby.

This means that the parenting a child receives is not solely down to decisions made by their parents. It is also down to the child and how they respond to their environment. The causal relationship goes both ways.

This is something that is not captured by parenting styles. Maybe those children who got authoritative (supposedly ideal) parenting were those who were naturally quite cooperative and compliant, and that's why their parents were able to be authoritative, rather than the authoritative parenting causing their children's temperaments. Maybe many parents 'choose' (or more likely, find) their parenting style in response to their child's differences, rather than their child's differences being a result of their parenting style. Just like in the diagram. Parents influence their children but children also influence their parents.

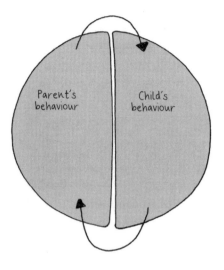

Why am I going on about this? It's because the belief that parents (although let's be honest, it's usually mothers rather than fathers) cause their children to be a certain way through their parenting is deeply rooted in the way that we see the parent–child relationship in Western society. If a person grows up to commit terrible crimes, people ask what their mother did wrong. If a child is behaving in a challenging way, parents feel blamed by both professionals and other parents. And those whose children are calm and compliant often assume that it's due to their parenting. This starts from babyhood, when those whose babies are sleeping through the night and playing independently are prone to give advice to others, assuming that it must be due to their parenting rather than due to their having got lucky with their child's individual temperament.

This is deeply frustrating for parents of children who are not calm and compliant, because they can find themselves immersed in blame. Not only is their child very clearly not 'under control', they are not performing the cultural expectations of Good Parenting™ – and it's assumed that this is the reason that their child isn't under control.

The suggestion that it must be something they are doing wrong is everywhere, from the raised eyebrows at the supermarket to the play workers at Stay and Play asking if they've tried a sticker chart or Time Out.

(Not) producing the ideal child

In the last couple of decades, books and courses on different approaches to parenting have proliferated. Attachment parenting, gentle parenting, peaceful parenting, tiger parenting, free-range parenting – there is a bewildering array of information for the sleep-deprived new parent. Some of them can be really helpful. However, they often contain the same assumptions – that parenting is something that parents do to children (rather than *with* children) and that parents can mould their child into the person they were hoping for by getting the parenting right.

The values are still outcome focused. Many attachment parents hope to create emotionally secure and happy young people, and it can be a shock when their child is highly anxious or apparently lacking in confidence. There is a logic (often unstated) that goes like this: *children brought up this way will become this type of person.* Many approaches to parenting have assumptions about what 'all children need', whether that is lots of time outdoors, long-term breastfeeding or strict boundaries and routines.

This has unforeseen consequences. One is that parents believe the rhetoric, and are bemused when their child is not turning out as expected – and they usually blame themselves for not having parented 'correctly' or been consistent enough. They go back through their past, worrying about their traumatic birth, difficulty with breastfeeding or the arrival of their sister when they were two. Many parents worry incessantly about things that they (might) have got wrong as parents. Which makes them susceptible to those who promise ways to get it right.

Selling solutions

Felicia was pregnant with her second child when she decided to do a hypnobirthing course. Her first birth had been a traumatic emergency caesarean and she wanted to have a different experience this time around.

As she sat in the hypnobirthing class, she started to feel guilty. The hypnobirthing material said that a baby born in a calm and drug-free way (which hypnobirthing promised was possible) would be peaceful and serene, having not experienced a medicalised birth. Their first experience of life would be of gentle love and care, not the bright lights of an operating room.

Felicia looked around at the other mothers. They were all first-timers and they were nodding. They were imagining how calm their newborns would be after their peaceful births.

Felicia started to feel tearful. Her older child had never been calm and serene, not for a moment. Not even in the middle of the night. He had required constant holding for most of the first year of his life and as a two-year-old was what is somewhat euphemistically called 'a handful'. He had had one of the most medicalised births possible as Felicia had had an emergency caesarean and had been required to stay in hospital for two weeks afterwards. Maybe it was all my fault, Felicia thought. Maybe I've damaged my child for life because I didn't use hypnobirthing the first-time round.

She felt so awful about it that she started to find the hypnobirthing materials triggering. She was meant to lie and listen to the meditations, imagining the baby being born calmly and naturally. All she could think was, What if I'd refused to go to the hospital the first time round? Maybe he would have been born in a different way and maybe everything would be easier for him now. Maybe I've ruined his life.

Of course, there are many different things that could have happened for Felicia, and it might be true that the birth of her first child could have gone differently and been less traumatic. It's also true that it could have been worse. While Felicia was imagining this ideal alternative scenario where her baby's birth was natural and drug-free, there is an alternative scenario in which he or she was permanently physically damaged by his birth, or even where one of them did not survive it. She can't ever know which of those scenarios might have played out if she'd made different decisions or paid for particular courses. The one thing that is sure is that there are no guarantees in childbirth, just as there are none in parenting.

Those hypnobirthing books are marketing materials. They have a product to sell, and they are using parental anxiety to sell it. That doesn't mean hypnobirthing or other techniques can't be helpful or useful. They can be. But there is always a flip side to these marketing promises, because for every product that promises a result there is another, often unstated, message, 'if you don't buy our product, you won't get that result', and even worse (and what Felicia is picking up on), 'if you haven't had that result, it's because you didn't buy our product.'

Sometimes the hard sell is more explicit. I've seen adverts on Facebook for extremely expensive parenting courses that tell you that if you really cared about your child, you'd pay them thousands of pounds because you can't put a price on their happiness. Some of them even imply that if you don't pay for their course, your child might harm themselves, and you'll regret not spending the money. They play on parents' wishes to get parenting right and their love for their child.

These are sales techniques. No one can guarantee a specific outcome for your child. If they claim that they can (and particularly if they want you to pay them a lot of money for it), be suspicious.

When Good Parenting™ meets a pressure-sensitive child

Good Parenting™ is a control-based paradigm of parenting. Parents are told that in order to parent well, they must get their child under control. Pressure-sensitive children respond very badly to being controlled. And the worse they react, the more their parents are told to get them under control.

This is never going to go well.

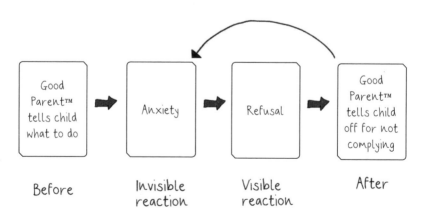

Here's a BIVA code breaker from Chapter 1 to show what happens when Good Parenting™ meets a pressure-sensitive child. There's a clash and very quickly everyone is stuck in a loop that becomes a trap.

And when there's a trap, all the effort everyone puts in just makes things worse.

A control-based parenting paradigm can't work with children who are sensitive to pressure. They need something different.

A paradigm shift

Good Parenting™ culture is all around us. Doing something different feels transgressive. You break social taboos all over the place – and people will show you that they noticed. But some children show us loud and clear that they need a different approach.

The question is, what does that different approach look like?

In the rest of this book, I'm going to explain something known as 'low demand parenting'. Low demand parenting steps away from the control paradigm. It rejects the idea that control over children is the ideal. Control is sometimes necessary for safety, particularly with small children, but it shouldn't be a way of life. It isn't good in and of itself.

Rather than behaviour being something to control, in low demand parenting we see behaviour as a communication of how the child is doing. A happy child is easier to live with, but it's not because they are 'under control'. A child will be easier to live with when they are surrounded by people they feel safe with and who understand them and when their needs are met. That is where low demand parenting starts.

Low demand parenting puts relationships and flexibility first, even when a child's behaviour is very challenging. Just as I talked about in Chapter 1, the aim is to help children stay in their window of tolerance so that they can learn and flourish. It is suitable for any child, but it is particularly useful with those who are sensitive to pressure or demand avoidant. For them, the control paradigm simply does not work.

The bad news? Low demand parenting cannot promise any particular outcome. Definitely not obedience or compliance. However, the hope is that you will find a happier and more balanced way to live with your child, and that this will have long-term benefits for you all.

Eliza and Naomi:
What's the right thing to do?

NAOMI: Hi Eliza. What do you think a Good Parent™ is in our culture?

ELIZA: A parent that is boundaried and consistent. Firm but fair. Doesn't spoil them. Doesn't give in.

NAOMI: Doesn't allow kids too much leeway, but is loving while they do it. Setting and holding those loving boundaries. That's tricky when your child makes it really clear that they don't think those boundaries are loving.

ELIZA: They make that clear quite early on.

NAOMI: Loudly.

ELIZA: There's a strong narrative about parenting that feels universal. I don't think you hear of other things.

You wouldn't go to your playgroup and say, 'It's great, she's sleeping with us every night.' The thing that would be celebrated is that they're sleeping through the night in another room.

NAOMI: Your early experience of parenting can just be a feeling of failure, can't it? It's like all these milestones that you're meant to have done, getting them to go to sleep by themselves. They're sitting there and saying, 'Put them down, drowsy but awake.'

ELIZA: I think there's a strong parenting narrative that is celebrated very early on that is seemingly a universal one.

NAOMI: Yes, it feels like everybody knows that this is what good parenting is. If you're not doing it, you are a bad parent. The thing about this idea of good parenting is it ignores the interactive relationship. Really, I think that good parenting happens *with* the child rather being something you do *to* the child.

ELIZA: Because the child isn't mentioned in this. They're all meant to respond the same way. Even though they're all products of their own cultural environment. They're meant to be this neutral thing that reacts exactly the same way every time.

NAOMI: It's as if there's a guarantee. If you do the right parenting, you'll get the right outcome. Which makes it really hard because it means when you do something different, people say, 'Well, aren't you worried that they're never going to do these things?' Low demand parenting really steps out of the main parenting paradigm because most of mainstream parenting is about effectively controlling your child.

With low demand parenting, we step out of that and we're like, 'Maybe the question shouldn't be *how do I control my child*? Maybe instead it should be about getting the environment right so this child can thrive.' Unfortunately, that doesn't really fit with mainstream parenting ideas at all.

ELIZA: I think for me, it wasn't about thriving. Thriving was later when I realised that we were creating something more than just getting by. At the beginning it was that we couldn't sustain the misery. It was, 'We can't live being this miserable and having this fractious existence.'

NAOMI: Survival, really.

ELIZA: I don't think we were thinking of it in terms of thriving.

NAOMI: I think most parents are trying to find a way that works, but we are hemmed in by the societal expectations of what we should be doing.

It's like, 'We found this way that works, we're sleeping with our baby, but now that's a bad thing. We shouldn't be doing that.' Or 'We found this way, we feed them to sleep. We shouldn't be doing that.' It's like everything that works, you're told that it's not what you should be doing, which means you just continually feel terrible.

How do you think low demand parenting is different?

ELIZA: I think low demand parenting is really ripping the old book up. It's listening to your instinct with your child and what feels right for them. It's about connection with them and their needs. It's about the evenness of us and our response to whatever is thrown at us.

It's listening to what our children are seeking first and foremost.

NAOMI: It's what makes them feel safe. It's our presence and emotional consistency rather than consistency of imposing stuff on them.

Too much to read, too little time?

1. Parenting culture is all around us, but it's only when you break some of the rules that you become really aware of it. As a shorthand, I have called this Good Parenting™ (the "™" is to make it clear that I do not really think this is good parenting or works for everyone).

2. Diana Baumrind carried out hugely influential parenting research which found that parenting fell into three main types: authoritarian; authoritative; and permissive. Authoritative was her preference and that is what her research found was best. (Just in case it isn't clear, I don't agree with Baumrind's way of seeing parenting.)

3. Good Parenting™ culture tends to focus on the child as a passive recipient of parenting. A Good Parent™ has their child 'under control'.

4. Research shows that children affect their parents' behaviour as well as parents affecting their children's behaviour.

5. Parenting in a way that falls outside the Good Parenting™ norm is socially transgressive and will often provoke the judgement of others.

More to read if you are interested

Dream Babies: Childcare Advice from John Locke to Gina Ford – Christina Hardyment

The Myth of the Spoiled Child: Challenging the Conventional Wisdom about Children and Parenting – Alfie Kohn

Unequal Childhoods: Class, Race and Family Life – Annette Lareau

3

The Principles of
Low Demand Parenting

HUMOUR
COLLABORATION
ACTIVE INVOLVEMENT
ENVIRONMENT
RELATIONSHIPS

Right, you may be thinking. This is all very well. You (and my child) have convinced me that we need something different, but how does that actually work? What do we do?

There's a certain irony at the heart of this book. The very nature of low demand parenting is being responsive to your individual child, rather than applying a set of rules – and this doesn't lend itself well to a manual. Certainly not to prescriptive lists or techniques. What works with one child may not work with another and you will need to be open to experimentation. Lots of the things I talk about in this book might not be problems for you – in which case, that's great. There's no need to change something that's working.

Low demand parenting is fundamentally a change in mindset. Rather than thinking about how to change our children, we need to start by thinking about how to get the circumstances right for them to thrive. A flexible responsiveness to the individual child is at the heart of it all. One good metaphor for this is to think of parenting as analogous to gardening.

Mainstream parenting techniques (and Good Parenting™) are typically outcome focused. They are about how to mould the child into the product you want – how to get them to be obedient, academic high achievers, social, articulate, well-behaved, well-rounded – all the things that parents want for their children. Do *this*, parents are told, and the result will be *that*. You can grow the children you want, in exactly the place you want, and they will turn out how you imagined.

This takes a lot of ongoing effort. You plant the seeds, but then you need to keep guiding the growth in the way that you want it to go. Maybe you want the plant to grow around a trellis, and so you're tying branches to the frame and clipping off the parts that are growing in the opposite direction. A lot of the job of Good Parenting™ is to try to get children to do an increasing amount of this work for you – you have the vision, but you want them to carry it out. You'd like them to do their homework without fuss, to help clear the table willingly and to stop hitting their siblings. You'd like them to cooperate with your plans. Parents often come to me frustrated. 'Why won't they just do what I ask!?' they ask.

It's as if parents are there in the garden, and they have this amazing vision for the future. They want the plant (or child) to be the most beautiful ever. Perfectly suited to the surroundings, healthy, lustrous, a perfect specimen in every way. Why can't the child see that this is such a great plan and get on board? Why can't we all work together? Why can't the children see that you just want the best for them?

The problem is that this is a child, not a plant. There's a crucial difference between plants and children. You don't get to choose your child nor their characteristics – and nor does the child come labelled with whether they prefer a shady or sunny spot. While you can go to the garden centre and decide that you want to plant daffodils rather than geraniums, with a baby you don't get offered the different seed bags so you can pick the child you planned. As you have probably already discovered, children have their own minds and their own opinions. They are born with their own genetic make-up, their own temperament, and while you can try to provide the best opportunity for them to thrive, exactly what that looks like will be to a large extent determined by the child's unique characteristics. If your child is an orchid they are never going to grow into a carnation (and you can do a lot of damage trying to make them do so). Of course, perhaps the hardest part is that no one is going to tell you what works best for your unique child. You have to work that out for yourself.

One of the hardest lessons of parenting is that what your child wants for their life matters more than what you want. Even if you think they are making a terrible mistake. Not just that, but sometimes what you want can get in the way of your child working out what they want if it feels like pressure.

When the vision of the child you imagined you'd have looms larger in your mind than the actual child you have, then you're going to run into trouble at some point. This is a natural part of parenting, and while for some it happens in babyhood, for others it doesn't happen until their children reach their twenties or even later.

When you can't let go of the ideal child, then the vision of the child you wanted is going to blot out the child you really have. They'll get in the way, as you imagine life in this other universe where your child is a different person. It's like having a shadow child, a 'might have been' – and it's deeply unhelpful to think about your child in this way. Your child is the person they are, and the job of the parent is to help them to thrive in the best way that they can, not to make them into someone else.

Come back to the gardening analogy. Good parenting™ can be like cutting and pruning in order to shape a plant into the form you wanted – like topiary. It's all about what it looks like on the outside. You're moulding and shaping the perfect child. If you could only get them to agree and stop complaining.

Low demand parenting starts from a different place. It begins with recognising that each child is different, experiences the world in a different way and needs different things. While parents can do a lot to give their children opportunities and love, the evidence from large-scale genetic studies seems to show that they don't actually do very much to fundamentally change who their children turn out to be, what they are good at and the preferences they have. We talk about parenting as something parents do to children, but low demand parenting sees it as something that happens in the interaction between the parent and the child. When parenting is going well, it's responsive to the individual. It's different for different children, even in the same family.

Getting kids under control

Good Parenting™ is controlling. The parent knows what outcome they want (even if they don't admit it), and they keep pushing (or coaxing, or nudging) the child in that direction. This pressure can take all sorts of forms. Some parents are very explicit about it and tell their children (for example) that they expect them to do well at school and they will punish them if they don't measure up, or they'll reward them for getting good grades. Or the pressure can take the more subtle form of showing interest and approval only when children do the things that their parents want them to do – for instance providing money for swimming lessons or helping with piano practice – but saying that video games are a waste of time, and refusing to buy new games or play with the child.

The explicit type of control is obvious, and many children pick up on it early on. They either go with it or they fight back. The more subtle type of pressure takes a bit longer for some of them to notice and it sneaks past many as children. Being controlled is just how things are, it doesn't occur to some children that things could be different. Then when they are teenagers, many of them start to resent it and to resist.

Some children – and you may well have one of these if you are reading this book – see through all these types of control from early on and refuse to play their role. These children can detect controlling agendas a mile away. Controlling parenting (even subtly controlling) just flat out doesn't work when children refuse to cooperate. Because it turns out that while you can make your child very unhappy if they don't do what you want, you can't actually control them if they refuse to let you (beyond a few circumstances when they are small and portable, like picking them up when they are about to run into the road).

The children who refuse to be controlled often seem impervious to disapproval and just keep on playing video games when told that if they don't stop now, there'll be no supper. They are the ones who get up off the Naughty Step and walk off. Coming back to the garden metaphor, these are the plants who keep growing in unexpected ways, and won't bend in the way they are being pushed and prodded. They keep breaking free of the twine that's being used to tie them to the trellis.

Most parenting starts with the question 'How do I get them to do this?' Low demand parenting starts with 'How can I help them to flourish?' – and that means, 'How can I provide the right circumstances for growth?'

This is all about getting the environment in the garden right. The right amount of water, sunlight, soil, fertiliser, preventing cats from scratching the bark off. . . all of that. Getting the environment right, and then trusting that the plants will grow without a lot of micro-intervention.

Putting in the groundwork

In Chapter 1, I introduced the BIVA code breaker, a way of understanding what is going on in specific situations and how things might be getting stuck. BIVA is about the in-the-moment problems and identifying traps. It's not enough, however, to focus only on the things that are going wrong. That can feel relentless, as you lurch from problem to problem. Low demand parenting works on two levels: the moments and the background. The background is the conditions in the garden, which require ongoing maintenance. The moments are reacting to things happening in real time – like the time that a large bush in my back garden pulled the fence over and uprooted itself during a storm. I had to do something to get it back into the ground and repair the fence. This means that as well as changing how you respond to the moments, you need to be cultivating a low demand atmosphere in your house. For this, there are some general principles. These are the fundamentals of low demand parenting. The groundwork. These are not problem- or solution-focused. They are positive. They are about making the atmosphere in your home a nurturing one.

There are five essential principles to our low demand parenting approach – Relationships, Environment, Active involvement, Collaboration and Humour – and we've put them together to make the acronym REACH. Hopefully, they will enable you to reach your child and work together with them, rather than continuously fighting against them.

The idea is that by creating a nurturing and low demand environment, the child will feel safe enough to grow, develop and learn. This takes a strong nerve on the part of parents, because we're told that parenting is all about getting them 'under control'. We're told that children feel safe when their parents set them 'firm boundaries' and are 'consistent' (both often really meaning 'inflexible'). Maybe some of them do, or maybe they just give up protesting when they realise that there is no point and we mistake their silence for feeling safe.

Just think about yourself for a moment. Do you feel safest and happiest when you're with a boss who decides what you are meant to do and says 'no exceptions' when you ask for some flexibility about picking up your child from school – and who makes sure there are consequences if you're late to work? Or are you happier when you have a boss you think values you, believes in you and you know will work with you to create a flexible way of working?

Giving up that need to control feels hard until you realise that control over another person is an illusion. For the most part, we can't control our children, and nor should we hope to do that for their whole lives. Even those children who appear to be under control as young children are going to wake up one day and realise that they want to make their own decisions. If they don't, then there will be trouble down the line when they reach early adulthood with very little idea of what they want for themselves, but lots of hang-ups about what others want them to do.

We want them to learn to take control of their own lives, while we create a safe enough environment for them to grow in.

In the next section of this chapter, we'll talk you through the five REACH principles and what the key mindset shifts are as you move towards low demand parenting. These principles are the groundwork, no matter what situation you are dealing with.

Relationships

Most parent–child relationships are based on conditionality. Parents say to their children, 'If you do this, then I'll do this.'

'If you hit your sister, I'll put you on the Naughty Step.'
'If you do well in your test, I'll buy you a present.'
'If you don't put your shoes on now, we won't get ice cream.'

The hidden (and often unspoken) part is what the child is meant to do next – which is change. The whole point of things like the Naughty Step, or rewards like ice cream, is to change the child's behaviour.

Many parents think that this is what they are meant to do in order to be a Good Parent™, and many parenting programmes and books reinforce this. I've even met parents who have their children on 'clicker training' programmes – they click a clicker when their child does something good in order to 'reinforce the behaviour', like you might when training a dog to perform tricks. Enough clicks of the clicker, and the child gets a prize. Not enough clicks, and they lose something they value, like time on a games console.

This perspective sees the job of parents as moulding the child through their interactions, nudging them towards being harder working, sticking at things rather than giving up, being more resilient – the list goes on and on. It's that perfect child again, always in the distance. If only they'd just be a little bit more. . .

All of this can be very tiring (and upsetting) for any parent. It's particularly difficult when a child doesn't fit into the path laid out by their parents. Life can become an endless series of the child not quite measuring up, not quite doing well enough, and of the parent always seeming slightly disappointed. Children hear a lot of negative messages about themselves as their parents try to nudge them into line. It's not unusual to hear a string of comments from parents with their young children out in public.

'Stop that.'
'Come here now and stop annoying her.'
'Why did you have to do that?'

'Now look what you've done!'
'Honestly, you are so forgetful you'd forget your own head!'
'Just sit still for a moment, can't you?'
'What is wrong with you?! Stop it now.'

Children hear a stream of correction from the adults in their lives and those whose behaviour is disruptive or hard to manage hear it more. They hear that they are a problem, that they aren't doing well enough – and they believe it. What we hear as a child can stay with us for life.

So how could this be different? The opposite of a conditional relationship is unconditional positive regard, an idea Carl Rogers, the founder of person-centred (or humanistic) therapy, put at the heart of his therapeutic approach. The idea is that there is something very powerful about knowing that someone has your back, *no matter what you do*. They will continue to look upon you in a positive way, even when you do something terrible.

This unconditional positive regard is a fundamental part of low demand parenting. Love is not withdrawn because of the child's behaviour. In fact, we assume that they need the love most when they are at their worst. Children often show us how much they need love by engaging in their most terrible behaviour.

The low demand approach requires a leap of faith. It means stepping away from using your relationship as a means to change or train the child, and instead focusing on establishing emotional safety and trust. This means that the child needs to know that you've got their back and that they are a worthwhile person, whether they have failed their science exam or marched out of their tennis lesson. Or even punched someone in the head.

This doesn't mean that you need to agree with them, or condone their behaviour. It doesn't mean you should pretend you haven't noticed that they punched someone. Unconditional positive regard does not mean that you lose your ability to stand up for yourself, or to say what you think. It just means that the first step should be understanding and empathy, rather than reminding them of what they haven't done or how they haven't measured up.

Building lasting relationships

A useful rule of thumb here is to remember that this relationship is going to be one of the most important relationships in your life as well as your child's life. It will (hopefully) outlast all the other relationships they have outside the family. Whatever school thinks, whatever other parents in the playground think, is less important than the relationship with your child. Other parents may tut when you don't lay down the law, but the question to ask yourself is what is going to build your relationship with your child more. In ten years' time you're unlikely to have much contact with the tutting parents, but you hope that your child will still be a major part of your life.

Mindset shift

Instead of 'I'll be nice to you when you're nice to me', try 'I'm here for you, whatever you do.'

Environment

For many children who don't respond to mainstream parenting techniques, there is a knock-on effect. Their world gets smaller and less interesting. They won't put their shoes on to go to the park, so they don't go to the park. Managing their interactions with other children is hard, and so their parents stop inviting them round. If they have trouble attending school their parents may be told to make their life at home less interesting – with the result that they become chronically bored and under-stimulated.

Very soon, their world becomes more limited – sometimes even limited to a corner of the front room or their bedroom, but even if it's not that extreme, there are fewer opportunities in their life. It's hard to go places, so you don't go. Each awful trip to a local attraction rules that place out for the future, and soon your local community is mostly full of places you can't go to because of what happened last time.

This isn't enough. Even if your child is refusing to do anything else, it's not enough. Children need opportunities to grow into. There need to be interesting and varied things happening around them for them to learn even if right now they are not ready to engage. This is tough for parents because it can mean steeling yourself for rejection, turned down suggestions and outings that end with no one getting out of the car at the car park. The way to help you here is to start to see making the offer as enough, even if it's turned down or doesn't actually work.

The environment needs to provide opportunities, particularly if your child can't currently leave the house, or comply with the rules for a game. To achieve this, parents need to think about how their child is right now, and make that their starting point.

Bringing the world to them

When children find life hard, a lot of parenting ends up being focused on 'if only they could do X, then we'd be able to do Y.' Families can exist in a sort of suspended animation, waiting for the day when things will be different. Children who can't do X end up missing out on things they might enjoy, because of the barriers that mean they can't access it.

Low demand parenting means we need to try to break that link. We need to work on the environment right now, and work out how to make it more interesting. Parents tell me they worry that if they make home too comfortable, children will never leave, and so they avoid doing things that could enhance the environment at home. They say they don't play video games or buy new games for their child, because they want them to do things that aren't on a screen.

I think this is a mistake. When children are unhappy and bored, they are less likely to want to do things – so making them more unhappy and bored is likely to keep them stuck rather than persuading them to change things.

Parents need to think of ways to create an environment of opportunities, whenever possible without conditions like 'We've got to go out for that' or 'You've got to behave for that.' It means starting where the child is, and working on making that more exciting. It might mean working out ways that you can visit venues when they are quieter – going to outdoor attractions in the rain, for example, or going at unusual times of day. It means finding the things that they really love, and doing more of them. Some families have bought annual passes so that they can go somewhere just for the last hour of the day, when things are getting quieter and others are leaving.

If the child really dislikes leaving the house, this means bringing things into the house. That could include people as well as things. Other adults, if other children are too much to manage. Some parents ask relatives to come and spend regular time with their child; others might have friends who have some time. Sometimes these other adults can be people who are ostensibly music teachers, sports coaches or tutors – but really, their role as another involved and interested adult is just as important as their role as a teacher.

Ways to enrich children's lives when going out is hard	
Physical activity	Gorilla gyms, mini-trampolines, exercise balls, door frame swings, soft play and sofa dens in the front room.
Social relationships	People who can come and take an interest in your child – relatives, coaches, tutors. Some families have even recruited older teenage volunteers from local schools to come and spend time with children who have few friends their own age.
Intellectual activities	Board games, video games, books, online escape rooms, word puzzles, podcasts, TV shows, documentaries, Dungeons and Dragons, coding.
Sensory activities	Various bath concoctions, experimental cookery, slime making, paddling pools, kinetic sand/sand play, water play.
Creative activities	Making music using apps, musical instruments, listening to music, art apps, art materials, YouTube art videos, creative writing prompts.
Peers	Online gaming, board games, familiar visitors (if they can manage, with spaces to retreat to).

Many parents make their houses into places that look quite different to a conventional set-up: pull-up bars in the doorways, mini trampolines in the sitting room, wobble boards in the kitchen. Ordering subscription boxes can mean that something interesting arrives in the post. (Although for some children, the arrival of these boxes can feel like pressure and so they won't open them. You might need to order a subscription box for you, and open it yourself.)

The aim is to create an environment where it's easy to stay active, eat well and do interesting things – even if your child finds it hard to stop playing video games or do new things. Break the connection between 'you have to do this, so that we can do interesting things' and work out how to bring interesting things to them, wherever they are.

It is normal for pressure-sensitive children to refuse all suggestions, particularly if you are new to low demand parenting. They don't yet know that they are truly able to say no, and so they defensively say no to everything (more about this in the next chapter). That means that sometimes reading a table of ideas can be a dispiriting experience, as you think, Oh, they'll just say no to all of that. Part of low demand parenting is that while you need to respect those 'no's, you also need to keep opportunities open. Just because it's a no today doesn't mean it will be a no forever.

Your task here is to make your home environment interesting and reduce barriers, so that it is easy for children to try something new. At first that might involve doing things yourself, without the expectation that they will join in.

Mindset shift

Instead of *'If you can't behave, we can't do that'*, try *'Let's make life more interesting and do things together, no matter how you behave.'*

Active involvement

Much of low demand parenting involves *not* doing things other parents do. Not putting pressure on, not setting conditions, not using rewards and punishments. Instead of 'telling off', parents focus on adjusting expectations so that the child can meet them.

That can leave many parents wondering what they actually *do* do. What is parenting, if it's not this process of nudging and pushing children into compliance? Some parents back off so far that they aren't really involved in their children's lives at all. It's low demand all right – but it's achieved through nothing very much happening at all. Parents say that their children sit in the living room all day, hardly talking – or their teenagers spend the days shut in their bedrooms and they've given up.

Sometimes it is important to have a time of recovery like this when there are really no demands at all, but in the longer term it isn't enough. You need to keep on expanding the world and working out ways in which you can help them to come out of their comfort zone so that they can get the experiences they need in order to learn.

This means meeting children where they are, whether that means playing *Plants vs Zombies* or going to the swings together – or just sitting together on the sofa and looking at Lego sets they'd like to put on their birthday list. It means being there and being interested, without conditions. Even if their interests bore you to tears, you can still be interested in what they get out of it and enjoy their enjoyment.

For younger children, this can involve play, but for older children and teenagers it's usually more about listening without pressure and showing an interest. It might be about being available, even if they are apparently not interested. It might mean hanging around the kitchen together. It might mean watching them play *Hollow Knight* and looking up walkthroughs when they are stuck. It could mean thinking of things they'd like to do, and working out the ways in which those can be done with minimal demands or conditions to manage first.

Mindset shift

Instead of *'They won't do anything I suggest, so I've given up trying'*, try *'Let's see what they enjoy, and do more of that together.'*

Collaboration

If we can't use control, pressure or conditions – what happens instead? Do parents just have to sit back and do whatever their children say? Lots of parents say that their efforts to be low demand leave them feeling controlled by their children, and sometimes that the whole family's life is controlled by one child. One child decides who goes out, when they go out, what they can do and where they can do it. This is a problem for parents, but it's even more of a problem for siblings. They can seriously miss out on being able to make choices, because their sibling is making choices that prevent them from doing so.

Collaboration means working together towards a mutual goal, and collaborating with children is a key element of low demand parenting. The pioneer of collaborative problem solving with children is Dr Ross Greene, and his books outline a detailed methodology for using the approach with children. It's a good approach, but it requires some adaptation for pressure-sensitive children. There are a lot of questions and 'drilling down', which for some children will feel like pressure. Naomi describes a low demand method of collaboration in detail in Chapter 9 of her book *A Different Way to Learn*.

The basic principle of collaborative problem solving (from Dr Greene) is that *children do well when they can*. So if they aren't doing well, then we need to think about why this might be, rather than trying to punish them for not doing so. He sees much child behaviour through a lens of 'lagging skills' rather than 'bad behaviour'. Some children take longer to develop skills than others, and this can be frustrating for them. When they show this frustration, it's seen as negative behaviour, and so they are often punished for it. The punishment does nothing to address the problem, which is the lagging skills.

Sometimes parents think that collaborative problem solving means sitting down and having a discussion. They say, 'We try, but the children won't do it!' For lots of pressure-sensitive children, sit-down discussions are absolutely not an option. They feel put on the spot and they clam up, refusing to talk about it any further.

Collaboration doesn't have to mean asking children outright for their ideas – depending on the child, this may or may not be possible. It means parents trying to involve their children in decisions, and if something is non-negotiable, thinking about how it can be made easier for all involved.

Low demand collaboration starts with accepting the child's position, and working from there.

We're going to talk about this more in further chapters – right now, it's more about thinking about the sort of attitude that you want to foster towards your children. It's 'We're in this together' rather than 'You have to get used to doing what you're told.' It's 'I'm listening to how you feel' rather than 'Stop making such a fuss.' And finally (possibly as a future distant goal), it's working out how to make things work for everyone, how we can get everyone's needs met, including yours as the parent.

Mindset shift

Instead of 'You need to do what I say', try 'Let's work out how we can both get what we need.'

Humour

And finally we come to humour! The part that makes everything more fun. Bringing humour into your life with your children means letting yourself be silly, and laughing at the ridiculous things you do. It doesn't mean making fun of your children, or mocking them or others. It means laughing with them – if fart jokes and toilets are what they find funny, then that's where you are right now. It won't last forever.

Playing music and dancing is a great way to let go and feel genuine joy – even if your children won't join in, do it anyway! Finding songs to go back to again and again can help form family traditions, and you can work out your own silly dance moves.

This isn't about contriving anything. Everyone has a different way of being humorous – for some families it's all about slapstick, for others it's more about dry humour. It's about keeping things light, even when they are really tough.

Mindset shift

Instead of *'There's nothing funny about this'*, try *'One day we will look back on this and laugh.'*

Eliza and Naomi:
REACHing up the stairs

NAOMI: Hi Eliza, what do you think low demand relationships are like?

ELIZA: I think they're non-hierarchical. I think they are consistent.

NAOMI: Emotionally consistent. But not consistent in the sense in which the word is often used, which is 'I've told you what to do now, and you've got to do it.'

ELIZA: I think part of that consistency is that availability, being there as much as you can be. That can mean even at 10 o'clock at night being available to do something with them.

NAOMI: Quantity time, just being around. It's like the opposite of the 'quality time' idea. You try to be around even if you're just hanging out in the same house, without the expectation that your presence will mean they must be doing something active with you. There's something about the non-reactiveness in a relationship that's important, the safety of 'You can say whatever you want to and it's going to be okay.' I've got your back no matter what, really.

What do you think we're aiming for in a low demand parenting environment?

ELIZA: The impact of the environment is a huge one. It's getting completely in tune with the child and what they need, rather than asking the child to change.

NAOMI: Thinking about what environment works for this child. Either making it more interesting (for example, if you're stuck in the house), but also just thinking about things like, Do we need a place for them to retreat to? Even if you're in an environment that you can't necessarily control, like if you're visiting somebody else, it's about thinking, How can we make sure that there's a space that they can go to?

ELIZA: I feel like that's when people talk about reasonable adjustments and needs. I actually think that once that environment is adapted to what they need, then you'll see very little of them needing anything else.

NAOMI: It's a bigger-scale thing, isn't it? It's like you can't make little tweaks necessary to the environment, you need to restructure the way that everything works.

ELIZA: It's not about some noise-cancelling headphones.

NAOMI: Children need to spend a lot of their time in an environment that does work for them. Even if they sometimes need to be somewhere that doesn't work so well for them, if they know that they can come back to somewhere where they can just be themselves then that can make all the difference. I think that can be things like having their own bedroom or having their own space where they can shut the door and get away from everybody else.

ELIZA: Active involvement is the one I feel passionate about because low demand parenting can sometimes be seen as a lack of parenting. People think that you're not doing anything really or you're just leaving them to it. It's not that. Involvement comes from your presence, from talking, your interest in them. There is a lot going on that you're doing while being low demand.

NAOMI: You're not just leaving them to it. It's more like, I'm here if you need me, but I'm not going to pressure you.

What do you think about collaboration?

ELIZA: That comes down to being non-hierarchical as well. You're working with them. You're always working together. You're always figuring stuff out together. They've got that space to come to you so you can think things through and thrash things out. It's the same with whoever's involved with your child. It goes wider than just between you and the child. It starts to be the community around you.

NAOMI: That's a tricky one. How do you get the community around you to collaborate? If they don't want to?

ELIZA: Well, you need to find the ones that will.

NAOMI: I think it's something about working with, isn't it, rather than doing to? We're working together here. It doesn't necessarily mean that you're telling the child that they need to collaborate with you, particularly with younger children.

I think people sometimes expect the child to play a part that maybe the child can't play. They expect it to be a discussion and lots of children don't want to discuss how things are going to work. It's not very collaborative if the adult is trying to insist that the child does it. It's more about taking their needs in mind and thinking about how you can help them get their needs met, rather than it being, 'You need to work with me on this', which the child is going to experience as pressure and so it won't work.

Finally there's humour. Why do you think humour is so important?

ELIZA: Because it lightens the mood. It reduces tension. It takes off a lot of the demand if you can make things seem lighter and less heavy.

NAOMI: Just remembering that you're going to be able to laugh about it at some point, I think, can really help. If you're able to think to yourself, 'At some point, I'm going to laugh about this. It will be a funny story.' The worst moments are the funniest stories. Like the time that my son threw all the laundry baskets full of dirty laundry downstairs and then jumped in all the clothes. He was just having lots of fun.

ELIZA: That does sound like a good game.

NAOMI: It's a great game but not so fun for me because it meant all the dirty clothes had been distributed around the house.

The other thing about humour is that you can sometimes say things in a humorous way that you can't say in a serious way.

ELIZA: Mucking around about things like having a bath and comparing the odour in the room to a fruit bat has been quite successful in our house.

NAOMI: A fruit bat?

ELIZA: There's a zoo near us that's got fruit bats.

NAOMI: They smell really horrible?

ELIZA: Yes.

NAOMI: If your child likes that humour, that could work. I can see it might go the wrong way with someone else.

ELIZA: Obviously, you have to use the right humour for the right person.

NAOMI: You have to know your audience.

ELIZA: You have to know your audience.

Too much to read, too little time?

1. Low demand parenting is about turning around the underlying assumptions of more mainstream approaches and creating the circumstances for children to grow and thrive.
2. We've identified five principles which are the pillars of low demand parenting: Relationships, Environment, Active involvement, Collaboration and Humour – the REACH approach.
3. Low demand parenting isn't a set of techniques to be applied. It's about redefining your relationship with your child so that control and conditionality are no longer the main focus.
4. This will involve a lot of unpacking and questioning for most parents, as it's likely that you were parented in a controlling way, and that you have always assumed that 'good parenting' equals effective control of your child.

More to read if you are interested

Different Way to Learn: Neurodiversity and Self-Directed Education – Naomi Fisher

The Explosive Child – Ross Greene

Playful Parenting – Lawrence Cohen

Unconditional Parenting – Alfie Kohn

4

Communication

Rashida was in despair. 'Whatever I say, it's wrong,' she said. 'I try to be gentle and understanding, but my daughter reacts as if I'm the most horrible strict and brutal parent, making her march around at gunpoint. Whatever I suggest, she says no, and when I asked her politely to come and sit at the table she swore at me. What am I getting wrong?'

Communication

How we communicate with our children (and how they communicate with us) is one of the things parents worry about most. For some parents, it seems so hard to talk to their children without triggering anger and frustration. Parents sometimes tell me they feel they can't open their mouths because they just know that whatever they say, it will be wrong.

So far in this book I've talked about children for whom the usual parenting techniques just don't seem to apply. Those who don't respond well to firm boundaries and an authoritative tone of voice. Those for whom strategies like counting to three and Time Out seem to make it less, rather than more, likely that they will cooperate. I've talked a bit about the idea of 'parenting' and where it came from, and how it is often assumed to be something that parents do to children, rather than something that happens in a relationship.

In Chapter 3, we outlined the principles of low demand parenting and showed you how they were different to those associated with Good Parenting™, the prevailing parenting culture most of us are immersed in without even realising it. In this chapter, and the next few, we'll be getting down to the nuts and bolts. We're going to talk about what the detail of low demand parenting actually looks like, and how you can change the way that you relate to your children in order to create a low demand environment.

We'll focus on communication, behaviour and emotions, and then there are two chapters about real-life situations that parents often ask about. These separations are artificial, because in reality all of these things are tangled. Life doesn't fall into neat boxes. But it would make the chapters too long and confusing if we put them all in together.

In Chapter 1, I introduced the idea of the BIVA code breaker and how we can identify loops that become traps in which parents and children get stuck. This chapter looks at some of those traps in greater detail, for loops aren't always easy to identify, and it's never easy to get out of a trap.

Communication from their child is usually the thing that first signals to parents that they need to do something differently. Adults tend to think of communication as words, but the way that children express themselves is typically through their behaviour. With a baby, it's how settled they are and when they cry. As children get older, they show us through their behaviour that things aren't working for them – and sometimes that makes no sense to their parents.

Parents tell me that whatever they say, they seem to get a response from their children that is totally out of sync with their intentions. They say 'Put your shoes on' and their children react as if they've yelled at them. Parents are full of good intentions to let things go and not fight over the small stuff, but then they find themselves having an out-and-out fight with their nine-year-old about whether shoes belong on the sofa, or whether they can eat the whole packet of biscuits. Everything becomes a struggle and life is no fun at all. 'We didn't want it to be like this,' parents tell me, 'but it's like *Groundhog Day* around here. We are stuck.'

The reason that you feel stuck is because you are falling into some well-established communication traps. The way that you are communicating with your child isn't having the effect that you want – but more than that, it is actually making things worse. You are trapped in a negative feedback loop. When you're in a loop, the harder you try, the worse things get. It's like one of those finger traps where the harder you pull, the less likely you are to get out. You are putting in so much effort, and none of it is helping; in fact, all your efforts to solve the problem only end up making it worse.

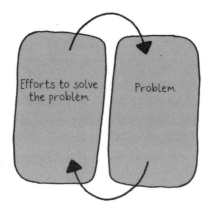

Getting out of these traps isn't easy, because your efforts to get you out push you further in. We need to work out how to release the trap so you and your child can get out.

In order to do this I've developed a basic three-step process you can apply each time. First you have to identify the trap – use a BIVA code breaker to work out where your feedback loops are. Then tune into your child's perspective and turn down the pressure, using some tools I'll explain shortly. Your traps might be similar to those described here, but they will also be unique to you.

Springing your traps

1. Identify the trap.
2. Tune in to the child's perspective.
3. Turn down the pressure.

Before I start, a caveat: sometimes books about communicating with children are really about how to get children to do what you want without a fuss. This chapter is not like that. The aim of low demand parenting is not compliance. The way to release a trap cannot be the child changing in order to do what you want – if your aim is that, then you've fallen into another trap. You'll get stuck again.

Falling into traps

Traps are situations where everyone is trying to get things to change – but somehow, the strategies that they are using make things worse rather than better. Sometimes those strategies work okay in the short term, but in the long term they make things worse. Think about something like having trouble sleeping. You can't sleep at night so you're really tired during the day. To solve that problem, you drink lots of coffee to keep you awake. In the short term, that works okay. You get through the day. But when it comes to the evening you are still hyped up on the caffeine and you can't sleep again. In the long term it makes it even harder for you to sleep, and the large amounts of caffeine start to cause anxiety and irritability – and so your efforts to solve the problem have made things worse.

Parenting is filled with traps like these. And if your child is pressure sensitive, then the one that generally causes most problems (and underpins most of the other traps) is what we'll call the 'Pressure Paradox'.

The Pressure Paradox

Jason's mother had told him that he could only have one sweet, but when she was looking the other way, he picked up another one from the open bag. She turned and saw him.

'I said you can't have another sweet, put it back please,' she said.

Jason protested, 'But I really want it. Please can I have it?' as he started to unwrap it.

His mother didn't want to back down. 'If you eat that sweet, they'll be no sweets tomorrow,' she stated.

Jason looked sadly at the sweet.

His mother said, 'Tomorrow we are going to the shop and there will be a sweet for your sister and not for you if you eat that one now.'

Jason moved the unwrapped sweet towards his mouth and licked it. 'Okay,' he said. 'I won't eat it now. I want one tomorrow.'

His mother was stuck. 'No, you've licked it now,' she said. 'It's too late to change your mind.'

Jason was furious. 'But you didn't say that!' he yelled. 'You never said I couldn't lick it. Only that I couldn't eat it!'

His mother held the boundary. No sweets tomorrow because of the licked one. And Jason should stop shouting too.

The meltdown lasted two hours.

It started again the next day when his sister was given a sweet and he wasn't, and this time it lasted three hours.

This time his father stepped in by saying that he wouldn't be allowed sweets for a week if he didn't stop immediately.

Jason didn't stop, and they had meltdowns about sweets every day for the next week. By the end they could hardly remember what had started it all off, and they had no idea how to get out of the cycle they were in. His parents kept threatening Jason with more severe consequences if he didn't stop – and then the consequences resulted in more intense and longer meltdowns.

Each day they would remind him of the consequences of his behaviour, and each day his behaviour got worse. He started kicking and punching them when they told him that he wasn't allowed a sweet that day. He would wake in the morning and ask if he could have a sweet, and when they said no, would immediately become furious. They tried restricting his access to his tablet until he stopped kicking them, but again, that just made his behaviour worse.

His parents started to worry that his behaviour meant that he was addicted to sweets, and discussed whether they needed to impose a complete sugar ban. They told Jason what they were thinking in the hope this might improve his behaviour. The meltdown after that one lasted for most of the day and into the night. Everyone was exhausted.

What's happened here? It all started so small. Jason's mother tried to stop Jason from eating an extra sweet by adding consequences, and Jason tried to find a way out for himself that didn't involve him being totally compliant with her request. He could see what he wanted – the sweet – which makes it particularly difficult for children to resist their desire. Jason's mother thought he had to learn to accept her limits and so she stuck to what she said. She thought that if she allowed Jason to have another sweet, he would learn that he didn't have to do what she said. The worse his behaviour got, the less likely she was to back down, because she didn't want to encourage that behaviour. She was becoming more inflexible, the more challenging his behaviour became.

They are all trapped, because the strategy that Jason's parents are using to try to change his behaviour – putting on pressure via a punishment of 'no sweets tomorrow' – is making things worse. And the worse things get, the more they are applying this strategy. They are ramping it up rather than turning it down. Jason is also trying to change the situation, and he's doing it by showing his parents very clearly that what is happening is not okay with him. These two different reactions interact to form a trap. Both he and his parents are becoming more rigid rather than more flexible – and it's not clear what the way out is. This is the Pressure Paradox in action. The code breaker diagram below shows what is happening – and how Jason and his mum are stuck in a loop.

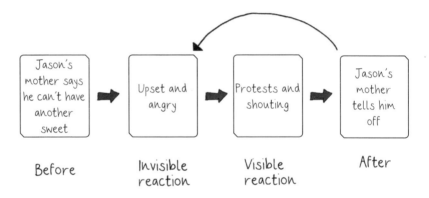

| Before | Invisible reaction | Visible reaction | After |

The Pressure Paradox is one of the most powerful traps in parenting, and once you start to notice it you'll see it everywhere. Stated in a few words, it's this:

> The more you pressure your child to do something, the less likely it is that they will do it.

The reason why this is so difficult for parents to get their heads around is because the Pressure Paradox is the opposite of how we are told that parenting works.

Good Parenting™ is typically about how to use pressure effectively. The idea is that a good parent will train their child into 'good behaviour' by a series of strategies, and then over time this will be internalised and the child will no longer need to be directly controlled by their parent. The parenting books call this 'authority' or 'being in control' or 'firm leadership'. But to the child it can feel like pressure.

Sometimes this pressure is very obvious – shouting and punishments – and sometimes it's much more subtle – shaming and disapproval – but the basic paradox remains the same. The harder the parents try, the worse the problem gets. Everyone gets entrenched.

When pressure makes things worse, none of the usual parenting techniques are going to be helpful. Not star charts, not clear consequences, not counting to three, not Time Outs. They are all based on pressure. They will all make things worse. It never gets to a point where the child goes, 'Okay, I'll give up and do what you want.' It starts to feel as if you are banging your head against a brick wall.

Parents usually discover this by themselves. It starts to go wrong when a child doesn't comply with what seems like a minor parental request. The parent responds by laying down the law, in the hope that this will lead to compliance. The result is the opposite. The child becomes even less compliant, and the only thing the parent knows to do is to push harder.

That pressure can be communicated in a subtle or overt way. It includes how we talk to children (a firm tone), what we say to children ('You'll regret this') and what happens when the children don't comply ('If you don't stop then you are going straight to bed'). Children can also feel pressured by what their parents think of as positive attention, including rewards, approval and praise. It really doesn't matter what your motivation is. If your child feels pressured by you, then doing more of what you are doing is likely to make things worse. Everyone gets trapped. As the loop goes round and round, the pressure rises and both the child and the parent get more explosive.

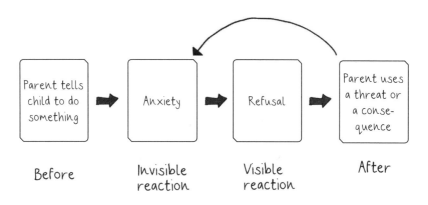

The Pressure Paradox in action

Many parents fall into the Pressure Paradox trap when using common parenting techniques. Parents tell me that when they tried to use the Naughty Step or Time Out, the instructions say that the child should stay there until they have calmed down. A few minutes, this is meant to take.

Some children do not calm down in Time Out. Thirty minutes later and they are still expressing their displeasure very loudly. Forty-five minutes, and nothing has changed. An hour in and no one is anywhere near 'calm'. Their distress gets more rather than less. Two hours in and it is starting to feel like no one knows what to do. You can see the trap visually in the BIVA code breaker below. The parents are left with a dilemma – do they 'follow through' and keep their children there until they stop, or do they give up and 'let the child win'? The parenting books rarely address these scenarios.

If parents decide to stick with what they originally said, then a full-on battle of wills ensues. And it's usually true that children have more time and energy to invest in battles of wills than their parents. They aren't worried about cooking the tea, or dealing with other children or earning a living. They can put their whole heart and soul into it, for as long as it takes. They can be devastatingly consistent.

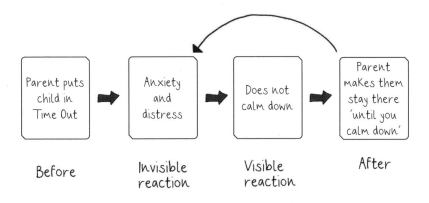

| Parent puts child in Time Out | Anxiety and distress | Does not calm down | Parent makes them stay there 'until you calm down' |

| Before | Invisible reaction | Visible reaction | After |

This pressure cycle is at the heart of a lot of the problems between children and their parents. Parents tell their child to do something, the child does not comply, parents put on more pressure and this makes the child less likely to comply. There is no way out because the parents' strategy is based on increasing pressure, and increased pressure increases anxiety, which makes the child less rather than more compliant. This can happen all the time, about almost anything. (And it isn't actually only with children that the Pressure Paradox trap can be activated. I know many parents who tell me that they are stuck in this trap with other adults too.)

Releasing the Pressure Paradox trap

I know you just want to know how to get out of this trap and what to do. You want the answers. That's completely natural when you feel stuck. The bad news is that there are no short cuts. I can't tell you what to do for your unique child.

All I can do is offer some principles and examples you can use to make your own plan.

If you remember, the three steps to springing the trap are these:

1. Identify the trap.

2. Tune in to the child's perspective.

3. Turn down the pressure.

We've identified the trap using the code breaker – there's a clear feedback loop between Jason's behaviour and his parents'. The next step is tuning in to the child's perspective. In other words, you need to become aware of the way your child experiences what is happening and what the world feels like from their perspective. Only then can you start to turn down the pressure. This applies even if you think that their perspective is completely unreasonable and unjustified (and you may well think that).

Tuning into hidden pressure

Most of us are unaware of all the ways in which we use pressure on our children. If you're unaware of pressure, then it's very hard to stop using it. You can't get out of a trap if you have no idea of your part in keeping you stuck.

Much pressure in parenting is invisible. We don't talk about parenting approaches being controlling or pressuring. The books are not called *Effectively Control Your Child* or *Make Your Child Do What You Want without Complaining*; instead, they talk about 'authority' and 'leadership' or 'discipline', or even 'obedience'. We see other people parenting in a controlling way all around us. Control is an accepted way to interact with children. Parenting books suggest new and more effective ways to pressure children into compliance – but without mentioning pressure. The fact that the purpose of this is how to get children to do things, whether they want to or not, is assumed rather than stated openly.

This means that parents are often blissfully unaware of the pressure and expectations hidden in the way that they communicate with their children, which means that they haven't a clue how to start to do it differently. They were pressured to comply as children themselves, and so they do the same with their children. If they do think about it, they think of 'pressure' as authoritarian or strict parenting – shouting, commands, instructions or physical punishment – but pressure is much more widespread and subtle than that.

Here are a few examples of how subtle pressure shows up for some of the parents I've worked with:

Type of pressure	What it looks like	The hidden pressure from the child's perspective
Comparisons	'Your cousin plays the piano so well.'	She thinks I should play the piano.
Rewards	'I'll get you an ice cream if you come to the park with me.'	He's trying to make me come to the park.
Persuasion	'Come on! It'll be fun!'	I can't say no without disappointing her.
'Innocent' questions	'Were you just going to play on the iPad all day?'	She wants me to stop playing on my iPad.
Teachable moments	'Look at that monument. Did you know that there are war memorials all around the country. . .?'	He expects me to be interested in what he's saying and remember stuff about the war.
Gentle reminders	'Can you get your coat on?'	She wants to make me go out.
Telling off	'You must never do that again. That was outrageous behaviour.'	He's disappointed in me and I can't manage how that makes me feel.
Making it personal	'I've been preparing this for you for ages.'	I have to behave as if I like it.
Adding emotion	'It would make me so happy if you did this.' Disapproving face.	I don't have a choice.

Take some time to observe how you communicate with your child over the next day or two, and see if you can pick up on the subtle pressure. You need to become more sensitive to your child's perception of pressure and tone down your defensive internal voice, which is almost certainly saying 'I'm not pressuring her!' or 'I'm not a controlling parent!' What matters is your child's perception, not whether you think you are pressuring them or not.

Exercise: Detecting pressure

Write down the things you say that your children react badly to. See if you can work out where the pressure is coming from. Use their reactions as a clue.

What are the openly pressuring things you say to your children?	
What are the hidden ways that you pressure them?	
What are the things in the environment that they find pressuring?	
What are things other people say that they find pressuring?	
Are there people and things that they find low-pressure?	
When are the times they seem to feel least pressured?	

Turning down the pressure

When you've tuned into the child's perspective and found the sources of pressure, the next step is to turn down the pressure. Here, your most important tool is flexibility. When a rigid adult meets a rigid child, things go very wrong fast.

Communication tool 1: Flexibility

Let's go back to Jason. When Jason said 'Please can I have another sweet?' the most flexible approach would have been just to say 'Yes.' His mother could have asked herself if it was worth it and decided that it is just a sweet and not worth a conflict. She could have exercised her right to change her mind and it would have been a non-event.

His mother also had a second chance to say yes when she realised that this was becoming a battleground. Even when the meltdown had started, she could have apologised and said yes. It might have been too late for that day, but she would probably have been able to save the next day by not sticking to the consequence. Flexibility could have redeemed the situation.

What stopped her from saying yes was her fear that this would be 'giving in' to Jason, and that she would be 'reinforcing bad behaviour'. Maybe she's worried that Jason will eat so many sweets that he won't eat anything else and that she will lose all authority. For her, there is so much more at stake here than just one sweet. It represents what type of parent she is, because restricting sugar is one of the things Good Parents™ do.

This fear has trapped her, because the worse his behaviour gets, the more she doesn't want to give in. This means that both Jason and his parents are trapped in inflexibility. I'll talk more about these fears in the next chapter, but suffice to say that in low demand parenting 'giving in' is often the better choice, and the earlier the better. Save the 'firm boundaries' (and therefore the battles) for the things that really matter, the non-negotiables of life. If it doesn't really matter, then be flexible. And one more sweet does not really matter.

Communication tool 2: Levelling

Closely aligned with flexibility is getting alongside your child – working with, rather than telling to. The basic idea is to see the issue as a shared problem that needs to be solved together.

Getting on the same level is about showing the child that you are in this together. Your aim here is to find solutions that meet everyone's needs. Any in-depth discussion about this may be a long way off, however, particularly with younger children (by which I mean those under twelve). Don't get discouraged if your children do not seem at all interested in talking about things with you right now. You can still take a more equal approach to your relationship with them.

Levelling is about your relationship with your child. Most Good Parenting ™ involves being authoritative – in other words, parents say what they expect from children in a firm but loving way, and the child is expected to cooperate. This is what Jason's mother was doing when she told him he couldn't have another sweet. She wouldn't have said that to another adult, and Jason can't say that sort of thing to her (or if he does, she'll probably laugh at him and take the sweet anyway). Their relationship is hierarchical.

Most relationships between children and adults are hierarchical. Adults are clearly in charge; they decide what happens – the child's job is to do it. There often isn't much, if any, real consultation. Of course, parents are also often in hierarchical relationships. They may feel pushed around by their boss, by teachers at school – they may feel that they themselves have very little power.

Humans like to feel powerful, particularly if they don't feel very powerful in other areas of their lives. So when parents feel controlled by work and school, they react by trying to control their child, who reacts by trying to control whoever they can – siblings, neighbours, the dog, anyone who is available. It's expected that those who are further down the hierarchy will do what they are told.

When a relationship is hierarchical, this affects everything. Think about a situation at work when you were the most junior person – for me, it's when I worked in a shop as a Christmas temp. I was only there for three months and could be asked to leave at a week's notice at any time. There was a group of us, and at the end the 'best' of us might be offered longer-term work. In theory, the staff team were consulted about things like what music played in the shop and when our breaks were, but in practice, the senior staff with permanent contracts made all the decisions. I knew that they had power over me and so I didn't want to do anything to upset them. When I was asked for my opinion, I told them what I thought they wanted to hear, not what I really thought. I was super-compliant and 'well-behaved'. It didn't work: I didn't get offered a job at the end.

Hierarchies do that to people. Fear of getting something wrong or upsetting people means that you can't really give your opinion. There is some fascinating research on how hierarchies affect team functioning – essentially, if a team is very hierarchical, then it can't really operate as a team because no one is free to say what they think. Junior people can't bring up problems because they know they risk being shamed or ignored. More senior people have to appear to be in control and so they can't accept feedback. It can appear like something is a whole team decision, when actually it is just the decision of one person. Some very bad business decisions and scandals have happened in hierarchical structures where people knew that things were going wrong but felt unable to speak up.

When it comes to children, adults tend to think that hierarchies are good. We think that children should know their place and do what they are told. Schools make children stand up when adults enter the classroom to 'show respect' and sometimes children are told not to 'answer back', meaning 'don't disagree with me'.

These hierarchies are power structures in which the voice of the child really doesn't matter. They are also a form of pressure, and many pressure-sensitive children pick up on them (and refuse to play their part) even as other people think of them as 'just the way that things are'.

Levelling means making space for children's views without shaming or judgement. With Jason, this would have meant taking his request for another sweet as a valid question, just as you might with an adult. It might have meant saying 'That's up to you' if there really wasn't any good reason why one more sweet was a problem, or if there was a problem (like, those sweets were for both children and Jason's sister hadn't had any yet), enlisting Jason's help with how to resolve that.

Levelling isn't just about what you say – it's also about how and when you say it. Sitting side by side is usually easier than facing each other. Talking while you are facing the other way (for example while cooking in the kitchen) can be another way to reduce the pressure in a conversation, as can sitting next to each other in the car. The following table gives some examples of how to find a more equal level in your communication.

Instead of. . .	Try. . .
'Time to stop playing that game now.'	'Are you ready to stop now, or is there a better time coming up in your game?'
'We are going swimming now.'	'You don't have to go swimming but your brother is going. We can sit and watch him with your tablet and I'll bring your swimming things just in case.'
'Put that coat on now or you'll get cold.'	'You might not need it but your coat is here. Yes I know you're not cold.'
'You have to come, there's no choice.'	'You don't have to join in but I can't leave you here alone. Would you prefer to bring your tablet or a game to play together?'

'If you lick it, you have to eat it because otherwise it's a waste.'	'Licked sweets sometimes get dirty because they are wet. How could we keep it clean until you want it?'
'Stop. You can only have one of these cakes.'	'There are six cakes and six people. How many do you think we should each get?'
'No, you can't have another sweet. You've had enough.'	'There are a few sweets left and they are here. I know you can decide when you've had enough.'
'You'll be sad later when everyone else has had fun and you've just stayed at home.'	'You can stay at home with Daddy or you can come to the park with us. Both could be good and you can decide which you prefer.'
'You better stop doing that right now before you hurt somebody.'	'We have a problem. You can't do that here because it might hurt someone but I can see that it's fun. Any ideas?'

Of course there are times when you need to take charge and make decisions as the adult. Levelling doesn't mean that you aren't still the grown-up. But it means that you don't always have to be the one calling the shots or controlling petty details. You want your child to feel that you are there to help them reach their goals, not there to stop them getting things they want.

When it's more complicated

With something like Jason's request for sweets, it's fairly clear what the conflict is. Jason wants a sweet, his parents have said no. Jason is trying to find a way around that, but the more he tries, the more rigid his parents become. The pressure comes from his parents' belief that they must stick to what they have said, and that Good Parents™ are inflexible when it comes to issues like this. They think that Jason 'has to learn' to do what he's told when it comes to sweets and food. It's all out there. It's a clear example of the Pressure Paradox trapping a family. They could get out by taking a more flexible and less hierarchical approach.

Many traps parents find themselves in are much harder to see and to detect, and that's where your tuning-in skills are essential. The next trap I'm going to talk about is trickier to detect. It's the Automatic No.

The Automatic No

Some parents tell me that their children say no to everything. They say that they don't make suggestions anymore, because they know what the answer will be. Some parents say that they don't even have to say anything, just taking a breath in is enough to get a very vehement 'No'.

This is where communication gets complicated. For it's not just what you say that matters, it's the way that you say it.

What do I mean? Well, when we suggest something to a child, we generally assume that they are reacting to that suggestion.

So if we say, 'Would you like to go to the park?' and the child answers 'No', we think that means they don't want to go to the park. It seems obvious. But in fact, surrounding that suggestion are lots of demands. There's the need to respond to a direct question, there's the tone of voice the suggestion was said in, and there's the anticipated response if the child says yes (or no). There might also be the worry about what a sibling might say or do if they don't want to come. The actual suggestion 'going to the park' is deep inside a layer of demands. Whether they want to go to the park might be the last thing a child is actually thinking about.

For many children, the pressure of how things are said feels so intense that they react to that rather than to the actual suggestion. So a parent says, 'We're going to the park now. Quick, get your shoes!' and the child reacts and says 'No' because the urgency feels too much for them to manage. They can't even think about whether they want to go to the park, because the suggestion itself causes anxiety, which means they automatically react with a no. They can't make a real decision. They can't say yes.

This can mean that a child gets stuck behind a wall of demands and expectations, unable to do things they might actually enjoy. The expectation makes them so anxious that they react with an immediate refusal. This is the Automatic No, and it's a particularly pernicious trap.

The trap

The Automatic No is when children (or adults) say no out of overwhelming anxiety or another emotional reaction. That no is not really a choice. It's more like a protective shield, held up in front of the child to protect them. The Automatic No comes from a deep need to get away from difficult emotions and to stay safe.

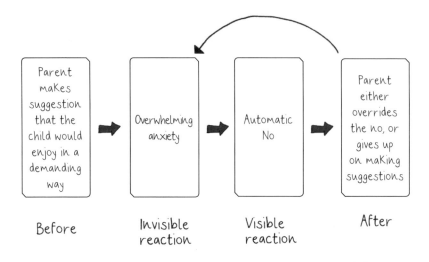

| Before | Invisible reaction | Visible reaction | After |

The Automatic No means that parents could suggest something that their child would love to do, but because of the way that it is framed, the child can't do it. More than that, the child can't even think about whether they want to do it, because they are out of their window of tolerance. The emotions feel dangerous and so they are acting to defensively protect themselves.

Both children and parents get trapped by the Automatic No. Children because they can't actually do things that they want to do, and parents because it's easy to mistake the Automatic No for a genuine no. Many parents think that their child just doesn't want to do anything. They stop offering things and they stop trying to make life more interesting. But the problem isn't the actual suggestion – the child might want to do the thing that's being suggested – the problem is that the anxiety it generates is so high that the child can only say 'No'. Sometimes, ironically, parents do this while thinking that they are supporting their child's right to choose what they do. They think that the child's Automatic No represents what they genuinely want, rather than a need to defend themselves against demands. This leads very quickly to a highly restricted life for families (and a lot of frustration).

The other way that an Automatic No can trap families is when parents believe that they must override the no by pushing through it. This leads parents to force their children to do things, which then makes children feel more threatened, which then makes Automatic Nos more frequent and more forceful. These families end up with lots of battles.

The alternative to an Automatic No isn't an Automatic Yes, or in fact any type of yes. In fact, some children do give an Automatic Yes out of fear and that can be just as much of a problem as the Automatic No. They are super-compliant and will say yes to whatever they are asked to do in order to get away from the distressing feelings that come up when they say no.

The opposite to both the Automatic No and the Automatic Yes is being able to make a genuine decision. It's being able to think, Do I actually want to do this? and to make that decision for yourself. It's being able to give a genuine no, or a genuine yes. It's being able to make a decision that isn't driven by a need to protect yourself from distressing emotions.

Tuning in

Some children always respond with an Automatic No because they are so overloaded. If living with your child is like walking on eggshells, it's likely that their nervous system is on high alert all the time.

If this is you, you need to think about your child's life and what is going on each day. Are they getting enough down time? How do they decompress and can you make more space for that? Is their time too structured and how many demands are they dealing with? Do they spend much time with people who 'get them' and, if not, could you increase that time? You need to go back to Chapter 3 and think about the REACH principles – the groundwork.

Before a child can lower their Automatic No shield, they need to feel safe. This means they need to know that they won't be forced to say yes, and that if they need to say no, it will be respected. In order to be able to risk a yes, they need to know that the no is possible.

Hemanth was ten and he had a very strong Automatic No. It came out all the time, even for suggestions like 'Would you like an ice cream?' He was so defensive that his mother's tone of voice was enough to trigger a no before she had even got further than 'Hemanth. . .'

For his birthday he had asked for an expensive Lego set, which his grandparents had bought him. When he saw the wrapped box and knew what it was by the size, he couldn't open it. He said no. His mother sadly opened it later, and put it on his shelf along with all the other unopened kits and games he had been given.

Hemanth was bored and under-stimulated, while being surrounded by apparently interesting things to do. He had a cupboard full of unopened Lego sets he wanted to play with, but couldn't start.

His parents had stopped offering activities because everything got a no, and Hemanth spent most of his time fighting and bickering with his little brother. His parents didn't know where to start, but they knew that it wasn't working as things were. No one seemed happy and yet they thought they were doing what Hemanth wanted. 'He can choose what he does,' they said. 'We don't put pressure on him. We don't understand why he's so irritable and why things feel so unbalanced.'

Turning down the pressure

Releasing the Automatic No trap takes a major change of mindset. You need to stop thinking, How can I get them to. . . and instead ask yourself, How could I make this opportunity as low pressure as possible? It's about making something available in a way that doesn't activate a child's shield. As long as that shield is up, they are unable to access all the fun things going on just over the other side of the barrier. It's not a happy place to be.

The strange thing about releasing the Automatic No is that you will need to lean into that 'no' when up to now you've been pulling against it. Leaning in releases the tension that makes the Automatic No feel necessary to the child. Often, the more able a child feels to say no, the more able they are to actually think about it and say yes (or no).

This can feel really counter-intuitive. You're used to fighting that Automatic No, but now you need to almost befriend it. You need to show the child you're not scared of it or trying to fight it, because this will trigger their threat system. There are two tools you can try for this: adjusting the pressure and using scales.

Communication tool 3: Adjusting the pressure

Pressure builds up over time in a relationship, just like in a machine. In order to change that, parents need to consciously lower the pressure in everything they say and do. It's like releasing a pressure valve to let the air out.

This often involves saying less. It means tuning into what is hard about the situation – and deliberately acting against it. If the problem is urgency, then be less urgent. If the problem is the expectation that they will enjoy something, suggest that they might not enjoy it and that's okay! Even if it seems a bit strange.

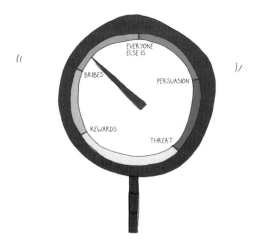

This will feel unnatural at first and you might worry that your child is going to think that you don't care if they do something or not. Try it out and see how they respond. If things aren't working as they are, then you haven't got much to lose.

Pressure up	Pressure down
Emotional pressure ('You'll make me so disappointed if you. . .')	No emotional pressure ('I will be happy whether you come or go.')
Rewards ('If you do this then you can have a sweet.')	Unconditionality ('You can have a sweet whatever you decide to do.')
Threats ('You need to get here now or there's no food.')	Declarative language ('There's food on the table.')
Urgency ('Come here right now!')	Drop the urgency ('When you're ready we can leave.')
Enthusiasm ('You've done that painting so well, that's amazing.')	Playing it cool ('Oh, your picture is over there?')
Too many options ('Do you want the blue one or the orange one or the green one?')	One option at a time ('The blue one is there.')

Adding blame ('You broke that cup, why can't you be more careful?')	No blame ('Everyone breaks things sometimes. We have other cups.')
Making it about them ('Do you have to leave now? But we only just got here!')	Make it about you ('It's pretty busy and loud here, I'm ready to leave with you.')
Talking lots.	Saying less.
Asking questions ('How was school? What did you like best about today?')	Making statements ('You're back from school. My day had some good and bad moments and I'm happy to see you.')
Asking for their participation ('Will you come and do this with me? Will you come and play?')	Starting an activity and making it available for them to participate without comment.
Verbal reminders ('Come on, I've told you one hundred times.')	Non-verbal reminders (List on wall of things to do before going out).
Direct ('You need to get your school bag packed right now.')	Indirect ('That school bag is empty.')

Related to this is another tool: scales.

Communication tool 4: Scales

Whenever adults ask children a question, there are always different possible answers – but usually those answers are not at all equal in terms of how the adult approval is weighted. Usually one side is 'good' and the other is 'bad' (or at least 'less good'). Just think of an apparently innocuous question like 'Would you like to read a book together?' Both parents and children know exactly what answer the parent is hoping for. It's not 'Go away; I'm playing on the Nintendo Switch.'

However, when it comes to parents and children the scales are weighted beyond just parental preference. Many parents believe that their own preferred choice is not just a preference, it is objectively better than what the child wants, and if only the child understood that then they would agree. Parents feel that their choice is more worthwhile or productive and that the child must be made to see that. Practising the piano is more worthwhile than playing with Pokémon cards, for example. Playing outside is more worthwhile than *Mario Kart*.

Some children are very sensitive to their parents' agendas. Rather than thinking about what they really want to do, they start thinking, *What is the answer I am meant to give?* and that makes them feel under pressure. They get particularly stuck when they are thinking, *The answer I want to give is not the one that they want.* It's like they are teetering on a seesaw, knowing that their parent wants them to go in one direction.

Think of it like this. Often, without meaning to, parents are communicating to children 'I want you to say yes, say yes, say yes.' Children who are sensitive to pressure pick up on that; the pressure acts as a barrier and so they just can't.

I have even heard of parents giving their children 'good decision stars' for making the choices that their parents want them to make. If a child makes a decision in order to get a 'good decision star' then they aren't really making a decision at all. They are doing what they think other people want them to do. They aren't thinking about their own values and priorities. Some children don't notice how much they are being controlled – while others are very sensitive to it. For all of them, they aren't learning how to make their own decisions. They're learning how to do what other people want them to do.

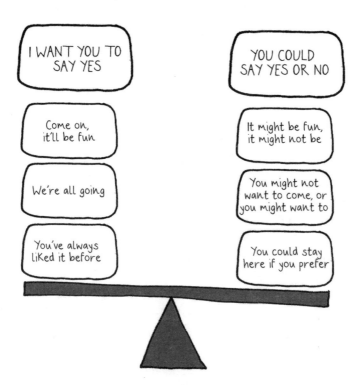

Balancing the scales means deliberately making it clear that there are two options, and both are okay with you as the parent. Take your emotional response out of the situation, and don't make your happiness dependent on your child agreeing to do something.

Ways to balance the scales

- 'You could do this – but you don't have to.'
- 'It might be fun to go out, but it might not be at all.'
- 'You probably won't want to do this, but we do have the option of. . .'
- 'When you're ready we can go or we could stay here instead.'
- 'There's some food over there but you don't need to eat it.'
- 'I think I might go over there and see what is going on. You don't have to come.'
- 'I'm interested in this so I'm going to go and have a look. You're fine to stay here, I'll be able to see you.'

Hemanth's parents had a think about what was activating his Automatic No. They realised that there was often a lot of pressure on Hemanth to visibly enjoy something and perform well. He was the eldest child and the eldest grandchild. With the Lego set, there was the expectation that he would open and be pleased with the gift, and then the pressure to actually open the box, follow the instructions and make the model, which he might get wrong or which might be frustrating. Then there was the feedback to grandparents who would want to see the finished model and who would ask if Hemanth did it himself.

All of that felt anxiety-provoking to Hemanth, even though he wanted to do the Lego set. So he raised his Automatic No shield to protect himself.

Hemanth's parents decided to be flexible and to release the tension in whatever way they could. They stopped buying him presents, and instead bought things they thought he might be interested in for themselves. His father bought himself a Lego set. He didn't ask him to open it, nor did he make a big thing out of having bought it. He opened it himself and started making the set in the front room while Hemanth was watching TV. His grandparents thought he had lost his mind.

Hemanth was surprised and at first he just sat nearby and watched. Then his father started (genuinely) finding a particular part difficult and put in several of the pieces back to front. Hemanth came closer by and made a suggestion. His father played it cool and didn't show any excitement but showed him where he was stuck. Hemanth helped him out and they started to build the set together. The next day when he got the set out, Hemanth came over and sat closer in. On the third day, Hemanth left the room when he got it out and his father worried that the progress he thought they'd made had been lost, but he didn't give up. By the fourth day they were actively collaborating and Hemanth's father was desperately trying to think of what they could move on to next when that kit was finished.

Finally, let's take a detailed look at one more trap. This one is about the way in which adults often respond to children's emotions. There's a whole chapter on emotions coming up, but this trap is about the way in which adults often communicate in response to children's emotions and how that can make things worse. I call it the Push Back.

The Push Back trap

Adults tend to push back on how children feel. This means that when children tell us they feel a certain way, we tell them that it's not really like that. Again this is a strategy adults use in the hope that it will convince children to feel better – but actually what happens is that they feel that no one understands, and so they feel worse.

It's another trap. The more we push back, the less heard the child feels and the less likely they are to tell you how they feel the next time. They still feel the way that they do, but now they feel bad about it, or like they shouldn't feel like that.

Noticing the Push Back

'I don't want to go.' – 'Oh you'll enjoy it when you get there.'

'I hate Molly.' – 'Oh, but you love her really.'

'I don't like going to the theme park.'– 'Oh, but you always have fun and we've already paid for it.'

I don't know about you, but when someone says something like that to me it doesn't make me feel better. Never have I gone 'Oh yes, you're right' and then felt happier. I feel better when someone shows me that they have heard me, even if there's nothing that they can do about it.

Push back creates tension between children, who are telling you how they feel, and parents, who are saying that they don't want to hear it. Feelings don't go away just because someone else doesn't want to hear them – often they actually get more intense. Pressure-sensitive children push back harder, and things get more entrenched.

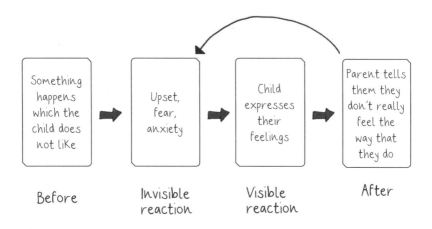

'I don't like it.'
'Oh go on, just have a try.'
'No.'
'It's delicious, you'd love it.'
'DIDN'T YOU HEAR ME SAY NO?'

Turning down the pressure

The way to release this trap is simple. Stop pushing back. Listen to what they are saying and empathise with how they are feeling, even if you don't agree. Stick with the feelings rather than the content. That's communication tool 5: holding the space.

Communication tool 5: Holding the space

'I don't want to go to school.' – 'Right now, you really don't want to go.'

'I hate Sunika.' – 'You really don't like your sister sometimes.'

'I want to stay at home.' – 'You are happy at home.'

Parents often feel that this is a risky approach. They worry that it will make the feelings worse – and it's true that often a child will feel more able to express their feelings if you reflect them back to them. They might cry or shout or they might explain why they said what they said. If you've been pushing back up to now, they might be surprised. They don't expect you to respond like that. They expect you to push back.

It might seem like the feelings are getting bigger. That's because they feel safe to express them to you, not because you have actually made things worse.

The aim in releasing this trap is to allow the child to really feel their emotions without feeling judged for them. The long-term aim is that the child is able to think what they really feel and how they react to the world – and that the world starts to open up to them.

Parents often find this very anxiety provoking. Even when the push back doesn't work, they feel safer doing it. It's like we're afraid that if we allow children to say that they don't want to do something, they'll stop doing anything at all and it will be the end.

Counter-intuitively, making sure that we have time to sit with how they feel (and helping them see that these feelings aren't frightening) can free up children to make decisions their parents thought would never be possible. And that is what low demand parenting is all about. Relieving the pressure so that children have space to grow.

Exercise: Day-to-day communication traps

Below are some traps parents often tell me about. See if you can identify some of your own.

These traps aren't traps for every family. There is nothing universally wrong with any of these approaches unless they don't work and form a feedback loop. The person who is best placed to identify the traps in your family is you.

	What it looks like	Why it happens
Praise	Jim praises Alfie for their painting – and Alfie responds by never painting another picture and ripping up the painting that Jim praised.	Praise can cause anxiety just as a punishment can. It can also create an expectation that they will do the same thing again. It introduces adult evaluation into whatever the child is doing, and for some that feels intolerable.
Gentle reminders	Emma gently reminds Finley to get ready for school. Each time she does so, Finley burrows deeper under his bed. By the fourth reminder, he is shouting at her and throwing his school uniform down the stairs.	Reminders can feel like pressure, whether gentle or not. Increasing pressure increases anxiety, which reduces the chance that the child can cooperate.
Serious talks	Maria sits Lilia down for a talk about her behaviour. Lilia starts hiding under the table and then kicks Maria's ankles.	Being sat down for a talk feels like pressure before you've even said anything.

Lots of warnings	Alice wants to help her son Marcel so she gives him lots of warning about the school trip. They go through every-thing each week for a month beforehand. Marcel grows more, not less, worried about it. On the day, Marcel refuses to go.	Lots of anticipation can increase anxiety for some children, which reduces the likelihood that they will be able to do something. Going over it repeatedly can make it worse rather than better.
Rewards	Pete wants to improve Olivia's behaviour, so he promises her the big-gest Lego set in the shop if she goes to school every day for a month without complaining. Each day, Olivia's behaviour before school gets more difficult and mentioning the Lego set seems to make things even worse.	The Lego set has added more anxiety into an already difficult situation. Now, if Olivia is struggling she's also thinking, *I won't get my Lego set*, and that is making her more anxious.

Five communication tools: FLASH

The five communication tools have the mnemonic FLASH. They are all ways to turn the pressure down rather than up – and ultimately release the traps you and your child have found yourselves in.

Flexibility
Levelling
Adjusting the pressure
Scales
Holding the space

Eliza and Naomi:
But you're doing so well!

NAOMI: Eliza, one of the things that parents often seem to find most tricky about communication is that they say they're being really enthusiastic and positive with their child, but it backfires. It doesn't work in the way they were expecting.

ELIZA: I think that's one of the hardest things because our assumption is that when you are positive the other person will be positive in response. That can be difficult for a young person. Someone being positive can be another demand. It can feel like if that person is really positive towards you, then they want something out of you.

NAOMI: Parents are often told to praise and be really focused on positive reinforcement. It's hard to get your head around how positive attention can feel like pressure as well.

ELIZA: I think it's very difficult if you are positive to someone and that is met with negativity or rudeness or a shut-down. It feels really personal.

NAOMI: I was working with one family and they said their little girl really liked drawing until she won a prize for it. They told her and they were excited and pleased. And then she was like, 'That's it. I'm not doing it anymore.' I can understand that because it's like her relationship with what she was doing had changed. Now she is no longer drawing just because she wants to do it.

ELIZA: I'm someone who does struggle with praise, and I think that, for me, it feels that it's taken away from me slightly.

NAOMI: It's not yours anymore. You've introduced somebody else's gaze.

ELIZA: When I was drawing as a child, I was often doing that quite privately on my own in my own space. I think if someone came in and said, 'That's brilliant', it's almost like they've snatched that piece of paper out of my hand and taken it into another place.

NAOMI: I think it can bring the pressure on. It's like thinking, Well, what if the next one's not as good and you don't say it's brilliant?

ELIZA: I think sometimes as parents we're trying to find something positive. That child might be doing something away from school and, as parents, we're desperate for something. We take that thing and we want to positively highlight it because they're not doing other things, but by doing so we introduce pressure.

NAOMI: We think of it as building them up, don't we? We're encouraged as parents to use praise and we're told that it's good for children. We don't actually notice that there is manipulation there as well, that we only praise what we want to see. We're communicating something very significant to our children through our praise, and they notice.

I remember as a child I loved reading, but there were certain books that I was praised for reading and other books that I wasn't praised for reading. Non-fiction books were good and books that were too hard for me were good. But just reading books I liked, that wasn't as good.

ELIZA: It's like, is it okay for children to have a space of enjoyment where we as parents have very little input in that?

NAOMI: And where we just trust them to want to do this and we don't have to bring our views in.

ELIZA: It's our own pressure we put on ourselves as parents because we feel that we should always be noticing this stuff.

NAOMI: Maybe we think that active involvement is praising kids. We wouldn't necessarily think that with another adult, would we? When I am working with you I don't feel that my role is to praise what you do or to encourage you to do more. I can be appreciative but I'm not trying to motivate you.

Too much to read, too little time?

1. Parent–child communication can be full of traps.
2. A trap exists when the things that a parent or child are doing to try to make things better actually make things worse, meaning that everyone is stuck.
3. Three common parent–child traps are the Pressure Paradox, the Automatic No and the Push Back.
4. The three-step process to release the traps is to *identify* the trap, *tune in* to the child's perspective and then *turn down* the pressure.
5. There are five communication tools to help you turn down the pressure: flexibility, levelling, adjusting the pressure, scales and holding the space.

More to read if you are interested

Declarative Language Handbook: Using a Thoughtful Language Style to Help Kids with Social Learning Challenges Feel Competent, Connected and Understood – Linda Murphy

How to Talk So Kids Will Listen and Listen So Kids Will Talk – Adele Faber and Elaine Mazlish (also available in editions for Little Kids and Teens)

5

Behaviour

Matilda got in touch with me about her daughter Evie. She was frustrated.

'She makes everything so difficult, nothing is ever easy, and my other three are missing out. I don't want to, but I often shout at her and she gets very sad and says that she is a bad person. I just don't get it,' said Matilda. 'Why does she have to be like this? Why can't we just be a happy family?'

Evie was the third of four children, and she had always been more challenging than her siblings. In particular, she had extreme reactions to things her siblings hardly seemed to notice – wearing coats in winter, for example, or smells of cooking. She would rip tights off herself or refuse to put them on at all, and sometimes would have furious rages when things didn't go her way.

Her father Chris told me that they had read many parenting manuals, and had tried all the strategies when Evie was younger. Time Out:

she refused to stay 'out' unless they held the door closed the whole time, and by the time she was let out she was so angry that it took all day to calm her down. The Naughty Step: she kicked and bit them and said they'd never be allowed to try that again or she'd push them down the stairs. Star charts: she was completely uninterested in the stars and ripped the charts off the wall. Any hint of telling off and she went 'completely ballistic', they said. It seemed to make no difference anyway – she did the thing she had just been told off for again straight afterwards.

Not only did their techniques not work, but Evie was also learning from all their attempts at control and using the strategies right back at them. After a failed attempt to get her to cooperate on the count of three, Evie had started counting to three herself when her parents weren't doing what she wanted and getting very angry if they didn't do what she said. The stricter the boundaries, the more Evie refused to stick to them. The more consistent her parents were, the more consistent Evie was. And she didn't ever give in. They were exhausted and constantly fighting.

Her parents got in touch because they wanted anger management for Evie or maybe, they said, cognitive behavioural therapy or mindfulness. Something that would improve her behaviour. Evie, in contrast, wasn't keen. She didn't think *she* had a problem, she thought everyone else had the problem. They were so annoying and they kept trying to make her do things.

This is what makes working with children so different to working with adults. With adults (in most cases) the goals are theirs. They want help. An adult who comes for anger management typically wants to learn how to manage their anger (unless the therapy has been mandated by a court, which does sometimes happen). With children, it's generally other people who see a problem. This means that changing things isn't as simple as acquiring some new skills or techniques, because the child doesn't think they need them. They aren't looking for ways to keep themselves calm. They're looking for ways to make other people stop being so unreasonable and be nicer to them.

Behaviour

Behaviour is what we can see someone doing. In the BIVA code breaker, behaviour comes under V – the visible reaction. It's often the most obvious part of any situation. When it comes to children, 'behaviour' is often used as a synonym for 'unacceptable behaviour', but in psychological terms, behaviour is far wider than that. Humans are behaving all the time. Sometimes that causes problems for others, and sometimes it doesn't.

We have a strange way of thinking about children's behaviour in our society. We tend to talk about it as something children do on purpose, without acknowledging the things that drive it. We tell them that they need to try harder, or we say that their behaviour means that they are 'challenging' or 'out of control'. Children are 'well-behaved' when they do what is expected of them, and 'badly behaved' when they don't.

How we think about behaviour has consequences for how we respond. We seem to believe that the behaviour itself is the problem

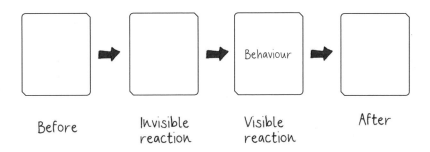

Before   Invisible   Visible   After
reaction   reaction

(as opposed to the visible reaction to a problem). The UK government is setting up 'Behaviour Hubs' to advise teachers on how to control children's behaviour. It's as if we believe that we can change behaviour, and poof, the problem it indicates will be gone. Our culture has a collective belief in the science of behaviourism. But what actually is it?

Behaviourism

I have two cats. If I go near to the drawer that contains their food, they immediately come running. If I open that drawer, they run over to their food bowl. If I don't feed them, they start miaowing at me. I don't think they understand the process of how food gets to their bowl and they certainly don't understand my mental processes around feeding them. They don't have to. What they know is what behaviour of mine predicts feeding. I have (inadvertently) trained them to associate the food drawer with their food. Their brains and bodies expect food when they hear the drawer opening.

I have also deliberately used this ability of theirs to my advantage. Whenever I feed them, I whistle. They associate the sound of the whistle with food, and this means that I can use the whistle to call them in the evenings. They come running to their food bowls when I whistle. I have conditioned them.

I did this because in my undergraduate psychology lectures, I learned about just this sort of thing. At the tail end of the nineteenth century, Ivan Pavlov, a Russian physiologist, started experimenting with dog behaviour. He discovered that, just like my cats, his dogs could learn associations between food and other events. He rang a bell every time he fed the dogs, and after a while, the dogs started to salivate whenever they heard a bell. They had associated the bell with the food – just like my cats have done with the drawer. Pavlov had discovered what is now called 'behavioural conditioning', and a new field – behaviourism – was born.

Behaviourism can be thought of as the place where psychology started to exist as an independent subject. Before that, it wasn't really separate from medicine or philosophy. Early psychologists were keen to establish their field as a scientific discipline, which meant measuring and observing what could be seen. Thoughts and feelings were subjective and hard to quantify, so they focused on visible behaviour. Behaviour could be observed and recorded. And, it turns out, changed.

Dogs were just the start. Scientists in the first half of the twentieth century discovered that they could change the behaviour of many animals by manipulating the consequences of their behaviour. They rewarded the behaviour they wanted (usually with food or sugar water) and punished the behaviour they didn't want (often with electric shocks), and the hapless animals would learn to run through mazes, peck at boards, and other (not so) useful things. Rats and pigeons turned out to be particularly good subjects for this sort of training, and so much time was spent training rats to run around mazes, and pigeons to peck at boards. Pigeons were so responsive to training that they were used to deliver messages across long distances during both world wars.

By the 1920s, this new science was being applied to children. Behaviourist John Watson wrote parenting manuals in which he recommended that children should be treated as small adults and that hugs and kisses should be discouraged. He saw effective parenting as a training process. Crying, asking for attention, food preferences, difficulties sleeping – all could be framed as 'behaviour'. That meant that they could be changed by the use of rewards or punishments. If a child cried too much, the behaviourist explanation for this was that they had been rewarded for this behaviour in the past by their parents paying attention to them when they cried. The answer was to stop paying attention to the crying – the child would learn there was no point, and the crying would stop.

John Watson's ideas were extreme. He saw childrearing as an emotionally detached training process. Few would agree today. However, the principles of behaviourism are still there in our present-day approach to parenting. When baby manuals suggest that babies should be left to cry to 'learn to go to sleep by themselves', this is behaviourism. The crying has been defined as 'unwanted behaviour' and so the way to deal with it is to ignore it, and the child will stop crying when they see that this doesn't get the desired reaction. Time Out, the Naughty Step, sticker charts, class behaviour tracker apps, prizes for attendance – they are all behaviourist. They focus on modifying behaviour rather than thinking about why it has happened.

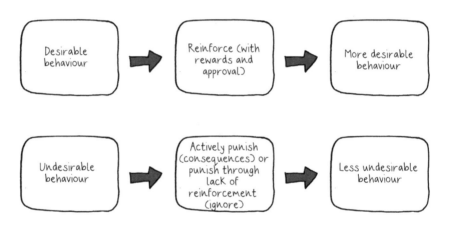

In the illustration you can see a basic flow chart to show how behaviourism is meant to work. The idea is that by changing what happens after the behaviour occurs, the adult can change how the child behaves. Almost anything can be defined as 'behaviour' in this model, which focuses on manipulation through rewards and punishments rather than what caused the behaviour.

Once you become aware of the behavioural model, you'll see it everywhere. When people say things like 'You can't let them get away with that' or 'No surprise she behaves like that, if you give in to her' they are (usually unconsciously) channelling behaviourism.

Echoes of behaviourism

- Baby training.
- 'Cry it out.'
- The Naughty Step.
- Time Outs.
- Ignoring 'bad behaviour'.
- Sticker and star charts.
- Class behaviour tracker apps.
- Behaviour charts/peg charts.
- Whole class reward systems.
- 'If you give in to her now, of course she's going to do it again.'
- 'Attention seeking'.
- 'You'll spoil her.'

What's the problem with behaviourism?

All very well, you might think, but it seems to work. Shouting at my children is the only thing that stops them hitting their sister. Threatening to take away their iPad works like nothing else.

Behaviourism does work *on its own terms*. That's why it's so popular and why it continues to be used. Behaviour does change when children (or adults) are scared enough of the consequences. A class of children who are scared of missing their playtime if they get moved off the Sun to the Raincloud might well be quieter than a class who don't have a public behavioural chart on their wall.

However, behaviourism is a (very) limited way of looking at children. Controlling behaviour through fear is not the same as children learning to behave. Behaviour charts don't ask why a class might be behaving the way they are – they instead use fear and shame to control behaviour.

In the real world, a child's reasons for behaving the way they are do matter. 'Bad behaviour' can have a whole set of different reasons and if we aren't curious about these reasons, we risk making things worse. Think back to the BIVA code breaker from Chapter 1. Sometimes behaviourist approaches try to eliminate the visible reaction, without understanding either the context or the invisible reaction that is driving it. This means that behaviourism can have hidden consequences, even while it appears to 'work'. Sera's story, in the text box, illustrates this.

Sera was always getting in trouble at school. She spent days sitting outside the headteacher's office. The main issue was that she just didn't stay seated at her desk. She would get up and move around, and this disrupted the class and annoyed the teacher. Her name was written on the board, and if that happened three times then she was sent to see the headteacher who would tell her off. This is a behaviourist approach. The idea is that Sera will want to avoid being told off, so she'll stop getting out of her seat.

What it doesn't look at is why Sera is moving around so much. There could be a number of reasons for this. Sera might be a person who needs to move more than the average, and she isn't getting enough movement in her daily life. Sera could be finding the work of the class too difficult, and so she is moving around instead. Sera might be agitated for a reason unrelated to school – perhaps there are things going on at home that are making her anxious, and one of the ways in which children show their internal state is through behaviour. Maybe she has undetected food allergies and has stomach aches that feel a bit better when she is moving around. Or Sera might be developmentally out-of-sync with the requirements of the class, and still be at a stage of life where she needs to be learning through movement, play and exploration. Or it's possible that the girl who Sera sits next to is poking her with a compass and Sera doesn't feel safe sitting next to her.

Sending Sera to the headteacher seems to work. Sera is frightened enough to stay put outside the headteacher's office. But it hasn't solved any of the reasons why Sera was behaving the way that she was. It's just stopped Sera from moving.

If Sera gets scared enough, she may well appear to be 'better behaved'. She'll stop moving, but not because she doesn't need to move anymore. In fact, now she is both uncomfortable and afraid. This isn't a good mindset for learning. She hasn't 'learned to behave'; she is too scared to express herself through behaviour.

What we think of as 'good behaviour' can be an absence of behaviour. While Sera seems to be better behaved at school, at home things quickly get worse. She starts crying in the evenings and saying she doesn't want to go to school in the mornings. Her parents don't know what to do.

We may not be able to see the reasons for a child's behaviour but they will always exist.

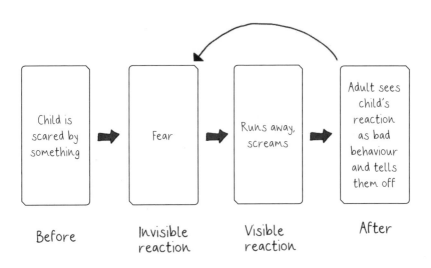

Before	Invisible reaction	Visible reaction	After
Child is scared by something	Fear	Runs away, screams	Adult sees child's reaction as bad behaviour and tells them off

When behaviourism doesn't work

Behaviourism runs deeply through Good Parenting™. So deeply that most people don't notice it's there at all until they come up against a child who doesn't play by the rules. For there are assumptions to a behaviourist approach – primary of which is the assumption that if you make the consequences severe enough, the child will comply and change their behaviour. The assumption is that children must be made to behave.

Some children don't do this. The more severe the consequences that their parent comes up with, the more the child refuses to comply. No iPad for a week? Fine. No supper? I wasn't hungry anyway. No holidays this year? That's fine, I prefer staying at home. No sweets? I don't care.

What happens then is that parents think they must make the consequences more severe in the hope that the child will give in. They're sometimes told to find 'something that they really care about' and take it away. I even know a parent who was advised to buy a games console for her children with the idea that she would then be able to take it away as a punishment.

Remember the communication traps from Chapter 4? When a parent's reaction to a child creates a loop in the code breaker, it

can form a trap. The behaviour trap is a particularly vicious one because what it can mean is that parents become harsher and harsher with their children, in the hope that their behaviour will change. It's not so much a simple loop as a downward spiral. The child ends up surrounded by negativity and feeling terrible about themselves. They hear many more negative things about themselves than positive things.

I have never yet met a child who, as the punishments became more severe, became more cooperative and easier to be around. They do sometimes give up and become more compliant on a particular issue, but they are usually furious about it. And who could blame them? If my husband prevented me from doing things I enjoy because I had failed to empty the bins, it would not improve our relationship or my happiness.

Getting stuck in the behaviour trap also happens to some children at school, like Sera. They end up surrounded in negativity and disapproval. Everyone is behaving as if being nice to them would be 'rewarding their behaviour'. If a school uses a whole class behaviour system (where the whole class is punished if one child doesn't comply), then this negativity can come from their peers as well as the teachers. The children who are having the hardest time find themselves in a hostile environment. This does not improve things and can affect how they think and feel about themselves into adulthood.

The low demand approach to behaviour is underpinned by something Dr Ross Greene explains in his book *The Explosive Child*. It's the assumption that runs through everything:

Children do well if they can.

This means that if children aren't doing well (by which I really mean living a life that fulfils them and makes them happy) then we need to work out the reasons why and start there.

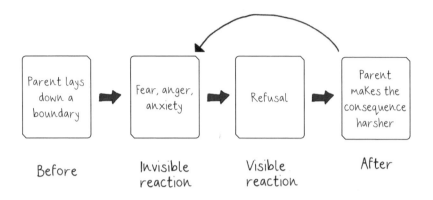

Before — Invisible reaction — Visible reaction — After

The behaviour trap

How do you release the behaviour trap? You'll know by now that the low demand approach to parenting works on two levels. There are the immediate, visible, obvious events. This is the 'What do we do now?' level. Then there is the groundwork, which is the ongoing work to change the way that your family works so that the child's arousal is reduced, and they can start to become less reactive. This is where the REACH principles come in.

I'm going to start with 'In the moment' scenarios, which is for those times when everything is going wrong, the 'unacceptable behaviour' moments. Then I'll move into thinking about the groundwork.

This will include changes in day-to-day things like transitions, difficult conversations and non-negotiables.

In the moment – the behaviour cycle

The most important thing to remember about the low demand approach to behaviour is that we aim to release the behaviour trap that keeps many children mired in negativity. This means not responding to 'bad behaviour' with punishment. It means not using negativity about the child to try to control their behaviour.

When a child's behaviour is driven by anxiety or distress and an adult reacts in a way that increases anxiety and distress then there is really no good way for this to end. The child gets more distressed, the parent puts more pressure on and before you know it someone has got hurt or is in meltdown. You can see how this works in the illustration.

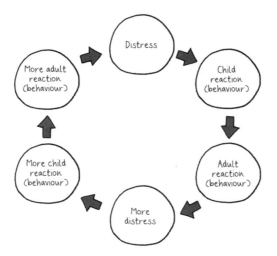

Generally everyone wants to know how to change the child's behaviour – but in fact the quickest way to stop the cycle is via you, the parent. You are far more motivated (look, you're reading this book!) and you hopefully have more control over your behaviour than your child does over theirs.

This approach is for the times when everything has got out of control, when your child is kicking and screaming on the floor or telling you that they hate you. It isn't, however, a way to stop them doing this – there isn't anything apart from extreme fear that will reliably stop an overwhelmed child, and I do not suggest using fear. Fear appears to work in the short term but in the long term it will make things worse.

At the point where a child is behaving like this, they are completely out of their window of tolerance. They have been pushed beyond what they can manage. Their emotions are overwhelming. They aren't really processing information, they are not thinking rationally and they are not doing this on purpose. They are often so sensitive at this point that everything will feel like pressure, even things they can usually tolerate.

There are three main steps.

1. Don't do anything that makes it worse. This is the most effective way to stop the behaviour cycle from turning.

It sounds strange, but I often meet parents who think they *must* do things that escalate a child's distress – like tell them off, use a delayed consequence ('Because you did that yesterday you can't play on the iPad now') or hold a boundary that doesn't really matter ('You must turn off the game *now*, not in five minutes'). They think that this is Good Parenting™. They don't want to reinforce the behaviour.

This is not a teachable moment. The child is out of their window of tolerance and they will not be effectively processing information. Your task at this moment is to get through this without doing anything you'll regret later. Discussions can happen at another time when everyone is calmer. Right now, be flexible. If it's not important, just let it go. If it is important, then say less and don't do anything aggravating. Don't ask lots of questions. They will not have the capacity to answer.

Not making things worse can be hard with a pressure-sensitive child, particularly if they are already overwhelmed. Just standing nearby or looking in the wrong direction can be enough to get you shouted at. You will come under a lot of provocation, and you will have voices in your head saying things like 'They can't be allowed to get away with this' and 'They need to learn.' Bite your tongue. They don't 'need to be told.'

2. Keep everyone safe. If that means removing younger children or making sure that your child doesn't have access to knives or other things they might use as weapons, then that should be your priority.

This is an exception to the 'don't make things worse' goal. Even if it makes your child angrier, you need to do what you can to make everyone safe. If your child can be aggressive, then you need to make sure that the things they might use to hurt themselves and others are inaccessible. Lock things like knives away if you need to. Make a safe place that your other children can go to. Plan ahead and be proactive.

3. Wait for the storm to pass.

When you have stopped doing things that make it worse, and everyone is safe enough, then it's about waiting for the storm to pass. *It will pass*. Even if it takes hours. Providing food and drink might help at this stage, but I'd do that by placing them near to the child and letting them help themselves if they want to. Don't ask them what they want or make suggestions as that will add more pressure to the situation. By removing yourself from the behaviour cycle, you've taken a lot of the fuel out of the fire. You may not be able to make things better, but you are making sure that you aren't making it worse.

> # In the moment aims
>
> 1. Don't make it worse.
> 2. Keep everyone safe.
> 3. Wait for the storm to pass.

You

It is highly stressful parenting a child who doesn't respond to behavioural strategies. It will bring up all sorts of thoughts and feelings. You'll be critical of yourself, critical of your child, and this will make it harder for you to respond calmly and non-reactively in the moment. A threat is frightening, even if it is your beloved eight-year-old who is threatening you. And you cannot leave, particularly if just leaving the room makes your child more distressed and hence their behaviour worse. It's easy for parents to feel trapped by their children's behaviour.

Most of us have a set of automatic thoughts (as well as feelings and body sensations) that pop into our heads at times of stress. These are often negative. We don't choose to have these reactions, and they can make it really hard to respond in a calm and consistent way to distressed children.

Exercise: Automatic reactions

Take some time to do this when you are not looking after your child.

Have a think about what happens when your child's behaviour is at its most challenging. What are your reactions? What thoughts about yourself pop into your head? How does it make you feel, both emotionally and in your body? Allow yourself to be honest.

Write some of them down if you want to. Do not write them down somewhere where your child or other family members might find them.

It can feel strange to write these things down, but once they are written down you can often look at them more dispassionately.

The table below gives some of the thoughts, feelings and body sensations that parents tell me about.

Thoughts:	*They should have grown out of this by now.* *What did I do wrong when they were little?* *Are they insecurely attached?* *I'm a failure.* *I'm not good enough.* *What if it's like this forever?* *I shouldn't feel this way.* *I should be able to stop this.* *I'm a bad parent.* *I never signed up for this.* *I don't want to do this anymore.* *They'd be better off with a different parent.*
Feelings:	Despondency. Despair. Fury. Worry. Frustration, anger. Powerlessness. Hopelessness. Fear.
Body sensations:	Stomach aches, headaches, weird feelings, wanting to run away, numbness, shutting down, prickliness over your body, dizziness, vertigo, buzzing in ears.

All of these thoughts and feelings are natural responses to stress-ful circumstances. They come and go. If they aren't going, then that's a sign that your life isn't sustainable and you need to think seriously about how to look after yourself going forwards.

In the next section I'm going to talk about some ways to move on from those automatic reactions but I'd also encourage you to think seriously about how to make your own wellbeing a priority. These automatic reactions are manageable if they come and go, but not if they are dominating your daily life. In the short term, you can push yourself beyond what you can take, but parenting is a long game and you will crash if you aren't getting time to recharge yourself.

You need some space where you can decompress or at some point you will burn out, and that will help no one. This space can be very difficult to achieve if your child is only happy when you are there, or if you are a single parent with no support. I talk more about how to do this in Chapter 11.

Directing your attention elsewhere

You have probably already discovered that fighting your automatic reactions doesn't help. In fact, it can make things worse. If you start with a negative thought – for example 'I'm a failure' – and then try to fight that with another thought – 'You shouldn't feel like that' – then that first thought often comes back even stronger than before. You can get into an internal battle that makes you feel even worse.

Instead of fighting your automatic reactions, think about side-stepping them. Observe those thoughts as they come, and then deliberately direct your attention to something else. You can imagine yourself stepping sideways if you want. This is not easy to do; you will need to practise it and I suggest that initially you practise it at times when you are not under a lot of stress. Just like when you learn to drive and you don't start off on the main roads.

I'm going to outline two different ways to side-step: the first is a behaviour mantra, and the second is an 'I've got this' imagery exercise.

Behaviour mantras

One way to side-step your automatic reactions is to find yourself a 'behaviour mantra' to repeat. Choose yourself a short phrase or sentence that resonates with you – these ones might work or you might have something else you prefer. Write it down on your phone or stick it on your wall.

Behaviour mantras

'This too will pass.'

'They aren't giving me a hard time; they are having a hard time.'

'This requires my absolute best parenting skills to get through.'

'We will come out the other side of this.'

'One step at a time.'

'I don't have to solve this, just get through it.'

When we did this exercise in a webinar, some parents said that they had songs they played in their heads when things were really hard. *I Will Survive* was one, *I'm Still Standing* was another.

You can repeat your behaviour mantra to yourself when things get hard. As you repeat it, breathe in and feel it through your body. You don't need to use it to fight the automatic reactions, just let them be and direct your attention to the mantra.

'I've got this' imagery

Images are very powerful. Most of us are very much caught up with our thoughts when we are in a time of crisis, and yet the part of our brain that is triggering our danger reaction is a part we share with almost all animals. Our automatic reactions are not really on the level of language. We can't talk our way out of them. Images are much more effective.

The idea of this exercise is to find an image that reminds you that you have got through difficult things before, and you will get through this too.

Exercise: 'I've got this' imagery

Choose a metaphor or analogy for keeping your cool when things get hard. It doesn't have to be something that you can really do. It can be fantasy.

Some that other parents have thought of are:

Putting on a performance on stage
Ice skating
Flying overhead like a bird
Juggling
Sailing
Dancing
Skiing

Now I'd like you to imagine yourself doing this and let yourself focus on how it feels in your body. Take some deep breaths. Notice how it feels when it's all going well.

Give it a phrase or name – maybe 'I've got this' or 'I can do it.'

When you have connected with that sense of it going well, then introduce a challenge to the image. Maybe there's a bump in the ice, or you fly through a rain storm.

Notice how that feels in your body. Focus on your emotions and the sensations. Keep imagining yourself moving and repeat the phase 'I've got this' to yourself.

You might find it helps to cross your hands in front of your body and gently tap alternatively across your chest in a 'butterfly hug.' Some people find that this enhances their positive feelings.

Special circumstances

A crisis is not the moment to be worried about setting precedents, or breaking rules. You need to get through it without anyone getting hurt, and if that means watching TV after you usually have it turned off, or making food when the kitchen is usually closed, you do that. Do whatever makes it easier to get through the moment and tell the children that this is a special circumstance and that you are allowed to be flexible, even if you said something else at first.

Some families have had success with making that really clear using an external sign. I know one family who used to go 'Vehicle reversing, vehicle reversing' and make the beeping noise that some cars make when they needed to back out of a corner and do something different. Another would say 'Okay, time for a U-turn' and mime turning the wheel on the car. Another family whose child liked card games made actual 'wild cards' that they carried with them and would produce in a time of emergency to show the child that things were going to be different for a while. Think about how your children understand change and what sort of props might help them understand that this is different.

Of course, you have to be prepared for your child to use these signals too when you might not be thinking that it's a special circumstances type situation – in which case, don't use your Automatic No. Stop for a moment and think – they might be right.

Then don't beat yourself up about it.

Emotional hangovers

After things have gone badly wrong, it's common for children to apparently bounce back and to seem completely unaffected within a matter of minutes, while their parents are left reeling with the emotional impact of what happened. Some parents tell me that they are left feeling the aftermath for days afterwards, particularly if children say things that feel personal and distressing, like 'I hate you' or 'You're ruining my life', or if they have hurt someone vulnerable.

This can feel like an emotional hangover. Parents can be particularly affected when they regret how they behaved in the heat of the moment. Parents tell me that when, despite all their best intentions, they find themselves shouting things like 'You'll end up in prison if you don't stop this' or 'What is wrong with you?' they experience a sense of relief and a release in expressing those thoughts. They regret it when they see the fear on their child's face. Afterwards they feel deeply ashamed and like they have blown it all.

It's okay to get it wrong. You can't always be calm and consistent, no matter how hard you try. You can apologise to your child and move on – but the trickier bit is often forgiving yourself.

At this point, you need the compassion for yourself that you'd like to bring to your child. If you're going to model forgiveness with your child, you need to practise doing that for yourself as well. A lot has been written about compassion, and there are some good self-help books that can help you to develop compassion for yourself. The classic is *The Compassionate Mind* by Paul Gilbert. The exercise below is inspired by one from his book.

Exercise: Compassionate friend

Start with focusing on your breathing, find your rhythm. Just let yourself accept the moment for a few breaths.

Then allow yourself to think about a caring, compassionate image. Let lots of images come into your head.

Would you like your compassionate friend to feel old or young? Male or female? Human or non-human?

What colours and sounds are associated for you with the qualities of compassionate friendship?

Let those come into your head.

Now is the time to choose.

How would you like your ideal compassionate friend to look?

How would you like them to sound?

What other sensory qualities would you like them to have?

How would you like your ideal compassionate friend to relate to you?

How would you like to relate to your ideal compassionate friend?

What name would you like to give your compassionate friend?

What would your compassionate friend say to you at your most challenging times?

Practise bringing this image to mind at times when you feel okay and relaxed, and then as you get more practised at this you can bring your compassionate friend to mind at the times when you feel most self-critical and judgemental.

Putting in the groundwork

So far, I've been talking about behavioural emergencies. Getting through the crises. But this isn't enough. The overall aim is to reduce the number of crises, and you won't manage that through emergency management. The long-term aim is to enlarge your child's window of tolerance, so that there are fewer crises and meltdowns. This is where the REACH principles (which I introduced in Chapter 3) come in. Just like in Chapter 3, the REACH principles are about mindset shifts rather than specific techniques. They are about the atmosphere that you are aiming to create in your home.

Relationships

In the longer term, your relationship with your child is the key to getting out of the behaviour trap. The aim is to stop using your relationship as a behavioural control tool. You want the child to feel that your relationship with them is unconditional. You have their back, no matter what.

UNCONDITIONAL

Sometimes adults find it hard to imagine what a parent–child relationship looks like if it isn't controlling. They are so used to thinking about their interactions with their child through the lens of behaviour management that the question in their heads is always 'Should I be letting them get away with this?'

What does this mean? You don't need to be less nice to them when their behaviour is challenging, or nicer to them when they are behaving 'well'. Your relationship with them is a source of emotional security and safety, and they need that just as much when they are struggling as when things are going well.

If you're like most parents, you have behaviourist ideas going around your head that will affect your relationship with your child. Here are some ideas that will make it hard – and alternatives.

Behaviourist ideas about relationships	Low demand relationships
Being too nice to a child will spoil them.	Being nice to a child is likely to make everyone happier.
Doing what they ask for when having a meltdown will result in more meltdowns.	If they're having a meltdown, the priority is de-escalation and safety.
You need to stick to boundaries or they will walk all over you.	Making boundaries flexible models flexibility for our children.

Children need to know who's boss.	Children need to know that their voice matters.
If you give them an inch they'll take a mile.	Children do well if they can.
Parents need to show tough love.	Showing our children that we listen to them makes them feel valued.

You could try doing this as an exercise – what are the unhelpful ideas that you are carrying around with you about parenting, and can you think of some alternatives?

Mindset shift

Instead of '*I mustn't be nice to her when she is behaving badly as that will reinforce the behaviour*', try '*The worse the behaviour, the more she needs connection and empathy.*'

Environment

Context matters when it comes to behaviour. Behaviour that is a problem in one environment can be an asset somewhere else. One immediate way to reduce the problems caused by your child's behaviour is to modify your environment to play to your child's strengths right now.

If they are at a stage of breaking things, put valuable vases away. If they love jumping and rolling, consider investing in some mats or a trampoline. Find places where they can really run around if that's what they need. One inspiring family set up parkour in their (small, London) garden with old pallets. If your child finds groups of people overwhelming, focus on one-to-one meet-ups instead.

Let yourself really think about how your child manages different environments, and get rid of the idea that they 'have to learn' how to do things like stop breaking stuff or keeping still. They will learn these things as they grow up and mature. Right now, it's easier to change the environment than to change them.

Mindset shift

Instead of 'He needs to learn to behave', try 'We need to get the environment right so he can thrive.'

Active involvement

Many parents confuse active involvement with behavioural control, and so their involvement is laden with expectations. Children react accordingly (in other words, they say no) and parents are left not knowing what to do. 'They don't want me to be there' they say, and so they back off.

Active involvement doesn't have to be controlling. Instead of try-ing to get the child to join you, you can join the child where they are, even if that is engrossed in a video game or watching a TV show for the hundredth time. If your teenager won't play with you, then you can show an interest anyway. Learn how to play the games they are playing. Ask if you can watch them play. Start where they are. Resist the urge to make it a teachable moment or to judge them for how they are spending their time.

One common block to parents being more actively involved with their children is how difficult transitions are. Children find it hard to change from one activity or place to the next – and so everything feels like a struggle.

Transitions

Do you find transitions hard? Going from inside to outside, or from school to home? Sometimes children will refuse to do something, and the refusal isn't actually about the next activity at all. It's about the process of getting from one to another. Changing from one activity to another, or one place to another, can be very hard for some children.

Parents try to speed up transitions by putting on pressure, and the more pressure they put on, the more difficult the transition becomes. They get stuck in the Pressure Paradox trap.

The low demand approach asks, *How can I make this easier?* while accepting that transitions are often hard.

The following table has some strategies parents often use for transitions (and which can keep everyone stuck in the trap). On the right-hand side are low demand alternatives.

Adding pressure to transitions	Reduced pressure alternatives
Abrupt: 'Time to stop playing that game now.'	Choice: 'Are you able to stop now or is there a better time coming up in your game?'
Warning: 'I'm going to give you five minutes and then you need to stop.'	Choice: 'Would it work better for you to have five or ten more minutes?'
Nagging: 'Why haven't you put your shoes on yet? I've told you ten times. . .'	Letting it be: Take the shoes with you and say, 'Your shoes are here when you want them.'
Threats: 'Put that iPad down and put your clothes on or there will be no more games this week.'	Playfulness: 'Your clothes are here, I'll bet you can't put them all on without putting the iPad down for more than twenty seconds.'
Introducing uncertainty: (just about to head out) 'Are you really sure you want to go? We could go somewhere else if you preferred?'	Clarity: 'We're going there now; we can always leave if we want to.'
Frustration: 'Why didn't you get the lunch box when I told you to?'	Just do it: 'I'll grab your lunch box.'
Extended indecision: 'Shall we go? Shall we not go? Shall we go somewhere else? Maybe we should just stay at home?'	Clarity: 'We'll go. We can always come home' (or 'We'll stay here. It seems like a better idea right now').
Mind-reading: 'You must put your coat on before going out as you'll get cold.'	Flexibility: 'I'll bring your coat along just in case' (or do so without mentioning it).

Putting the load on them: 'You need to get your clothes ready and brush your hair earlier so we are in time for school.'	Taking whatever part of the load you can: 'Your clothes are here and I can brush your hair while you watch that film.'
Strictness: 'We are going to school right now and I don't want to hear any more fussing.'	Playfulness: 'I'm going to play that we're in *Minecraft* and that this is a new world we've just spawned in. Shall we take our minecart to school and see if James wants to play too?'

Mindset shift

Instead of *'They just won't do fun things with me'*, try *'What could I do to make it easier for us to have fun?'*

Collaboration

This is the big one when it comes to behaviour. And it includes the thing I get asked about most. What is the low demand approach when things *must* happen? What about the non-negotiables? Parents ask me if low demand parenting just means they have to do everything the child wants, even if they have serious misgivings about it.

No, low demand parenting does not mean that. You are the parent, and sometimes you need to make difficult decisions your child doesn't like. There is no easy and distress-free way to make someone do something they don't want to do – and part of parenting is doing this. There are always non-negotiables.

However, many of us aren't good at distinguishing between real non-negotiables and nice-to-have expectations. Seat belts in the car are a real non-negotiable. Brushing your hair is a nice-to-have. A lot of what you read about parenting doesn't really make this distinction.

They use the term 'boundary' for anything that the parent wants the child to do.

Is it a real non-negotiable?

Non-negotiables will vary from family to family and will change over time as the child grows up. Getting to a hospital appointment, moving from one parent to another if parents don't live together, allowing a parent to leave the house so they can go to work or get a much-needed break may all need to happen. Not watching pornography online or going alone to meet a stranger they met on the internet are non-negotiables relating to safety and the law. Something that is quite clearly making the child distressed but which they seem unable to stop (like continuously checking social media when they are being cyber-bullied) is about emotional wellbeing.

The first step is to ask yourself these questions:

- Is this really a non-negotiable or is it just something I would like them to do?
- What will the (real life) consequences be if they don't do this?

Some things seem like non-negotiables (putting on pyjamas at bedtime, practising the piano or sitting at the dinner table and eating your greens) but can be safely dropped in the short term. Don't panic; dropping them now doesn't mean that things won't change in the future.

Children are short-term thinkers. They do not have the experience to think through some of the consequences of their decisions. They make choices based on their feelings right now, which can be great but sometimes means that they don't see the bigger picture. This is one of the things that changes as they go through adolescence – but it changes gradually rather than overnight. Parents need to hold the long-term view for the family and that means that sometimes there are non-negotiables.

Safety first

Your number one guiding principle when deciding whether something is non-negotiable is safety. Parents have to keep young people safe. It is their responsibility to do so. Physically, but also emotionally and psychologically. Even if they protest.

Physical safety is often easiest to discern (if not to carry out). This means stopping them crossing the road in front of a car, and stopping them from hurting other people. It means providing enough good food for them, a stable warm place to live, and protecting them from bullies. Most parents find it easy to discern boundaries around physical safety.

Emotional and psychological safety is trickier, as it's more of a judgement call. However, if there is something your child is doing that is causing distress and they don't seem able to stop, you need to step in. This could include things like not allowing them to watch 18-rated films or monitoring their social media use. It might involve stopping them from being in WhatsApp groups that cause ongoing distress. It could include not getting them a smartphone if you don't think they are ready for it, or locking away the means to self-harm.

Low demand parenting is not about saying yes to everything. It's important that you feel able to say no. But, I hear you say, how do we actually do that?

First, some hard truths.

I cannot tell you how to get your child to agree to non-negotiables without protest. The only way that I know to do this reliably is to use fear. Really frightened children are often obedient. That doesn't mean that fear is a good parenting tool nor that this is good for the child. I don't suggest that you use fear. Not using fear means that your child is going to feel able to tell you how they feel – and they may well disagree with you.

This is one reason why it's really important to have it straight in your head that this really is a non-negotiable and therefore worth some distress.

If something really is non-negotiable, then don't give the child the impression that it is negotiable. Don't say things like 'Do you want to put your seat belt on?' or 'Would you like to go to Granny's?' when actually, there isn't a choice. It's easier (and less demanding) to say something like 'We all need to put our seat belts on before we can leave' or 'Shall we go to Granny's house now or in fifteen minutes?' Many children find uncertainty highly anxiety-provoking, and if they think that you are undecided about whether something is going to happen, it will make them more anxious. This will mean they are much less likely to be able to cooperate.

Next step, avoid coaxing or persuading. It's tempting to say things like 'If you put your seat belt on quickly we can get ice cream' or 'Please, please, please, put your phone down', but when parents start coaxing or trying to persuade a pressure-sensitive child, the child is likely to get entrenched in that position. The other thing not to do is lapse into telling them off or negativity. Saying things like 'Why can't you just behave like your brother?' will just get you into the behaviour trap. Instead, use the low demand communication tools from the last chapter.

If something is really non-negotiable, instead of the starting point being 'Please, please, please, will you do this?' it needs to be 'This has to happen, so how can we make it easier for you?'

Mornings

This stance of 'This has to happen; how can we make it easier?' shifts the conversation. The question is no longer, 'Are you going to do this?' but instead 'How are we going to make this possible?' It sometimes helps to appeal to a higher power than yourself – to say something like 'The government says that parents have to keep kids safe. I don't have a choice about that. Because of that, I can't let you walk down the middle of the road. Yes, I know it's annoying. How can we make it easier for you to walk on the pavement?'

With younger children, parents are likely to have to do most of the thinking about how to make things easier. Use what you know of your child. Adding any discussion makes it harder for some children – in which case, don't do that – while others like to know everything in advance and see pictures of where you are going.

With teenagers, there might be more of a discussion. But the key thing is that it's not a discussion about *whether* this thing will happen, it's a discussion about *how* this thing is going to happen. Ideally, it's proactive rather than reactive – in other words, you have the discussion at a time when you and they are calm and you are planning how to manage something together rather than in the heat of the moment.

Non-negotiables

1. Work out if this really is non-negotiable.
2. If it is, don't give the child the impression that there is a choice.
3. Don't try to coax or persuade or be negative about them.
4. Ask yourself or them, 'This has to happen, so how can we make it easier?'

Justin and Ayesha's story is a good example of a non-negotiable issue and how it can be dealt with.

When Justin's daughter Ayesha was young, he found her watching a pornographic YouTube cartoon. It had been auto-suggested to her by the algorithm on the basis of her viewing history of *Peppa Pig* and *Paw Patrol*. She couldn't read yet and she was just choosing the next suggested video. It was clear to Justin at that point that he could not keep Ayesha safe on YouTube. He knew Ayesha would not be able to understand the reason and he didn't want to scare her with stories of what she might see.

Justin thought, Okay, she needs to stop watching YouTube alone because I can't keep her safe. This has to happen, so how can I make it easier?

He decided that he would download alternative video apps that Ayesha could explore freely and where Justin was confident she would not find porn – children's versions of BBC iPlayer and Amazon Prime. Justin then said that they could watch YouTube together but she could not watch it alone and he removed it from her device. Ayesha was very angry and upset about this. Justin empathised and agreed that it was annoying but didn't negotiate or coax her. He knew this was a real non-negotiable. Justin could not keep her safe on YouTube and he was not prepared to risk her emotional and psychological safety in the hands of YouTube creators making cartoon videos designed to fool the algorithms. Keeping her safe had to be the priority and Justin was confident of that.

Ayesha was very upset. She felt it was unfair of her dad and that Justin had no right to remove apps from her device without her consent. Of course, she didn't really understand why it had happened and Justin wasn't going to explain in any great detail at this point. Justin said that he was sorry, but part of his job as a parent was to keep her safe. Justin didn't expect her to be happy about it and he didn't get angry with Ayesha for being angry. Ayesha was very angry for a day, a bit less angry the day after that, then she started to watch iPlayer instead and by a week later the 'No YouTube alone' rule had so much become a feature of the household that Ayesha wouldn't even watch YouTube at another person's house when she had the chance.

Making something non-negotiable isn't punitive. Justin was not punishing his daughter by removing YouTube. The reason was because he couldn't keep her safe. If something really is non-negotiable, then be consistent – don't say that the child can't watch YouTube because it's not safe and then later say they can for twenty minutes if they are well behaved.

Don't overuse your non-negotiables. Your children will respect your restrictions more if they know that you only do this when things really matter.

Making changes

Sometimes, you really need a change to happen, but you know that your child is likely to resist it. They might find any new suggestions anxiety provoking, and so it brings out their Automatic No.

This is the time for drip feeding. This isn't a short-term or immediate approach; you need lots of time and patience.

Essentially drip feeding involves mentioning something, stepping back and giving it time for the child to get used to the idea. You can predict that they will complain, say no, get angry – that's all fine and expected. It's part of the process. You just need to be there, listening and empathic, but not arguing or pushing back. Then you mention it again. And again a bit later. This is not a quick way to change. It's a slow and gradual process.

The hardest bit of drip feeding is stepping back and not pushing. I recommend you imagine yourself doing something slow and relaxing. Even better, go and make a nice cup of coffee.

The idea is that it takes many children time to get used to new ideas, and that they will often start off by saying no to any new idea. Introduced over time, a new idea can become more familiar, and the child is more able to think about it. They still might not agree with you, but they are no longer reacting from a place of fear. Moving from an Automatic No to a Genuine No (or Yes) is the aim (see Chapter 4 for more about the Automatic No trap).

Low demand approaches to behaviour

Question	Intervention
Is this really a non-negotiable or can I change my expectations or the environment so it's no longer necessary?	Change the environment or drop the expectation.
Is this an urgent safety issue (e.g. running out into the road)?	Step in and stop them. Expect anger, and deal with the fall-out afterwards. Empathise with their distress ('It was really annoying that I did that') but do not say you won't do it again. Appeal to a higher authority if that helps ('The government tells parents that they must keep their children safe and that's part of my job'). Be confident that keeping them safe is part of being a trustworthy parent.
Is it very important that this happens (e.g. medical appointments)?	*This has to happen, so how can we make it easier?* Don't try to persuade them (this will make them more anxious) or give the impression that this is negotiable. Use what you know of them to make it easier (e.g. does advance warning help or make it worse?) Apply any special circumstances that help. Predict that it will be hard just beforehand and then it will be over.

Is this about the transition and not the thing that is going to happen next?	*How can we make this easier?* Use low-pressure transition techniques. Predict that it will be difficult and use your mantra or imagery.
Is this something you'd really like to change but can't discuss as the child gets too distressed (e.g. moving furniture, buying new clothes)?	Drip feeding. Don't expect anything to happen fast. Don't give up. Let the idea become familiar.
Is it something you need to talk to your child about but can't because they get so distressed (e.g. internet safety, bullying)?	Ask for their advice about someone else with a similar problem. Talk side by side and while doing something else. Talk about yourself and your own experiences (possibly as a child/ teenager). Predict the distress and show that you aren't scared of it ('I know it's hard to talk about this but it's important'). Don't give up on important issues to avoid distress. Sometimes distress is inevitable and it is part of life.

With all of this, it's about accepting that this is hard but that it is also important, and sometimes important things are hard to do. When you get it wrong (and you will), then apologise and move on. It's okay for parents to get things wrong and it's okay for children to see that. The process of repairing a relationship after things have gone wrong is something children need to experience as they grow up.

Humour

Laugh about it all afterwards, particularly if you find yourself saying things you never thought you would: 'Don't wipe your fingers on the cat'; 'Please stop pulling your brother's toes' and of course Joyce Grenfell's classic (from *George, Don't Do That*, which is worth a listen for a reminder of nurseries in a time gone by), 'We never bite our friends.'

Make up silly songs about things that happen – and if your child can manage it, make jokes about silly expectations and what most adults would think if talked to like a child. If your child is very sensitive to humour and feels that you are laughing at them, then don't do this. However, it is okay to laugh about things to yourself or even to write them down to remember in the future when everything is less emotionally charged.

Eliza and Naomi:
Learning to behave

NAOMI: What was the mindset shift that happened for you around behaviour, Eliza?

ELIZA: I think the first thing is getting to a point where it isn't working. I know that the more that I ramped it up in terms of trying to tell them off then that created an angrier child, which then created an angrier me.

I think it just worked cyclically once I started to change that. I think it started with thinking about it and shutting out the outside voices. Then that's when the pressure reduced. Then I could just meet my child where they were at that time, but that very much involved not worrying about the outside world.

Then when I could see that it worked. . . It changed in me internally. It changed my nervous system so that I didn't feel reactive.

NAOMI: You focused more on attunement. In order to do that, you had to switch off the messages that you were getting from outside that what you should be doing was telling off. It's like you had to start to see what was really going on as opposed to what the world was telling you should be going on.

You have to start saying, Hang on a minute. When I tell them off, it makes everything worse. When I forced them onto the Naughty Step, it's awful. So why am I doing it? Whereas the message you get from outside is just keep doing it, and that's the only way.

ELIZA: This might not be the same for all parents, but certainly for me it felt like I was almost becoming an alien being as well. It didn't feel natural to be an authoritarian or angry person. I was becoming someone that wasn't me and I was introducing conflict into our home. It felt like I was the one who was introducing that. All of that felt very uncomfortable and unnatural.

NAOMI: Because if you've got a child who doesn't comply, then everything can become so negative so quickly, can't it? Everything is a problem. If you've got a child who's really reactive, then you just spiral really quickly.

ELIZA: It's a very negative place to live as well. To have that in your home isn't a very nice way to live.

NAOMI: And what's it for? What are we making everybody really unhappy for here? We're trying to control behaviour all the time and it's just not working. I think it's the difference between short term and long term. A lot of the times when people are talking about behaviour, they are talking about control of behaviour in the short term and they're not thinking about long term and wellbeing. Being in a negative environment all the time is not going to be great for anybody, for parents or children.

ELIZA: But as soon as you start talking about it in terms of long term, then you're taking that pressure off as well.

NAOMI: Unless you have that thought, If I don't get them under control now then. . .?

ELIZA: They'll be in prison.

NAOMI: Yes, this is just going to get worse. People say that a lot, actually, with the very young children, don't they? If you've got a three-year-old, people say 'Just wait until they're a teenager.'

It's a really weird way of seeing child development, this idea that the whole point as a parent is to get them under control and then to keep them there for life.

ELIZA: It's always that, isn't it? It's like negativity about children is a very strong narrative through parenting.

NAOMI: Particularly if your child's behaviour isn't compliant. Once you start to see behaviour through a lens of a struggling child rather than *This is a badly behaved child*, then it makes no sense at all to be punitive. You're basically saying the children who are struggling more should get more negative parenting. Somehow that's going to result in a happy child?

ELIZA: And a happy home.

NAOMI: It just doesn't make sense.

Too much to read, too little time?

1. Behaviour is a way in which people express their feelings and thoughts and react to their environment.
2. Behaviourist ideas run through mainstream parenting culture but are unhelpful with pressure-sensitive children.
3. We start with the assumption that children do well if they can.
4. It is easier to change your own behaviour than your child's behaviour – so start there.
5. There are non-negotiables, but these are usually fewer than parents assume.
6. If something really is non-negotiable, then the real question is how to make it as easy as possible.

More to read if you are interested

The Compassionate Mind – Paul Gilbert

Drive: The Surprising Truth About What Motivates Us – Daniel Pink

The Explosive Child – Ross Greene

Sulky, Rowdy, Rude: Why Kids Really Act Out and What to Do About It – Bo Elvén and Tina Wiman

6

Emotions

A trip to the park

No one sees the careful prep beforehand, making sure everyone knows what is going to happen, when and where. No one else hears the questions answered several hundred times, 'Yes we're going there; yes, we might see them; no, you don't have to join in if you don't want to; yes, you can take your tablet; yes, if you need to go home we'll leave.'

No one sees the bag with snacks, a complete change of clothes, several different types of entertainment and a charging lead. No one notices the way you are constantly assessing the situation – can we manage another five minutes, or do I need to find an attractive reason to leave right now?

No one realises that it didn't 'just happen' that one child is settled at a table, playing their spaceship game, while the other child plays on the climbing frame. They don't notice the multi-tasking skills it takes to respond to the cries of 'Did you see me?' and the questions about fuselage and fuel without getting them muddled up. You develop a default 'interested and attentive' face, which works fine until you answer the rocket question with 'Well done!'

In fact, when another parent *does* notice the effort, they are often dismissive. 'They're fine!' they say. 'Relax.' They make a comment about 'helicopter parenting' or how their approach is 'benign neglect'. They say that boredom is good, and they shouldn't expect you to play with them all the time. You think to yourself, Well, yes, it would be nice to have that option. But you don't say it, because how can you?

Now you have to manage another set of needs, as you pretend to the other parents that you aren't paddling desperately below the

185

surface to keep this all going. That this isn't all balanced on a knife edge. You pretend that you're just sipping a cup of coffee and chatting. You wonder if you're the only one who feels like this; if everyone else really is as relaxed as they seem. But you don't ask, because what if they are?

Then there's a quick end when it becomes apparent it's time to leave *now* and you negotiate with the child who doesn't want to go while packing up the snacks and the bucket and spade and the drawing tablets and the crisps. You try to postpone the meltdown for long enough to get away from the others or head it off with promises of ice cream on the way home.

At the end of it all you are exhausted, and what did you do today? 'We just went to the park. Nothing happened.'

You might recognise yourself in this story. Maybe you recognise your days and the sense of exhaustion but haven't acknowledged just how hard you work in these scenarios. You might have always blamed yourself for finding these things so hard when others don't appear to.

It's not your fault and you're not doing anything wrong. Some children need intense emotional and physical support just to manage everyday life. Providing that for them is hard, undervalued work. When it goes well, it's completely invisible to those around you, but when it goes badly, parents often get the blame.

Managing emotions is a demand (and a skill)

Keeping yourself emotionally balanced is hard work. We all have to cope with the events of our day, the trials and tribulations, make sense of them and integrate them into our life story. When something happens that overwhelms our ability to do that, we can become very distressed or we shut down.

In Chapter 1, I introduced the idea of the window of tolerance. This is the emotional zone within which we can manage the challenges and demands of everyday life. Keeping ourselves in this window of tolerance is skilled work.

As children grow up, their brains mature and their capacity to keep themselves in their window of tolerance improves. This doesn't just happen. As with so many aspects of brain development, it is dependent on experience. Children learn about emotions through many experiences of being helped to manage their emotions by caring adults. They learn to calm and soothe themselves through being calmed and soothed by others. If they don't get those experiences in early life (for example because their parents are not able to care for them properly, or due to growing up in an institution without ongoing caring relationships) then their capacity to regulate their emotions can be affected in the long term. Some children (and adults) find it harder to regulate their emotions than others, no matter what their earlier experiences. As with other aspects of brain development, our capacity to regulate our emotions depends upon a combination of genetic predisposition and ongoing experience.

Whatever the reason, it's the case that at any given age some children have a much smaller window of tolerance than others. These are the children who seem emotionally fragile, or who become angry at the drop of a hat. They seem to go 'from zero to a hundred' with very little warning. They are the ones whose parents are always on alert, waiting for something to go wrong. Or they are the children who are shut down, not seeming interested or excited by anything. The ones who seem to be frozen and are easy to push around, or who are extremely compliant, making them vulnerable.

Emotions are an invisible reaction, and as such it's easy to ignore them. We sometimes think that a child who isn't displaying emotions isn't feeling anything, but children demonstrate – and communicate – their emotions in very different ways. Managing emotions, your own and your child's, is a key part of low demand parenting.

From the day your child was born, you will have helped them to manage their emotions. When you rocked your baby to sleep, or bounced up and down on the spot while holding them, you were helping them to calm themselves. When you took them for a buggy ride so they would go to sleep more easily, you were helping them to regulate themselves.

As your child gets older, you have continued to help them with their emotions. Parents do this both by managing the environment and by helping the child soothe themselves through hugs, keeping calm themselves, providing food and drink, rocking or stroking – whatever the child finds helpful. They do it by showing their children that even though they, the child, think that their spilled drink is the end of the world, their parent knows that they will get through this. This dance between parents and children is called 'co-regulation' – helping another person regulate their emotions.

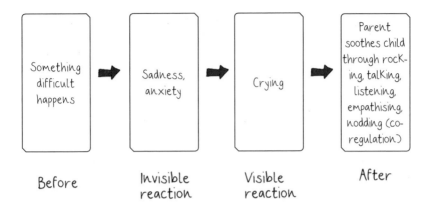

| Before | Invisible reaction | Visible reaction | After |

Much of the work of parenting in the early years is helping children to maintain their emotional balance (even if parents don't think about it like this). When parents notice that their toddlers are getting tired or over-excited and leave an activity early to head off a meltdown, that's emotion regulation. Regular food, drink and cuddles all help a child to manage their emotions. Staying close by is another way in which parents help young children regulate their emotions – just seeing a familiar person means that children feel they can take on challenges they would not be able to do alone.

Over time, children learn to manage more of their emotions. They internalise the soothing that the parents have been doing for them up to this point. They become able to tolerate the distress of a different colour cup. They no longer need to have their parent 'kiss it better' when they scrape their knee. This happens gradually, and at different times for different children. Tolerating distress is something many adults continue to find hard.

Sometimes parents are encouraged by others to step back too quickly, when their instincts tell them that their child isn't ready yet. Other people will tell them that their child is old enough to manage alone now, or that the only way that they will learn to manage is to be left alone to learn how to 'stand on their own two feet'.

The expectations that parents will step back get more insistent as children grow older. They become less like expectations and more like requirements. Many schools have residential trips for nine- and ten-year-olds, where children stay away overnight, sometimes refusing to let children talk to their parents at all in that time. These trips require children to manage their own emotions, managing day-to-day things like dressing themselves, sleeping, eating and their interactions with peers while maintaining their emotional balance. Some children are ready for this, others aren't – something that often comes under the banner of 'homesickness'.

Some children need co-regulation for longer than other children. Their emotions feel very intense to them, and they need continued help to soothe themselves and stay in their window of tolerance. As they get older, this need is often invisible to those who don't know them well, particularly if their response is to shut down rather than to be disruptive. The young person might appear to be 'fine' but this is only the case because the people around them are putting in a significant amount of work to keep them on an even keel. When that support stops, it can be like the safety net being pulled from under them and they fall apart. For some young people, this happens when they go to secondary school. For others, it happens at the transition to university or the workplace. Reduced support is combined with increased demands, and they can no longer stay balanced. They go into burnout or breakdown.

The parents of teenagers are often haunted by worries that they should not be providing as much support as they do, in case it is preventing their young people from learning to manage by themselves. They know that their adolescents still need a lot of emotional support, but they feel bad about providing it. As children grow up, they do need experiences of managing their emotions for themselves. I'll talk more about how parents can help with that in the second half of this chapter.

Children need opportunities to practise keeping themselves balanced – but these experiences should come when they are ready, not because they have reached an arbitrary age when other people think they should be ready. They should be small and gradual changes, with no sense of being dropped in at the deep end. For some children, these moments often come much later than for others. I know of children who couldn't manage being dropped off at a friend's house without a parent until they were thirteen or fourteen, for example, and for whom going to sleep without a parent present was not possible until they were well into their teens.

Making the invisible visible

You will be doing a lot of co-regulation with your child, probably without noticing it. Since birth you've been making adjustments to keep them in their window of tolerance.

Spend a day recording all the small things that you notice and then what you did about them. Here are some examples from Claudia, whose son Marty was ten.

What did I notice?	What did I do about it?
Marty was starting to rock and groan at breakfast and I realised that we had run out of his favourite cereal and he was finding it hard to adjust.	*Found something else he really likes for breakfast – waffles from the freezer – made them and then quietly put them on the table for him to notice.*
When we got to school Marty was scanning the playground anxiously. I realised he was looking for his friend and couldn't see her.	*Looked for his friend's mum and she was there. Pointed her out to Marty so he knew that his friend would be there.*
Picked up Marty from school and he looked glazed and exhausted. Ben's mum suggested we all go to the park. She likes to chat. I realised Marty wouldn't be able to cope but that once we were there it would be very hard to leave.	*I lied to Ben's mum. I said we had to go back because I had an important meeting later. I gave Marty a snack and got him to the car before he had a meltdown. Then I had to pretend I had an important meeting as the children heard me saying it.*

Marty was running around the house punching all of us. I realised he really needed to get out and expel some energy but he refused.	*I put some cushions on the floor in the living room and moved the exercise ball and mini-trampoline in there to make it into an obstacle course. Put on some feel-good music he likes as well. I left him to discover it and distracted his brother.*

The point of this exercise is for you to recognise (and value) all the things you are doing to help your child stay in their window of tolerance. You are an expert in your child – the things that worked for Marty probably won't work for you, but you will have a lot of knowledge about what does work for your child. This exercise is about noticing your own expertise.

The opposite of co-regulation

We don't tend to value the emotion regulation work that parents put in as children get older, but it's more than that. As children get older, Good Parenting™ culture encourages parents to use children's emotional reactions to control their behaviour. It's a bit like the opposite of co-regulation.

This is how behaviourism (which I talked about in detail in Chapter 5) really works. Behaviour might be what we see, but emotions are the invisible mechanism adults use to try to change behaviour. It's as if adults don't believe that children will have a strong enough reaction by themselves unless we hammer the point home.

What do I mean? Well, when things have gone wrong for a child, sometimes adults double down on their natural emotional reactions by telling them how disappointed they are in them or by telling them off. We make them feel worse about it by shouting or removing privileges. We call this 'consequences' and say that it helps them learn. When they do things we like, we make them feel good with praise, stars and prizes. We use our emotional connection with them, becoming more loving when they do things we like and less loving when they don't. We exploit the fact that they don't like it when we are angry or disapproving to steer them away from the behaviour that we don't want.

No matter which way you go, positive or negative, the underlying Good Parenting™ assumption is the same. It's this: *we need to magnify children's emotions so that they learn*. We need to augment their natural responses. We need to make sure that they associate feeling bad with doing things we don't want them to do, and feeling good with doing the things that we do want them to do. If we don't make them feel sad or frightened when they do something wrong, then they'll never learn to stop doing it, goes the logic. This forms a feedback loop – which, you'll remember from the earlier chapters, can easily become a trap.

Of course, we don't talk openly about the fact that we use our children's emotional reactions in this way. We talk about 'celebrating success', or 'holding them to account' and using 'consequences'. Adults often ask me how children would learn otherwise, as if the only reason that people are prosocial or motivated to learn is because their parents gave them enough stickers as a child.

Many schools do this too. They deliberately magnify a child's emotional reactions. They do this through public humiliation (which adds shame) using behavioural charts, and through strategies such as rewards for those who have 100% attendance records (which increase anxiety for children every time they are sick or have an appointment in school hours). They also pile on the pressure, telling young people

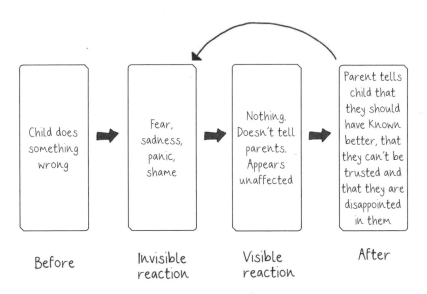

| Before | Invisible reaction | Visible reaction | After |

that unless they do well in their exams, they'll end up homeless and living under a bridge.

The idea seems to be that if we make children and young people feel bad enough, they'll do what we want in order to avoid those bad feelings. All of this is the opposite of emotional co-regulation. It's adults deliberately making things worse, in the belief that this is what the child needs in order to learn.

Many adults carry the legacy of this emotional magnification to this day. They are terrified of getting things wrong, not just because of the fact of getting something wrong, but because of how bad they will feel. They are more worried about telling other people that something has gone wrong than about the direct consequences. They hate getting feedback because of the feelings of humiliation and shame it brings up for them, even if it's constructive and friendly. We learned to feel this way through our childhoods, even if we were 'well behaved'.

I was well behaved at school. That didn't stop me from being scared that one day it would all go wrong. I remember the first day in a new school when I tossed my exercise book to the teacher because, in my previous school, my teacher had done this with us – she would playfully throw us our books and sometimes we would toss them back to her, with her pretending to do Olympic catches. The new school teacher didn't know this, and she was furious. Throwing exercise books was not part of her classroom routine and she thought I was being disrespectful.

I still remember the anger in her voice as she told me to come up to the front of the class and said that if I did anything like that again I would be going straight to the headteacher. I was utterly humiliated. In my previous school, book throwing had been a time of playful connection between us and the teacher, and now here it was a sign of just how wrongly I had judged the situation and how very far away my previous school and light-hearted teacher were. I had no reputation as a 'good girl' to protect me here. The other children looked at me sideways, this new girl who hadn't even learned that we don't throw books.

I didn't need to be controlled by fear. I wanted to learn. I wanted approval. But all the same I was afraid of what would happen if I put a foot wrong. Like most children, my own ability to correct myself if my error was pointed out was not deemed to be enough. I was shamed. I shut down some of the spontaneous and playful parts of myself in case I got it wrong.

How were you controlled as a child?

Do you remember adults making you feel bad (or good) in order to control your behaviour?

What was it like?

What impact did it have on you?

What did you learn about yourself in the process?

Emotion sensitivity

Most pressure-sensitive children are also emotion sensitive, even if they don't appear to be so. That is a reason why they react so badly to pressure. They find their own emotions harder to manage than others and it takes longer for them to develop the ability to manage their emotions. It might be that their experiences are more intense, or it might be that they are more sensitive to their internal experiences.

Pressure-sensitive children are often very well attuned to the emotional atmosphere around them. Parents sometimes describe them as human barometers. Everyone else might be pretending that there isn't tension in the air, but the child feels it far too intensely to pretend otherwise. Their behaviour (and sometimes their words) expresses the emotions everyone else is suppressing. They are often the one who says to the visitor 'You're talking too much', or 'Time to leave.'

Like almost everything about human development, sensitivity to emotions is highly variable. There isn't a discrete group of children who are very sensitive to emotions and a group of children who aren't. There is a gradual variation across the whole population. A child will vary in how sensitive they are to their emotions depending on the day, how tired and hungry they are, all the things that have happened to them in the past and how supported they feel by adults around them. We all have days when we are emotionally fragile, and days when we can cope with more.

Earlier I was talking about Good Parenting™, the cultural parenting practice of using children's emotions in order to try to control their behaviour. Sometimes this is really explicit – 'You should be ashamed of yourself' or 'Just wait until later' – but sometimes it is more subtle – 'I just want you to do well for your own sake' or 'I'm really worried about your grades.' When a parent uses emotional reactions in this way with an emotion sensitive child, it can go badly wrong fast.

For a child who is already very sensitive to their emotions, their parent's reaction can feel intolerable. This makes complete sense if you think about it. Something has gone wrong in their life – say they spilled a pot of paint on the rug – and they are already finding that difficult to cope with. Along comes the adult whom they trust; but instead of making it better, they are making it worse. Rather than helping them restore their emotional balance, the adult tells them off, or blames them, or tells them they need to be more careful and pay for the rug. Now the child's own emotional response has been amplified by someone else. It's not just spilled paint anymore, it's spilled paint surrounded by layers of shame.

This forms the basis of the Distress Multiplier trap, which is a downward spiral for many children and families. Emotions are already overwhelming, but when an adult makes them more intense the child learns to feel bad about their feelings – and this makes them feel worse.

Over time, the Distress Multiplier trap results in the child learning to expect that their parent will make them feel worse, not better, and so they avoid telling their parent about things that have happened for fear of how horrible it will make them feel. It cuts off the possibility of co-regulation.

Becoming afraid of our emotions

In my clinical work I meet a lot of children who are scared of their own emotions. Sometimes it's because, as young children, the way they expressed their emotions was very challenging for the adults around them. Maybe they hit other people, or maybe they shouted and swore. Maybe they said they hated people or even that they wanted to kill themselves or others. All of these things usually result in an angry or scared response from other people. The child learned that this was what happened when they were very angry or upset, and so they became scared of their own feelings.

Sometimes children become scared of their emotions because no one expresses emotions in their family. Everyone keeps it under wraps, and that becomes the family style. Children learn this sort of thing implicitly; they pick it up from the world around them. This might be something that you learned in your family of origin, and then you have recreated it in your own family without thinking about it. It gets passed down the generations without anyone really being aware of it happening.

There's another group of children who, in my experience, become scared of their own feelings. Some kids I meet are scared of their feelings after years of responsive and gentle parenting. Their parents have responded very quickly to head off and soothe any difficult feelings (or have planned thoroughly to avoid situations where children experience difficult feelings) and have hidden any negative feelings of their own. They have often been excellent co-regulators, smoothing the child's path to the extent that there haven't been many bumps or obstacles – and life hasn't thrown them too many curveballs.

The result has been that the child hasn't had much experience of managing difficult feelings and the feelings of uncertainty that brings. Their parents have managed it for them. When they feel anything negative, they don't know what to do, and one of the brain changes that happens around puberty is that their emotional reactions start to feel even more intense.

In my work, I meet a lot of children who become very angry with their parents around the ages of ten to thirteen, when they start to go through puberty and their feelings become more intense. They say things like 'I can't trust you anymore' or 'You've ruined everything' and parents find this really upsetting. What I think they mean is that their parents used to be able to make them feel better, and now that doesn't work anymore. They don't know how to manage the feelings that this brings up. It's a big developmental leap for young people when they realise that their parents can't always make everything okay. Some of them feel betrayed by this realisation and feel that their parents have let them down.

However it comes about (and there won't always be an obvious reason), fear of feelings makes those feelings bigger when they do show up. This makes sense if you think about it – fear of emotions adds more fear to the already difficult emotions. When a person is afraid of their emotions, they can never really feel safe, because emotions are always popping up.

This is the Distress Multiplier trap. It's like a particularly unpleasant emotional roller coaster with lots of loops. Each time you go round a loop, you're more scared of the next one – and that makes the next loop feel worse.

The more you think that your emotions are dangerous, the more frightening they will become. Some children are particularly vulnerable to the Distress Multiplier because their emotions feel so intense and their behaviour in response to their emotions often gets them into trouble or blamed.

Trying to feel safe from their emotions can lead to all sorts of behaviour to try to keep their difficult feelings away – children develop rituals like special cleaning routines, places that they must avoid, ways in which other people in the house must behave, to avoid uncomfortable feelings. They try to control other people, under the assumption that if other people behave exactly as they want them to, then their difficult feelings will go away. Sometimes when children won't leave their rooms it's because it feels too uncomfortable to go out. They are trapped by their feelings.

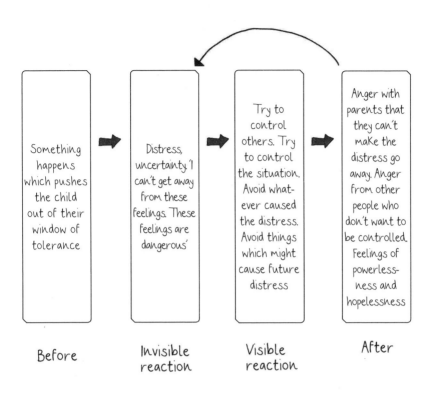

Before	Invisible reaction	Visible reaction	After
Something happens which pushes the child out of their window of tolerance	Distress, uncertainty. 'I can't get away from these feelings. These feelings are dangerous'	Try to control others. Try to control the situation. Avoid whatever caused the distress. Avoid things which might cause future distress	Anger with parents that they can't make the distress go away. Anger from other people who don't want to be controlled. Feelings of powerlessness and hopelessness

Children are usually working under the assumption that if they can make their feelings go away, they will be safe. It's an understandable assumption to make. From their perspective, the emotions are unpleasant, and so they must make them go away. Unfortunately, they are doomed to failure because distress is part of life. By trying to push our feelings away, paradoxically we make them more likely to stick around and become more intense.

Sometimes parents end up jumping right on that roller coaster with their children. They try to get the feelings to go away, or they behave as if the children's feelings are frightening for them too. Children take their cues from their parents when deciding if something is scary or safe. If you behave as if you are scared of, or angry about, your child's emotions, they will be too.

Identifying the Distress Multiplier

How does the Distress Multiplier trap show up in your family?

Think about a recent time when you or your child was distressed. What were the reactions to the distress that made the distress worse? What fuelled the downward spiral?

You could try filling in the boxes – it will be easier to do this for yourself at first.

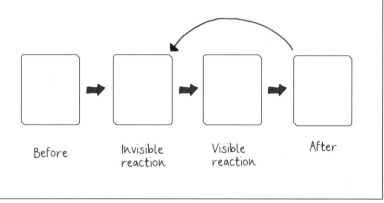

Releasing the Distress Multiplier

Christina heard a nasty cracking noise from the next room. 'Uh oh,' said her teenage son Cass. 'That didn't sound good.' He came through to ask Christina if she could come and take a look at what had happened. The new light fitting they had installed that morning in the cupboard was hanging off, wires exposed. He'd closed the door on it with something in the way, and it had been broken by the pressure.

The light was still working so there seemed an easy fix. Cass's brother got the duct tape and they reattached the light fitting. It wasn't quite as pretty as it had been before but it was functional. They all got on with their day. Nothing big happened.

Except that this is what Christina had always dreamt of. This is what she had aspired to as a parent, right since the early days. Something was broken, her children weren't scared to tell her, and no one got angry or blamed anyone else. The day wasn't ruined.

It didn't used to be like that. When Christina's children were younger, they were anxious about many things, but particularly about things getting broken or lost. This was so intense that they could never take a ball to the park in case it got lost, they couldn't throw away a broken cup in case it could be fixed. No other child who came to the house was allowed to touch anything. They lived on eggshells, waiting for something to go wrong because it would always be experienced as a disaster. She remembered the awful time that another child had come round to play and Cass had said they could touch nothing except a broken grey crayon. She had been stuck in the middle, trying to keep both Cass and the visiting child calm while Cass fiercely protected all of his possessions. He didn't feel safe with other people touching his stuff.

After this experience she started a cupboard of her 'own' toys, which visitors were allowed to touch and play with. Other parents thought it was ridiculous (and indulgent) that she had her own version of Cass's favourite knights and castle set – but having it meant that other children didn't ask to play with Cass's. And that had saved several playdates.

They had lurched from emergency to emergency. Just like many other families. But things had changed. So much so that it was hard to remember just how hard those earlier years had been.

Cass and Christina could have ended up in the Distress Multiplier trap when that light fitting broke. All it would have taken was for Christina to say something like 'Why were you so careless?' or even just a loud sigh and a comment on how much the fitting had cost. They'd been there many times before. But they didn't go there this time, and the reason they didn't was because of the years of effort Christina had put in to stop that trap from turning.

The Distress Multiplier starts with distress, but the trap is fuelled by reactions to that distress. Both adult and child reactions can add to the distress – and that sends the Distress Multiplier around another loop. Each time it goes around another loop, the distress gets more intense.

Parents and children try to get the distress to go away, but this has the paradoxical result of increasing the distress because the more we try to make feelings go away, the more they come back. This means that in order to release the Distress Multiplier trap, we need to change how we react to distress, rather than trying to change the distress itself.

To release this trap, children need to learn three things. It would be great if we could just tell them those things and that would be that. Unfortunately learning these things is not as simple as being told them. They need to experience them. These are things children learn throughout childhood and into adulthood, through many experiences of distress, seeing other people get distressed, and hearing how distress is responded to.

This means that these three keys are more about your mindset than what you explicitly tell your child. They should be your guiding principles when you can feel you and your child getting swept up in emotional distress and whirling around the Distress Multiplier.

These are the three keys to releasing the trap:

1. Everyone has emotions.
2. Emotions aren't dangerous (even when they are very intense).
3. Emotions come and go.

These are the keys to real emotional safety. We often confuse emotional safety with feeling okay all the time, but that isn't sustainable. Everyone has ups and downs. The only way to really feel safe in the long term is to be able to tolerate your emotions, and to know that even when things are bad, your feelings won't be the same forever. Things can get better.

With pressure-sensitive children, if you start trying to talk about their emotions they will almost certainly not be able to respond. They will feel put on the spot and they will be worried that you are going to make them feel worse. They may get upset immediately. The challenge for a parent is how to talk about these things without activating their anxiety. You definitely can't sit down for heart-to-heart conversations. You will need to think about how you communicate (look at Chapter 4) and how to make any discussion as low pressure as possible.

Everyone has emotions

Children compare their insides with the outsides of other people. They can feel how hard things are for them – but they can't see how hard things are for other people. They assume that the visible reaction they see is all there is.

Many children conclude that the difference between their intense internal experience and the apparent calmness of most other people must mean there's something wrong with them. They assume that if other people look okay, then they don't have the same emotional struggles. Adults can inadvertently make this worse by saying things like 'Everyone else is fine' or 'Look, no one else is scared.'

Your child knows about their own reactions (although they may not be able to describe them or tell you anything about them), and they can see everyone else's visible reactions – but they don't always know about other people's invisible reactions. You need to shine a light on them and make the invisible visible for them.

The way to do this is to talk about it. Not in a 'teaching way' but in a way that makes invisible processes visible. The easiest way to start is to talk about yourself and your emotions. Not with the aim of changing their behaviour, but with the aim of helping them see what is going on behind the façade. Don't expect them to respond, just make it part of how you talk to each other.

You could say things like 'We're going to a new group today and I don't know anyone. I feel a bit strange about it, my heart is beating fast and I'm hoping it will be okay.' Or 'I feel bad that I dropped that mug and smashed it. It makes me feel sad even though I'm not crying.'

The other thing to do is to find indirect opportunities to talk about emotions – TV shows are often great sources of emotional drama, or you can talk about other people's emotional experiences. You can ask your child's advice on something in an age-appropriate way – maybe if you have upset someone in your family, or if you said something you think made things worse.

Emotions aren't dangerous

Intense emotions feel very threatening. So threatening that many people (children and adults alike) devise elaborate rituals to avoid feeling their emotions. Emotions can feel dangerous, but the reality is that even very intense emotions are not harmful in and of themselves. Emotions are one way that our brains keep us safe – fear can be like a warning signal for dangerous situations. But the emotions aren't the danger itself.

When children have had repeated experiences of their emotions leading to them being told off, or shouted at or getting into trouble, they can become convinced that their emotions are dangerous and need to be avoided at all costs. The problem is that when you think your emotions are dangerous, you're trapped. You can never make your emotions go away and so you are carrying the source of threat with you always.

The way to change this is to deliberately show children that you are not afraid of emotions, even really intense ones. Some people find it helpful to think about befriending their emotions. Emotions are there to keep us safe, but sometimes they are over-protective and they try to keep us safe from things that aren't dangerous. You can think of metaphors for this – one of my favourites is a protective umbrella. We put up an umbrella to protect ourselves, but we don't always need it and it can stop us from seeing what is on the other side or when a rainbow comes out.

Some people like to draw or model their emotions as a small creature or person. Try it for yourself – your child might join in, or they might just watch you doing it.

You can also talk to your children about how intense your emotions are. Tell little stories about your life and your emotions – but don't overdo it. Don't make it frightening and make sure that each little story has a narrative arc – in other words, make sure that things get better at the end!

You could say something like 'I missed the bus today, I started to feel really angry because I saw the bus driver pulling away. I was *so angry* with that bus driver that my head felt like it might explode. Then I realised it was only five minutes until the next bus and I felt a bit calmer.'

'I went to meet some new people today. I felt anxious and worried because I wasn't sure what they would think of me. My heart was beating so hard that I could hardly hear what they were saying and I thought maybe I should run away. It was a bit strange but then one of them started talking about something I'm interested in and I felt better.'

'I had too many meetings on today. I booked in four meetings in a row and then I started to feel really grumpy and tired. I had no time to eat or drink. I will not be booking four meetings in a row again! It's better now that I don't have any more meetings.'

Stories about yourself as a child can also be powerful – again, find some stories where you were upset or angry about something but then things changed. You're trying to show them that you aren't scared of feelings, even really intense ones, and so they don't need to be scared of their feelings either.

Emotions come and go

When a child is in the midst of really intense emotions, it feels to them like it's going to be like that forever. They don't yet have the perspective to know that things will change. For them, how they are feeling right now could be it for life.

This means that parents need to bring in the perspective that these feelings won't always be there, even though it feels like that right now. This long-term perspective is something many children lack.

This does not mean telling them that their feelings are unimportant or wrong. It means acknowledging that we can have very strong emotions about something, and then we can feel differently later. That doesn't invalidate those strong emotions.

This means saying things like 'This is really hard' or 'This is so tough right now', without getting swept up in the idea that they will always feel like this. It means empathising with how they feel, even if part of you is thinking, Oh come on!

If you know that your child is likely to have a strong emotional reaction to something – for example, if they are likely to get to that Scouts meeting they want to attend and not be able to cross the threshold – then it can help to predict it. Say something like 'Often when we go somewhere new, you feel really anxious when we get there. Those feelings feel really big and it might be hard to go in. The next time we go it's often a bit better.'

Predicting emotional reactions can feel strange. Most parents are crossing their fingers and hoping it will go well, and it feels wrong to actually mention the possibility of it not going well. It feels like you will make it more likely. In actual fact, by talking about it, you make it less scary. Now feeling anxious at the door is just one thing that might happen, rather than the terrible thing that all of us are secretly hoping won't happen and not talking about.

If a child isn't able to do something they would like to do because they are anxious, then don't make it feel like a failure. Getting somewhere and deciding it's not possible today can be part of the process of trying new things. If you can frame it as 'Today we got to the door, next time that will be a bit easier' then you might be able to keep that option open for another time. Essentially you are showing them that strong emotional reactions are part of life.

Some kids will respond by telling you to shut up when you empathise with their emotions. That might be because you have got it wrong, or it might be just too much to deal with for them right now. It might feel like a demand. In that case, go back to talking about your own emotions and don't take it personally. You can predict your own emotional responses – say something like 'When we do something new, I often feel really worried at first and it can stop me from doing things. When I've done it a few times, I feel better.'

Mindset shift

Instead of *'We need to avoid our emotions'*, try *'We don't need to be afraid of emotions and they will come and go.'*

Meltdowns

So far I've been talking about long-term aims with emotions – things you want your child to learn as they grow up. I haven't focused much on managing extreme emotions in the moment, and in particular, meltdowns.

A meltdown happens when a child is overwhelmed by their emotions and they can't contain it anymore. They may be very angry or upset, and they are beyond the point where you can rationalise with them. They are way outside their window of tolerance, and their behaviour might well be what some would consider unacceptable.

First things first. Meltdowns aren't manipulative. Some people draw a distinction between tantrums (which are considered to be manipulative) and meltdowns (which aren't) but I don't know of any real evidence for this. Young children (who are often described as having the tantrums) are not capable of sophisticated psychological manipulation. I think it's more likely that both are a sign of overwhelm, extreme frustration and of a child being out of their window of tolerance. The child is no longer able to manage their emotions well enough to respond rationally.

There are two things to consider with meltdowns – firstly if there are lots of meltdowns, that's a sign that something in your child's life is too much for them to handle. You need to dial something back and reduce the demands. Your aim is to reduce their background level of stress and anxiety so that they can tolerate a little more without having so many meltdowns. This is the groundwork.

Then there's what to do when meltdowns actually happen – for they will happen, even if you are doing everything you can.

Meltdowns aren't a sign of failure; they just mean that at this time, the child has gone beyond what they can manage. You can learn from that and move on.

In the moment when a meltdown happens, the priority needs to be to make everyone safe and then to avoid escalation. You will know your child best. If talking to them escalates things, don't talk. If being there silently helps, do that. If you can offer food and drink without asking questions, that can be helpful – parents tell me that they just put a drink nearby in a bottle so the child can drink but it doesn't matter if it gets kicked over. If the child is violent make sure you get other children out of the way, particularly if they are younger or vulnerable. That needs to happen even if it makes the child in meltdown more angry or upset.

Children will often hold in their emotions when they are somewhere surrounded by other people, and then when it's all over and they are alone with their parents, they explode. This often happens after school. This can leave parents thinking they must be doing something wrong, because their children's emotions are so much more extreme with them. Parents sometimes make catastrophic predictions about the future – they imagine their child as an adult, behaving in the same way then as they are doing aged ten, and they panic.

You're not doing anything wrong. It takes an effort for children to hold themselves together, and then when they feel safe, they let go. Their parents usually get the brunt of it because they are the people with whom they feel safest.

Sometimes a meltdown is a release of tension, and means that a child can then move on with their day, having expressed themselves. Either way, a meltdown is not a disaster. They are going to happen sometimes; your task is to make it through with minimal harm in the moment and to move on without recriminations or blame.

That is not at all easy for most parents. Culturally we use emotions as tools in parenting and it takes a lot of tongue biting to stop. Deep inside most of us is the idea that children *must* be made to feel bad when we don't like their behaviour – or even that it is our duty to make sure they feel bad. And sometimes it feels good to get angry or to shame a child, because they have made us feel bad and (deep down) we want to get our own back.

Bringing it all together

This chapter has covered a lot. The box below summarises the most important principles when it comes to managing your child's emotions.

Four low demand principles with emotions

1. Stop using emotions to try to change children's behaviour. Stop adding anxiety or shame to difficult situations. This means breaking the association where adults make children feel bad when they get something wrong. Completely. Even when it comes to tone of voice or facial expression. Stop feeding them with anxiety and shame. It won't help. Take it calmly.

2. Safety. Get through the most intense emotional times with your child with everyone safe. Focus on staying calm, listening, and don't do anything to make it worse. Don't expect intense emotional times to be teachable moments. No consequences are necessary for distress, even when that distress is expressed as 'bad behaviour'.

3. Self-care. Look after your own emotional wellbeing. You are the lynchpin of all of this. A lot of emotional work is invisible, but draining and relentless. In order to be able to respond empathically to your children's emotions, you need people who can respond empathically to you. It won't be your children, at least not reliably so, so you need to find other adults who can hear you out and support you.

4. Support and scaffolding. Children learn how to manage their emotions by being supported to develop emotional awareness. Be there to listen to their emotions without judgement or telling them that they shouldn't feel the way that they do. Talk about your own emotions and internal state, to make the invisible visible for your children. Show them that emotions are not dangerous and that they come and go.

Eliza and Naomi:
Use your words

NAOMI: Eliza, you've drawn an illustration here of yourself in the kitchen with a mess. Tell me a bit about what you were thinking there.

ELIZA: I drew that because I thought it was quite a good example when there was a group of teenagers in the house and they had all cooked together. They had attempted to clean up, but there was quite a bit of mess.

I went into the kitchen and I could see the mess, but I had to think of the bigger picture here. My child orchestrated a number of friends to come around and they all cooked together and they all had a really nice time. So, I could think, is this something where I then reprimand or tell off about the mess? Or do I see that they've had a really good time and it's the first time they've all cooked together and made lunch?

That's a clear thing where we adults can spoil something that was really good, a really positive experience because we still think that we've got to put the moral tale within that. We've got to tell off.

NAOMI: Yes, we've got to make them feel bad about whatever they've done.

ELIZA: Because they haven't done it exactly how we think they should.

NAOMI: We can add negativity to a situation that wasn't negative, out of this misguided feeling that they have to learn. We think they're only going to learn if we make them feel bad about it.

ELIZA: I think it's a bit like when you see children running around having a brilliant time and you've got a parent shouting at them, 'Put your coat on.'

NAOMI: It's like putting a downer on it all the time.

ELIZA: It's like we feel that as parents we have to add input when maybe we don't.

NAOMI: It's like if a child does badly at something, for example, then we feel we have to tell them, 'Oh, you didn't work very hard on that' or 'You didn't put all the effort in', and we make them feel worse about it.

I find it really odd because it's as if we don't trust our children to have the emotional responses that everybody naturally does to things. We feel we have to ramp them up in case the child hasn't got the right responses. We have to make it more obvious for them.

So it's like, 'Oh, you didn't pass your exam. Well, you didn't study or you didn't put in enough effort there.' What if we behaved as if we didn't need to make anyone feel worse? What if we assumed that they will feel bad already?

ELIZA: Is it an assumption that they don't have those emotions?

NAOMI: Not enough of them, I think. We assume that children are careless or not thinking hard enough, therefore we have to make them think or make them feel the emotions so that they learn for next time.

For children who are sensitive to their emotions, they're already in an intense world where their emotions feel really overwhelming and then we make it more. We make everything more intense.

ELIZA: We add guilt.

NAOMI: Shame and guilt, I think. If you talk to adults, a lot of them will say that if something goes wrong in their lives, they'll say that the going wrong is bad, but it's the way that other people respond that is worse. That is what really makes it difficult. The layers of shame and guilt and worry.

ELIZA: There's the worry about how others will respond. You're worried. What will people think?

NAOMI: It's social judgement. We're training our children in that. Then at the same time, we're often telling children, 'Be yourself, just as you are. Be proud to be you.' But it's just words, because the way that we are interacting with them tells them that they need to be different to how they are.

ELIZA: It's like we're telling them they should feel this way and not this other way.

NAOMI: If you think about what rewards and punishments really are, they are basically saying this. If you do things that we don't like, we're going to make you feel bad about yourself. If you do things we like, we'll make you feel good about yourself. This is so manipulative when you think about it.

ELIZA: Something I've noticed as an adult is sometimes when I am looking forward to something, there'll be quite a lot of anxiety about that. I think that often that's because when I was younger, it's that thing of, 'Well, don't look forward to it too much'. In case it's a disappointment when there's something that doesn't go according to plan.

NAOMI: It's like we're scared. We're scared of being let down, of it not being as good as we hoped.

ELIZA: I think we're probably scared of doing things in the wrong way, perhaps not how we're meant to do it.

NAOMI: Got to get it just right. Our fear of how bad it would feel to get it wrong can end up boxing us in.

Too much to read, too little time?

1. Part of Good Parenting™ is manipulating children's emotional responses. We add our emotions to children's emotional responses.
2. For pressure-sensitive children, this is too much. It makes it hard for them to maintain their emotional equilibrium and they become afraid of their feelings.
3. Parents and children get stuck in the Distress Multiplier trap.
4. The way to release this trap is not to try to make the distress go away, but instead to change how we react to distress.
5. The three important things for children to know about emotions are that everyone has emotions, emotions aren't dangerous and that they come and go. These things can take a lifetime to learn.

More to read if you are interested

Brain-Body Parenting: How to Stop Managing Behaviour and Start Raising Joyful, Resilient Kids – Mona Delahooke

The Opposite of Worry: The Playful Parenting Approach to Childhood Anxieties and Fears – Lawrence Cohen

Raising Kids with Big Baffling Behaviours: Brain-Body-Sensory Strategies that Really Work – Robyn Gobbel

The Self-Compassionate Teen: Mindfulness and Compassion Skills to Conquer Your Critical Inner Voice – Karen Bluth

7

In the Real World

I had an email this morning from a 'parenting expert' who promised to help me with setting tough boundaries while keeping my kids calm. She said that her scripts would help my kids feel seen and heard – without compromising my boundaries.

She didn't specify what boundaries she meant, except that they were 'tough'. She didn't need to. She's speaking the universally understood language of Good Parenting™. Boundaries, we all know, are good. It's the answer to many parenting dilemmas – set those boundaries and hold onto them.

In Good Parenting™ lore, boundaries help children feel safe. The task of parents is to set boundaries and then hold to them lovingly, even as the child rages and cries, because that (we are told) will help children learn to manage frustration and anger and to see that their parents know best. When a child's behaviour is very difficult to manage, there's often muttering about lack of boundaries, and parents agonise over whether they have been 'too soft'.

It's always seemed odd to me that while there is a lot of talk about setting and holding boundaries (and abundant techniques for getting children to accept these boundaries with less fuss), there's much less talk about how parents should know which boundaries to hold. It's almost as if holding boundaries is thought to be a good thing for its own sake, *no matter what they are.*

This doesn't make sense. Because what are boundaries, after all? Sometimes it seems that they equate to 'what a parent says'. 'Boundaries' can include pretty well anything, including things a parent says and then realises are definitely not worth a fight ('No, you can't eat your crisps before your sandwiches'), but that they believe they have to stick to as otherwise they will be inconsistent (a Good Parenting™ sin). It seems that the ideal parent never changes their mind, never gets it wrong and is impervious to all arguments. But they are loving and calm while doing it, which makes the rigidity okay (remember Baumrind in Chapter 2?).

I wonder whether setting tough boundaries is just the twenty-first-century replacement for the nineteenth-century ideal of obedient children. Emotional security and safety holds more value in our culture than the religiosity and morality of the Victorians, and so that's the reason we give ourselves. This time, the morality is attached to parents rather than children. Good Parents™ set tough boundaries and keep them – and if they can't, they feel bad about themselves. They feel that it's all their fault if their children don't comply.

In the last few chapters I've covered the basics of low demand parenting. The principles on which it's based, and how these apply to communication, behaviour and emotions. How to use code breakers to identify the loops that you and your children are getting stuck in, and how to release common traps. It's been about fundamental principles and thinking about what you want your child to learn as they grow up. That's all very well, but what about the things that are making your life hard today? The details of everyday life – what do you do about those?

GOOD PARENT CHECKLIST

SCREEN TIME ☐

FIRM BOUNDARIES ☐

BEDTIME ROUTINE ☐

WELL BEHAVED CHILD ☐

This chapter is about some of the thornier issues that come up for families. Some of the things that cause problems again and again, and which make parents wobble and worry – and sometimes fight between themselves. The things that pull us in several directions and make us wake up at night, sweating. The things that make you wonder if you just need tougher boundaries.

But how do I get them to. . .?

You're reading this book, I assume, because setting and holding boundaries hasn't worked as you expected. Your child has not fallen in line, and you aren't sure what to do. Your expectations are far from the reality that you're living. You want to know what alchemy you missed out on, and whether there is some secret method other parents were taught. You want to know how to get your children to behave differently.

Maybe you want them to go to sleep on their own, stop complaining about going to school, stop fighting with their sister, put down the iPad when you tell them to, make less fuss about brushing their teeth. . . there are probably more things I haven't mentioned.

Most parents I meet are living their life in constant hope that their child will change and become easier to live with. Understandably, they want help to make that happen faster.

I think you already know the bad news. There is no parenting alchemy. You haven't missed out on the super-special high-level training that tells you how to get children to bend to your will, without complaint. The other parents for whom life seems to be easier? Either they are faking it (you have no idea what goes on behind closed doors) or they have a child whose temperament is naturally more compliant. As a psychologist, I have the privilege of a bird's-eye view because I talk to so many parents, and I can tell you for sure that a lot of them are faking it. You can't tell by how a family looks in public whether their children exist only on cheesy Wotsits, fight for hours every evening or which children still need their parents with them for hours every night in order to fall asleep.

Then the sort-of-good news, which you probably also already know. There is a way to do things differently – but it won't work in the way you think it will. Your child might not change. After all, they may well not see any reason to change at all, and it's always difficult to convince someone to change when they don't see the point.

That's the problem with the question 'How do I get them to. . .?' The real question that many parents are asking is 'How do I get them to *want* to. . .?' They don't want to force their child, they want their child to spend less time on their device, or more time practising the violin, or eating less sugar *because they themselves want to*. And you can't make someone else want to do something without manipulation. You can sometimes force them to do something, but making them want to do it is much more complex (and gets into the realm of mind-control or brainwashing, which really isn't somewhere that you want to go with parenting).

Some parents do of course go down this route and try to get their children to want to do something. They withhold affection so that their children work for approval. They tell children how very important it is to do what their parents want them to do. You've probably found already that these techniques don't work well with your children. I don't really think they work well with any children, but with pressure-sensitive children you can see quite quickly that you're on a hiding to nowhere. This is one great advantage of having a pressure-sensitive child – you can't get away with anything. They see straight through your efforts to control them.

Let's take a step back from this. I hear what you want, but let's start with thinking about how things really are. The question 'How do I get them to. . .?' is laden with expectations, which can mean pressure. And when we are talking about pressure-sensitive children, then pressure is a bad idea. It makes things worse not better. It gets everyone stuck in traps. You already know that.

I call the difference between how you would like your children to behave, and how they really do, the Reality Gap. This is a trap that happens inside parents' heads. They had an idea of how their family life should look, and it isn't how things really are. They spend a lot of their time feeling bad about this, and trying to work out how to get their children closer to their expectations. That's what the question 'How do I get them to. . .?' is about. Bridging the Reality Gap. The Reality Gap is the gap between what is really happening and what you expected.

EXPECTATION   REALITY

When you're in the Reality Gap and trying to change your child it feels like you're doing something, but what you're doing isn't working. You are trying to get your child to change in order to make your life more like that one you want – and the child isn't co-operating.

The Reality Gap is important because it can stop many parents from thinking about how to best manage the situation as it is now. They are constantly frustrated because life is not how they imagined and they just can't work out how to get their children to meet their expectations. They try being strict, being understanding, setting firm boundaries, more connection, empathising, rewards and punishments – to no avail. They are stuck in the gap.

The paradox of the Reality Gap – and yes, there are lots of paradoxes in low demand parenting – is that the more we focus on the expectations and how children aren't meeting them, the less we are able to problem solve about the real situation. We spend our time thinking, But it shouldn't be like this! or Why won't they just behave like everyone else for once? and the frustration leaks into everything.

The way to get out of the Reality Gap is to accept reality. To deliberately turn from trying to get your child to meet expectations, and instead turn towards where they really are.

Parents sometimes say this feels like 'giving up' but I see it very differently. Accepting where your family is right now means that you can focus on how to manage reality, rather than constantly striving after (and feeling bad about) a situation that exists only in fantasy.

The Reality Gap:
the difference between what you
expected family life to be, and your
family life right now.

Once you've identified your Reality Gap, you can move on to thinking about change. This means starting from where you and your child are, rather than where you think you should be. Essentially you are getting alongside your child, rather than trying to pressure them to change. This is the way out of the Reality Gap.

This is hard and many of us don't like the idea. Parents often tell me that they don't want to accept how things are in case that means they will never change. They strive towards expectations because accepting reality feels dispiriting.

I know it seems counter-intuitive, but there is something really liberating about seeing how things are right now and working with that. It can free you up to start moving forward, because you're able to start where you really are, rather than where you think you should be. A parent I know told me a story that illustrates the difference.

Alicia had two sons who were both very pressure sensitive and who found group gatherings overwhelming. She was a single mother. They were invited to the wedding of a close family member, and Alicia really wanted to go. She imagined introducing her sons to everyone, dressed up in little bow ties and jackets. She imagined them dancing with their cousins and being in all the photos. She thought about how proud she would feel.

Her fantasy (and she said to herself, this isn't unreasonable) was that it should all go smoothly. She'd be able to go to the wedding, have a good day, her boys would play with the other children and happily stay with her mother while she talked to her friends, and she would glow with pride. Everyone would compliment her on her well-behaved children.

Then she thought about the reality of her children, and how challenging they were likely to find the wedding. She thought about how they hated any clothes that weren't jogging trousers and disliked large gatherings. She thought about how they were unlikely to allow her to go up to the front to do the reading she'd been asked to do. This difference between what Alicia felt should happen and what was really likely to happen is the Reality Gap.

Thinking about the likely reality made her sad, but it also allowed her to problem solve. How could she get to the most important parts of the wedding, while acknowledging and planning for how difficult her children would find it? Instead of planning for an unrealistic scenario and keeping her fingers crossed, what about if she accepted fully how her children were right now, and instead planned for that?

For Alicia, this meant that she realised that her boys were very unlikely to make it through the wedding service and still be able to keep going into the reception – but they would probably enjoy the reception more than the service. She also realised that they would need intense support from her to manage the reception, and it was unrealistic to think that she could talk to anyone else while they were there. They would not run off and play with the other children. She asked a close friend whom the boys liked to come with her to the wedding, and they took electronic devices, ear defenders and snacks. The children wore their usual clothes. The boys stayed outside with her friend during the service. They stayed for thirty minutes of the reception, and then it became clear that the younger boy couldn't cope with much more, so Alicia took him off for an extended walk in which they played Pokemon Go while her friend stayed with the older child who wanted a piece of the cake. She got back in time for the toasts and the photographs, and then decided to quit while the going was good and to go home before the buffet meal. They all went home and had pizza.

Alicia could have felt sad about the gap between her expectations and the reality, but in fact she felt pleased that she had managed to do the most important things – get to the service, turn up and be in the photos – and also got the boys home before they were overwhelmed. It was a success; everyone had enjoyed some elements of it and the boys played 'weddings' for weeks afterwards.

This process of balancing the needs of children and the needs of parents is not easy, and takes a lot of practice. It's important to do, however, because this is one of the things that will drive change as children become adolescents. They need to start to see their parents as people with needs that must be balanced with their own.

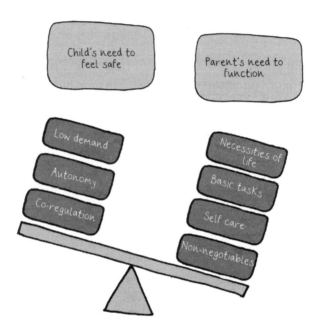

Exercise: The reality gap

This is an exercise to do when you are not going to be interrupted by your children. Ideally you could do it out of the house, perhaps while walking or exercising.

Expectations. Go back in your mind to the time before you had children. What did you expect your life to be like, by this point? What did you imagine your children would be doing and what life did you imagine you would be living?

What are the expectations of others around you of your family and children, and what they should be doing? Whether stated or not, what do you think they are saying or thinking behind your back? Do you hear critical judgements in your head when you are with your children?

Now give those expectations a name or an image. It could be 'fantasy family' or 'perfect' or something else that makes sense for you.

Just let yourself sit with those expectations for a while, without trying to push them away. Notice your relationship to them and where you feel it in your body. Do they feel sad? Do you feel shame or anger? Is there resentment or regret? Try to allow those feelings to be there without judgement or guilt. Just watch them.

Reality. Now bring your thoughts to how things are in reality. Allow yourself to be honest with yourself about how things really are even if your first instinct is to avoid or rationalise it. Let yourself admit the things that make you feel guilty or that you don't tell other people about. Acknowledge how hard it is for you sometimes. Just sit with those feelings for a moment without pushing them away.

Now give that reality a name or an image.

The Reality Gap. Imagine yourself standing between those two things, the expectations and the reality. For a moment, just see yourself in a gap or valley in the middle, looking from one to the other.

If you want, you can imagine that the expectations are in one hand, with reality in the other. Hold your hands out in front of you and see them both. Feel the pull between them and your different emotional reaction to expectations and reality. Just allow yourself to feel those sensations in your body. No need to judge or push any of it away.

Now I'd like you to imagine yourself turning towards reality. You can leave expectations where they are and just turn away, or you can do something to make them less significant. You could imagine them shrinking or you could cover them over with a blanket or turn them into a statue. If you have held your hands out, you could gradually lower the expectations hand while holding reality steady.

Turn your attention towards reality. Even if it's not what you expected and even if you wish it was different. Just turn your attention towards it and see things as they really are. Your family as it is, right now.

Take a few deep breaths as you look at reality. Notice where you feel it in your body. Notice if you have any urge to push it away.

Say to yourself, 'This is just how things are right now.'

This is where you can start, with a clear-sighted view of how things are right now.

When you've identified your Reality Gap, the next step is to decide what is really important, given where you are right now, and to think about how you might move towards that.

I'm going to introduce a new tool to help you do this. It is (somewhat ironically) called PLEASE – ironic because one of the questions I get asked most is how to get children to say please and thank you.

Together they make up a phrase reminiscent of the London Underground, which has 'MIND THE GAP' written all along every platform. Mine is a bit more polite.

PLEASE mind the Reality Gap

PLEASE stands for Prioritise Long-term Essentials, Address barriers, Step back and Encore.

PLEASE is a tool to help you first work out whether your expectations are really realistic, or whether in fact you are asking too much of your children. Ask yourself two main questions here. Is this something that will matter in the long term, or is it something that is essential now? Imagine yourself in a few years' time. Is it going to matter whether this happened now or not?

To give you an example, people are often very concerned about hair brushing. In the long term, hair brushing does not matter. You can cut your hair off and start again at any point. In the short term, hair brushing may or may not be essential. If your child has very short hair, it's not necessary. If your child is home educated, it may not be essential. However, if your child is at school then having neat hair is part of the deal – so then that might need to be a priority. Toothbrushing, on the other hand, matters in the long term because tooth decay causes other painful problems down the line.

Think of it this way. Each boundary you hold (or demand you make) uses up a bit of your child's capacity to manage, so you better make really sure that each one is worth the cost. Start with assessing whether it really is something you need to **Prioritise** as a **Long-term Essential** and you will save yourself a lot of energy wasted trying to hold boundaries that really don't matter.

LITTLE DEMANDS

LITTLE DEMANDS

LITTLE DEMANDS

LITTLE DEMANDS

LITTLE DEMANDS

Once you have decided that something is a priority, you need to **Address any barriers** that might be stopping the child from managing to meet this demand. This means, make it easy. Really easy. Rather than asking 'How do I get them to. . .?', once you've decided that a particular boundary is worth holding, the question to ask yourself is this:

How can we make this as easy as possible?

If it's worth doing, then it's worth making it easy. Making it easy means that you think about your child, and what makes it hard for them to do something – and try to reduce the barriers.

Eliza talks about how, when her daughter went to school, she would set everything out for the morning so that it was as easy as possible for her to get dressed and out the door with the least friction in her path. No faffing around. No 'Have you packed your bag?' or 'Have you got your PE kit?' Little last-minute demands like that can be enough to derail your child and will make it harder to get out the door – so cut them out. Letting go of any hang-ups you have about being late can be useful here. Visualise a fireman's pole – you want the child to be able to almost fall into their clothes. I do know children who have slept in some of their clean clothes for the next day to make the morning easier.

Then you need to **Step back**, which means, do it in a low demand way. Do everything you've learned in the previous chapters. Avoid the traps. Don't pressure them. Offer but don't insist. Drip-feed new ideas. Be casual about it. Keep everything on a steady emotional keel. Don't make lots of suggestions or ask them about something repeatedly. Don't poke them with endless questions or reminders. That will not help.

And then finally, **Encore!** – be prepared to do it all again. There are no short cuts. This is not a way to get children to accept what you say without question. The point of PLEASE is for you to make sure that if you are going to say that something needs to happen, you better make sure that it's both worth the effort (for you) and as easy as possible (for them).

Always start with the Reality Gap

Before you use the PLEASE tool, use the Reality Gap exercise to work out your Reality Gap, and to turn towards reality.

If you're thinking, But I don't have a Reality Gap – then think again. Most parents have a Reality Gap. Even parents whose children have turned out pretty much as they expected tend to be fixated on things like the way their children don't love reading as much as they did as a child, or that they spend too much time playing video games. Or they feel that their child isn't passionate enough about their projects, and seems too passive, or they don't help with chores with enthusiasm, or they bicker with their sister too much, or they aren't musical enough, or they don't put in enough effort at school.

Because parents feel bad about their Reality Gaps, they don't discuss it with other parents except in very specific circumstances. This means that most parents worry that it's just them for whom life is so hard, that everyone else is living the life they imagined with the perfect children they imagined they'd have. They compare their inside knowledge of how chaotic their life is with the outside gloss of what other families present to the world – and of course their life comes off worse.

Using PLEASE

In the next section I'm first going to use two examples of using the PLEASE tool. These will talk about how some families used it to address different areas of their life.

Then I'll talk through the questions you might be asking yourself in two other areas. Finally, there's a worksheet you can use on your own.

P rioritise

L ong Term

E ssentials

A ddress Barriers

S tep Back

E ncore!

Food

Lina was concerned about her eight-year-old son Dylan. She was worried about food. Dylan had a very limited diet and mealtimes were battles for everyone. Lina was concerned that she wasn't firm enough around food and was allowing Dylan to get away with not eating a healthy diet.

Expectations

Lina grew up in a family where food was scarce as they didn't have much money. There was little choice about what children ate and she had eaten what was put in front of her as a child. She had always expected that her children would do the same. In fact, she said that she had always felt that parents whose children didn't eat everything were spoiling their children. She took health very seriously and provided a balanced diet for her family. She saw her children's role in this as eating what she provided. She hated wasting food as it made her feel like a bad parent.

Reality

Dylan disliked strong-tasting foods – and to him, many things were strong tasting: salad, lentils and most vegetables. Even the smell was enough to make him feel sick. He also preferred consistent texture. He had come to dislike sitting at the table with his parents because he associated it with pressure to eat things he didn't like. Lina would sometimes tell Dylan he couldn't leave the table until he had finished his food and Dylan would get very distressed and throw his plate on the floor. Lina then punished Dylan by sending him to his room, but Dylan would refuse to go. Sometimes the entire evening was spent with Lina trying to get Dylan to go upstairs while Dylan got increasingly angry.

The Reality Gap

Lina is stuck between what she thinks should be happening – Dylan eating what is put in front of him without fuss and with gratitude – and what is really happening, which is that Dylan is refusing to eat most of what she offers and that mealtimes are battles. She's continuing to act as if, one day, Dylan might suddenly start behaving as she thinks he should. Mealtimes are arranged according to her expectations rather than reality. Dylan is constantly not meeting those expectations – and things go downhill from there.

Dylan isn't growing up in Lina's family of origin, and his relationship with food is going to be different. Lina grew up in a time of scarcity and her relationship with food was formed by that. Dylan has always been in a family with enough food. Food has become a trigger issue for this family, and the more pressure there is around it, the less Dylan is able to try new foods.

Many children have restricted diets and still get a good enough diet. There are big individual differences in how food tastes and feels, and food being familiar and predictable can be really important. If a child doesn't know that they will get enough to eat, then they are going to feel unsafe. Being hungry is also likely to make everything else worse.

Lina spent some time visualising the reality gap and turning towards how things really were – rather than how she thought they should be. She didn't like doing that, because she felt really strongly that things should not be as they were, but she gave it a try. She thought about what Dylan really did eat, and also how her behaviour was creating a lot of stress around eating and mealtimes. Up to that point, she'd thought about how Dylan's behaviour was causing stress, but not so much about the impact of her own behaviour.

Then it was time to move on to using PLEASE.

Prioritise. Lina identified that the priority really was improving the family relationships around food and reducing how much time they spent arguing about food and the high levels of conflict in the evenings.

Long term. In the long term, Lina wants Dylan to have a good relationship with food. She wants him to be able to eat when he is hungry and stop when he has had enough. She doesn't want food to be associated with pressure or anxiety.

Essentials. Dylan needs to eat regularly, and so does Lina.

Address barriers. Right now, Lina's expectations are a barrier to Dylan eating. She expects him to eat under pressure, and he can't do it. She also expects him to eat everything, which he can't do. Dylan isn't getting enough to eat at mealtimes, and it is making the family's evenings miserable.

Lina decided to rethink and prioritise.

She decided that she would accept that, right now, Dylan wasn't able to eat everything and she would make him the food he preferred (chicken nuggets), alongside the food that she preferred. She would make other options available but not pressure him. She decided to drop the expectation that everyone ate together at the table because this was also a barrier to Dylan eating enough.

Step back. Lina made changes immediately. She started cooking chicken nuggets without comment. She put them out for Dylan and stopped suggesting that he had a carrot as well. She made other food available but didn't insist.

And she bit her tongue. She stopped saying things like 'Is that all you're eating?' and 'You need to eat your greens to grow up big and strong.' She didn't suggest that Dylan ate 'just one more bite' or 'just try this one.' She stopped saying 'That rubbish isn't real food.' She stopped telling Dylan how lucky he was to have so much to eat and how she would have loved to have the food that he has. She didn't remind him of starving children elsewhere in the world.

Encore! Over a period of months, Lina succeeded in taking the conflict out of food as a family issue. Dylan started to feel confident that he would be able to get enough to eat and no one would pressure him. Lina continued to cook other foods but didn't make Dylan try them. She made her peace with some waste. She also allowed Dylan to eat alone with an iPad next to him as he found it easier when there was a distraction as he felt less pressured and watched.

Years passed and Dylan grew older. He did start to try some new foods. He didn't always like them but once he knew that he could refuse or even spit something out, he became more likely to take the risks. Lina didn't comment when he did this. She didn't make a big deal out of it. As he got older, he came to join them at the table voluntarily. Lina didn't comment but just laid his place.

What changed for Lina and Dylan? The main shift was starting with reality and letting go of Lina's expectations, for now. This meant that Lina could focus on what was possible, rather than on what Dylan couldn't yet manage. By doing so, she created enough space for Dylan to try new foods when he was ready.

Sleep

Sid was worried about his son Thomas's sleep. Thomas had always had difficulty getting to sleep, and now that he was nine, things were still very different to how Sid thought they should be. Either Sid or his husband Ahmed had to spend hours lying with Thomas every evening to help him get to sleep, and then once he was asleep, he would wake a couple of hours later and come into their bed. Ahmed was tolerant of this but Sid hated it. He got woken up every night, there wasn't enough space for three of them and he was tired and grumpy. He wanted to know how to get Thomas to go to bed by himself and stay there.

Expectations

Sid's expectations around sleep were that Thomas would go to sleep alone and would stay in his bed. He had slept alone himself in childhood from the age of two weeks, and while he remembered being scared of the dark, he thought that it had been good for him to cope alone. His parents had put him to sleep at 7 p.m. and had then watched TV downstairs. That's what he had expected parenthood to be like and he missed his evenings of peace.

Reality

The reality of the situation was that Thomas needed hours of help every evening to go to sleep and then would come through to them in the small hours. Ahmed and Sid did not have any evenings together and their nights were disrupted. Sid would get angry and frustrated because he felt that Thomas should be going to sleep alone and he and Ahmed would often argue about it. Every so often they would try to insist, Thomas would get very upset and would cry for hours, and then they would give in at about 1 a.m. and he would sleep with them. They were all very tired.

The Reality Gap

Most parents tell me that they thought their children would be sleeping in their own beds much earlier than is actually the case. It's common for parents to tell me that they spend hours lying next to their children at night to help them go to sleep and that their children find it very hard to wind down in the evenings. It's also common for parents to be sleeping separately because the children need to be with a parent all night, and there just isn't room for everyone.

Many children come and sleep in their parents' bed during the night, sometimes with no memory of doing so – sleepwalking to be with their parents. I've had parents ask me about their children coming through to them up to age fourteen and older after stressful events.

In the great majority of families I have worked with, children naturally start to stay in their own beds as they go through adolescence. They also become more able to go to sleep alone and they use strategies like listening to audiobooks to help them do so. Adolescents have a hormonal shift that means they usually start to sleep later in the mornings and often stay up later at night and they often want their own space in order to get the sleep they need. This is a biological change rather than something that has to be made to happen.

PLEASE

Prioritise. Sid and Ahmed agree that enough sleep is the main priority here, for everyone.

Long term. In the longer term, Thomas needs to get enough sleep and ultimately be able to get to sleep on his own. Sid and Ahmed want some time together again.

Essentials. With sleep, the bottom line is just that. Sleep. In the long and short term you want everyone in the family to be getting enough sleep. Anything else is secondary. Where, when, how. . . without enough sleep, everything will fall apart.

The first thing Sid and Ahmed need to do is work out how to make it easier for that to happen. How much sleep do they all need, and how are they going to get it?

Address barriers. What is stopping sleep from happening? Parents often think that the problem is the child and their reluctance to live up to the expectations – but if we accept the reality of the situation as it is right now, what is stopping everyone getting sleep?

In Sid's case, there are a few things stopping good sleep and one of them is their set-up. They have set up their life according to expectations, not reality. They have a double bed and Thomas is down the hallway. They expect Thomas to go to sleep in his room and stay there, but Thomas is showing them that he's not ready for that.

Sid and Ahmed think about how they could achieve better sleep for everyone. They try a few different things. The first thing they experiment with is putting a mattress for Thomas on the floor in their room so that he might be able to sleep without waking them all up. This doesn't work – they keep treading on him when they're trying to get to bed. So instead, they set up a sofa bed in another room, and agree that when Thomas comes through, one of them will leave so they can all get better sleep.

This helps. Everyone gets less tired and grumpy. They also get separate duvets for everyone so that no one is cold. Sid and Ahmed then start to plan for how things are in the evenings – it's obvious that the idea of adult evenings is not happening at the moment, so they decide to try to make some other time to spend together during the weekend when Thomas goes to football club. They decide to play audiobooks in the evenings to help Thomas stay in bed and to accept that right now he needs them there with him.

Over time, Thomas starts going to sleep in their room rather than his own, so he doesn't need to move. Then something strange happens – Thomas starts going back to his own bed in the early mornings. He says he wants the space. Sid and Ahmed say that their home feels a bit like a game of musical beds – but it's working much better. They're all getting more sleep, and they're arguing about it less.

Step back. Sid and Ahmed changed the environment, but they also stopped telling Thomas that he should be sleeping alone. They stopped the pressure. They resigned themselves to this phase of parenting being different to what they had expected – but also bore in mind that this would not go on forever and that as Thomas grew bigger it was likely that he would feel more comfortable sleeping alone.

And then,

Encore! Getting to a place where everyone was sleeping better didn't happen overnight for this family. It took experimentation and trial and error, and there was some resistance to this from Sid, who felt that if they made it too easy for Thomas to sleep with them, he'd never leave their bed. It helped him to think about this as a developmental stage: Thomas was developmentally out of sync with their expectations – but that didn't mean that he wasn't still developing and learning. Not sleeping alone now did not mean that it would be like this forever.

Parenting is a long game, a marathon not a sprint. If a change is important, keep trying.

Now it's your turn! Here are a couple of areas where parents often struggle, with some questions to ask yourself so you can try out the process.

Hygiene

Expectations

What were your expectations around hygiene? What did you expect your child to be doing? When did you expect to stop reminding them about teeth or washing? How often did you expect them to change their clothes or brush their hair?

Reality

What are they actually doing? Do they clean their teeth? Do they change their clothes or brush their hair?

The Reality Gap

Many children find teeth brushing and self-care demanding and aversive. They dislike the sensation of toothpaste and of shampoo. Mint, even mild mint, can taste very strong to some children. Toothbrushing can feel very invasive when done by someone else – you are sticking a hard stick into their mouths.

For others, washing is a problem. They don't like having to get undressed for the shower or bath and they particularly don't like being told to do it. I know families who go swimming regularly in order to rinse off their children, because it's easier than persuading them to have a bath or shower at home.

Other children are very attached to their clothes and the way they smell after being on for a couple of days. They may see no reason why clothes have to be changed and they might not like the feeling and smell of clean clothes.

PLEASE

Prioritise. Health and a minimum standard of cleanliness are the priority.

Long term. Toothbrushing is important and has long-term health implications. Headlice are very irritating and infectious. Other things may be short-term rather than long-term issues.

Essentials. What are the really important things here? Being clean enough so that you don't smell is important, but for pre-pubescent children it can take a long time before they start to smell bad once they are past the stage of playing in the mud. Being dirty, unless they are really dirty, might be something that you can let slide for longer than you might have thought. You'll need to decide for yourself what your minimum standards are.

Address barriers. How do we make it easy?

How can you make it really easy to brush teeth or stay clean enough? Would swimming once a week instead of showering be possible? Might it help with changing clothes if you just bought the same clothes so that their wardrobe is made up of identical items?

How can you make toothbrushing easier? You can get tasteless toothpaste, which many children find more tolerable than flavoured. You can also get soft toothbrushes, or some children like electric toothbrushes (others hate them). You can also get special toothbrushes that brush both sides of the teeth at the same time so that you need to do fewer swipes. You can use mouthwash, too – there are lots of children's flavours to try. Some children like timers rather than being reminded by their parents, while others hate timers – you know your child best. Where you brush teeth can also make it easier; some children prefer to brush their teeth in the living room or with other people around rather than in the bathroom. Brushing alongside them might help. Some children like a special toothbrushing song, others don't.

Sharing information with children about the importance of doing something like toothbrushing is fine, but don't keep reminding as a way of pressuring them. It will backfire. Share information if you think they don't have it, but don't keep repeating it to try to persuade them to comply.

Step back. Once you have addressed the barriers, go low demand. Put the toothbrush out ready and let them know but don't request that they brush. Make baths available and let them know.

Don't remind them again and again – remember, this will make it less rather than more likely that something will happen.

Encore! Don't give up. They might not brush their teeth or change their clothes every day, but keep trying and keep making things as easy for them as you can.

Siblings

Expectations

What did you imagine it would be like, having several children? Did you have visions of them playing happily together in the garden? Did you think they would be best friends? How did you imagine yourself with several children?

Reality

What is it really like in your family? How do your children feel about each other? What was it like for the oldest child when the younger ones came along? What is it like for the less vocal ones now?

The Reality Gap

Most siblings fight. Particularly if they are close in age. Many parents tell me that they can't leave their young children alone in a room together because the older child might hurt the younger child badly by doing something like pushing them off the sofa.

Many parents think that the quality of the relationships between children is down to their parenting, but whether siblings get on or not is largely down to luck and temperament. Many siblings do not like each other. Others do. This can change over the lifetime of a family.

It's common for families to feel that one child is dominant, particularly if that child expresses themselves more loudly than the others. It's common for there to be power struggles between children, and for parents to have to deliberately rebalance the situation.

PLEASE

Prioritise. Family relationships are the priority, and making sure that everyone has the chance to make choices and feel heard.

Long term. It's important that, within a family, each child feels that their voice counts. When one child expresses their needs much more forcefully than another child, it's easy for that child to become the dominant voice in the family. What they say goes because they say it so loudly.

This isn't good in the long term. Not just for the children whose voices aren't being heard, but also for the child who is dominating the rest of the family. The family is where children learn how relationships work, and they need to learn that they cannot always make decisions for other people.

Essentials. Preventing siblings from being hurt by each other is essential, as well as making sure that each child knows they are loved and valued.

Address barriers. Think about your family. What are the trigger points between siblings? Are children sharing space without privacy? Are they fighting over resources and could you make sure there are enough for everyone?

The expectation that family members will do things together is often a barrier – it may be more realistic to divide and conquer, using every moment when you have more than one adult available to split up siblings and do things that suit each of them. This is particularly important if the needs of one of your children are so high that they often override the choices of the others. Make the most of every moment when you have more adults available so that they get choices too.

This can mean getting help with the most flexible child, planning an escape strategy from any event (if you go in the car somewhere, is it possible for one child and adult to go back on the bus, for example, so that you don't all have to travel back together?), and taking along things like tablets and snacks so that if one child isn't enjoying an activity, this doesn't necessarily mean that you have to leave immediately.

For some children, it can be helpful to have a formal plan so that all voices are heard. You could have a structure so that one day, one child gets to choose what you do, and another day, another child gets to choose. Then the question becomes again, how can we make it easier for this to happen? If there are non-negotiables, like having to attend a medical appointment with a sibling, then all of your thinking needs to be around how to make it as easy as possible. That might involve taking snacks, treats, new games to play – whatever you can do to make it easier for the other children.

Parents often ask whether it's possible to be low demand parents with one child, but take a more mainstream approach with the others. I don't recommend it. Low demand parenting can work for all children, not just those who are pressure sensitive, and you are going to set up resentment and conflict in your family if there are obvious differences in how you treat them. You don't want your children to look back at their childhoods and say 'my brother was allowed lots of choices about his life but my parents came down on me like a ton of bricks.'

Having said that, differences in parenting are inevitable. Responsive parenting involves responding to the child you have, and it's fine to adapt. You can talk to your children about how different people find different things hard, and will need different things. For example, if someone is really into swimming they might need new goggles, while someone who is into cycling might get a helmet.

Step back. Try to lower the emotional temperature in your house around sibling issues. It might be better just not to comment sometimes, or to let small things go. Avoid catastrophising about sibling conflict – it's going to happen, it's part of life, and it's a place where children learn how to manage conflicts.

Encore! Sibling issues are going to change all the time as your children grow. Small children who get along well can turn into teenagers who hate each other, and vice versa. Some people dislike each other as children but really value each other as adults – and again, vice versa. This is one that is really never finished.

We're coming to the end of this chapter now, but there are some worksheets at the end of the book to help you use the Reality Gap and PLEASE tools. It will feel clunky at first, and you might find that you resist accepting reality because it feels uncomfortable. Try it for an area of your life you'd like to change.

Eliza and Naomi:
Our own Reality Gaps

NAOMI: Tell me about your Reality Gaps, Eliza. Where are the places where reality and expectations have clashed for you?

ELIZA: One thing I've talked about before is when other parents talk about their children reading Victorian Gothic literature. And I'm thinking, Wow, we haven't picked up a book in I don't know how long. It's things like that and then I break that down. I ask myself, how will that impact her life if she hasn't read those books?

Then I ask myself, did *I* want to read Victorian Gothic literature when I was thirteen or fourteen? I unpick my own situation and reference that back. I think that the Reality Gap is a difficult one to manage because we have those external influences telling us what they should be doing.

NAOMI: It's hard, isn't it? I think people often have the image of what it will be like to have children. When you have a baby, you have this expectation that you'll be able to do things like put them down to sleep and it'll all be sweetness and roses and fulfilment.

I think if your child is really different to you or really different to what you expected, that's particularly hard. I read loads as a child. I had a book with me all the time. Two books with me all the time, one to read, one in case I finished the other one.

Neither of my children read all the time. They do other things. I've got all my favourite children's books at home because I saved them and my children just aren't interested. In fact, the other day, my daughter was sorting out her bookshelf and she brought back down this big pile of books.

She said, 'I don't need any of these in my bookshelf. They're just taking up space.'

I was thinking, These are my most precious books. You can't just give them to the charity shop!

But they don't have the same significance for her that they did for me.

ELIZA: I think that's the difficulty, isn't it? Some expectations come from other people and external experiences, but it can come from our own and our internal expectations as well.

NAOMI: Exactly. We love these things and we want them to love the things that we love.

Sometimes when I meet parents whose children have very much been what they thought that they would be, it's like they've never had to confront this reality that this child is actually an entirely different person. They're going to have their own memories, their own things that they'll think about in the future.

ELIZA: That puts up quite a barrier, doesn't it, when we do that? Because we are not able to then meet them where they are.

NAOMI: We're thinking of our child as a projection of ourselves, basically. We never have to confront the reality of this different person with their own thoughts and feelings.

I think we can have that with an idealised childhood, too. We can be thinking, This is how it should be. We want them to be popular at school or we want them to do well at school, or we want all these things to fall into place for them. Maybe we wanted to be part of a community of families where the children are running in and out of each other's houses and growing up together. We had these dreams for their childhood and it can be really painful when it's not like that.

There's this gap between what you expected it to be like, and what it's really like.

Parents get stuck in between those two things because they're thinking, This is what I wanted and I've got this instead. This isn't what I signed up for.

Food is a really tricky one. It's hard to really change your expectations about food.

ELIZA: Well, we all know that a marker of a good parent is a healthy, balanced diet and meals around the table.

Maybe even three meals a day around the table. Three proper meals.

NAOMI: There's research I think that shows the families that sit around tables together have better outcomes and parents are told about this. It's such a pressure. Parents think, My child doesn't want to sit at the table. Does that mean I've got to force them? Does the research show that forcing children to have meals around the table is better for them?

ELIZA: It's the same with sleep, though. Isn't it called sleep hygiene? They never talk about forcing there either.

NAOMI: Yes, routines and going to bed at the same time and all that sort of thing is called sleep hygiene and it's considered to be a good thing too. There's no research that I know of that looks at whether forcing people to sit at the table or follow a bedtime routine has the same impact as it does on people who choose to do so.

When people say things like, 'Oh, families that sit around the table to eat together are happier', then I always think, is that true even if the family members don't want to be there and are forced to eat together? How does that make them happier?

There's often the assumption that when parents make the decisions and set the structure, the children will cooperate. There's the assumption that if the parents do it right, then the children will comply. The children themselves don't really have a voice. When it turns out that the children have their own opinions, parents are often left unsure what to do.

Too much to read, too little time?

1. Parents often get stuck because their expectations of how things should work in their family are so far removed from reality. This is the Reality Gap.
2. Accepting how things really are can feel like defeat, but actually it can start the process of working out how to move forwards.
3. Starting with how the child is right now and focusing on the long-term priorities can help you distinguish between what really matters and what doesn't.
4. If something really matters, then think about how to make it as easy as possible for the child; keep it low demand and keep trying.

More to read if you are interested

Kids, Carrots and Candy: A Practical, Positive Approach to Raising Children Free of Food and Weight Problems – Jane Hirschmann and Lela Zaphiropoulos

Raising Your Spirited Child: A Guide for Parents Whose Child is More Intense, Sensitive, Perceptive, Persistent and Energetic – Mary Sheedy Kurcinka

Siblings Without Rivalry: How to Help Your Children Live Together So You Can Live Too – Adele Faber and Elaine Mazlish

Sulky, Rowdy, Rude? Why Kids Really Act Out and What to Do About It – Bo Elvén and Tina Wiman

8

Screens

As I'm looking through Facebook, an advert pops up. It's a video, a person throwing a light-up ball back and forth. It's slightly hypnotising. The text is blunt, if slightly awkward: 'After I bought this toy for my child, he stopped wanting to spend time on his iPad, TV and console.'

I look closer. It really is just a ball. An expensive, flashy ball with batteries, but essentially a ball. I wonder just how long this child stayed off their iPad to play with a ball, and whether the parent really should be pleased. After all, there is only so much you can do with an electronic ball, while an iPad – its potential is limitless.

A few minutes later, another advert. This one is about an elaborate toy with lots of tiny pieces of plastic, which the child can arrange as a marble run. 'Screen-free ways to learn coding!' it proclaims. The children look engaged and excited. The relationship between the marble run and coding seems tenuous, and I can't help but be impressed by the brazen nature of the marketing – they are both playing on parents' fear of screens, while also playing on parents' desire for their children to learn coding skills that have high value in our world. Computers are both good and bad, in the same advert.

Parents are bombarded with adverts for things to buy for their children. Often there are hidden messages alongside the obvious one (which is usually, buy this product). In these cases, the messages aren't so hidden. Screens are bad, these adverts are telling parents. To be a good parent, buy our expensive screen-free toy, and tempt your child away from their device. They can instead spend their time throwing a ball or arranging a marble run. You can breathe a sigh of relief – until they get bored of the ball or marble run and ask for their console back again. And then you're back on Facebook, looking for the next expensive toy that might hold their attention for five minutes.

Perhaps unsurprisingly, I get asked about screens a lot.

'How do we limit them?'

'How much is too much?'

'Why do they want to spend so much time on their screen and is it going to damage them forever?'

'They shout at me when I ask them to come off their screens; does this mean they are addicted? What do I do if they are?'

Fear of screens is everywhere in modern parenting culture. I wonder if some of you turned to this chapter first, keen to know how you can stop fighting with your child over an extra five minutes of screen time. If that's you, I'd suggest that you go back and read the rest of the book first (although of course I can't tell you what to do and it's your choice). This chapter won't make much sense if you start here, since low demand parenting is a whole life approach: you need to understand the principles before you can apply them to specific situations.

If you're already trying a low demand approach, you wouldn't be unusual if you have found that screens are one of your main sticking points. You've given your child more autonomy – and then you've found that they are using it to spend almost all their time on a device. Your head is filled with worries and you aren't sure what to do. You know that putting on pressure won't help – but you are worried about what all this screen time is doing to your child's brain.

In this chapter we're going to take a deep dive into screens. Your relationship with them, your child's relationship with them, and what you can do to improve both of those things – and your relationship with your child.

Let's start with a quick look at the concept of 'screens'.

Screen time

I don't know when 'screen time' started to be a thing. I don't think it was when I was a child, because we only had the TV (although there was a fair amount of negativity about that too, with rumours of children developing 'square eyes' if they spent too much time watching TV and disparaging articles in the newspapers of not-good-enough modern parents using the TV as 'electronic babysitters'). But by the time I had my children, in 2008 and 2011, I could not avoid becoming aware of *screen time*. Parents discussed it, internet forums were full of it, health visitors asked about it.

Screens

When I became aware of screen time it was very quickly clear that screens had become a marker for what type of parent one was. Good Parents™ limit screens. Very Good Parents™ may completely stop their children from seeing a screen – I have met families who do not allow their small children to talk to Granny on video call and who keep their own phones out of view to prevent their children from seeing them. I met one mother who would only check her phone in the locked toilet to keep it out of sight of her children. Her children lived in a world of wooden toys and cloth dolls while their parents secretly used computers after they had gone to bed (and their father made his living as a computer programmer). The split nature of this world seemed wholesome to the mother, and pretty strange to me. We seem to think that children must be protected from exposure to the tools of our culture, even while we cannot get by without them ourselves.

This never made sense to me. When my children were small, I heard of course about the perils and risks of screen time – but my tendency when told that something is harmful is always to ask, 'How does that work? What is the process by which they are being harmed, and what role does the screen itself actually play?'

I looked at the offerings available for young children on screens. They were mostly pretty innocuous, it seemed to me. Why was *Fireman Sam* a bad thing when he talked and moved in the TV programme, but a good thing when he was static on the page in a book? Why was drawing on a piece of paper to be encouraged, but to be discouraged when done on a tablet? Why were the exact same card and board games good when played on the table, but bad when played on a device (with the bonus that on the device that you can't lose the pieces)? What was the problem with watching an animation while you listened to a song, as opposed to just listening to the song?

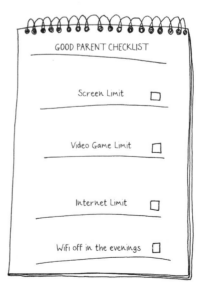

GOOD PARENT CHECKLIST

Screen Limit ☐

Video Game Limit ☐

Internet Limit ☐

WiFi off in the evenings ☐

It was quickly clear to me that touchscreens, in particular, ena-
bled children to access the world in a way that bypassed many of the
limitations associated with being so young. It didn't matter if they
couldn't read, or if their fine motor skills weren't very well developed.
It didn't even matter if they could talk. They could access things via
a screen that were more complex and stimulating than many of the
things available to them in the rest of the world. They could make
choices about what they did and watched that were not dependent
on an adult. They could feel competent in a way that often wasn't
possible in the rest of the world. And they noticed, you could tell.
They felt at home on an electronic device. Here was a place where
they could be independent. They were in charge.

I looked at the research. There was no research at the time into the
way that young children interacted with touchscreen devices, because
they were so new. The first iPhones came out around the time my son
was born, the first iPads around the time that my daughter arrived.

This means that the research that was being used to back up fears
about screen time was generally about TV. I looked at that research,
and found that it was often about the effects of TV on language development. Children from families where the TV was on a lot heard less
language and had smaller vocabularies, was the general drift. I found
the research frustrating because it didn't answer the questions I wanted
answered. I couldn't find any research on the difference for a child

between watching a TV programme designed for them, as opposed to an adult show simply being on in the background. I couldn't find any research on the difference between watching a programme with an interested adult and reading a book with an interested adult. There were none of the fine distinctions I was looking for. It seemed like it was all about the headlines. Big blanket recommendations.

My frustration has continued. Terms like 'screen time' focus our attention on the screen, and away from what is actually happening on screens. Screen time can now include reading a book on an e-reader, watching a documentary, playing an imaginative game, playing with someone else, making your own film and editing it, writing a story, solving a puzzle – I could go on and on. Screen time is such a huge and vague concept that it is essentially meaningless – and yet parents are encouraged to think that they should be limiting all the many things a child might do on a screen, simply because they are on a screen.

More than that, they are encouraged to be afraid of screens, and are told that being a Good Parent™ means they must set firm limits around screens.

Why do children love screens?

It is absolutely true that many children have a strong attraction towards computers and electronic devices. This is particularly the case for pressure-sensitive children, and if we think about it a bit, it's not hard to see why that might be.

An electronic device provides an environment where children can be far more autonomous than they are in the rest of the world. Think of a game like *Minecraft*, a sandbox game that can be played alone or with others. In *Minecraft*, you arrive in a new world, and it is up to you to gather resources, feed yourself, protect yourself from zombies and other enemies, and ultimately to explore the rest of the world. The child is in control of the whole world.

They can build their own house; they can set up a farm. They can go swimming in the sea or mining underground. They can quickly feel competent as they figure out how to put a pitched roof on their house (something I always struggled with) or how to pen in sheep and start breeding them. For children who find the outside world unpredictable and out of their control, here is a place where you know what will happen. If it all gets too much, you can put yourself on 'Peaceful' mode and turn off the zombies and creepers.

Games like *Minecraft* also give children chances to practise emotion regulation. The frustration of 'dying' and losing all your stuff is real (and often expressed very vehemently), but then, you can come back, regroup and continue with your game. Disasters happen and then can be overcome. Children learn that they can feel intense emotions and life goes on. Parents often see the intensity of emotions generated while playing games and see these as a problem – but another way to think about it is that this is a practice ground. Emotions are part of life. For children who find emotions hard to navigate, video games can give them chances to practise without the sometimes catastrophic consequences of the outside world. Even when your *Minecraft* house gets blown up, no one is really hurt (although you may be very, very angry about it).

Screens can also be an opportunity for connection. Many criticisms of screens for children focus on the risk of isolation, or of parents using the screens as replacements for interaction. There's no need for this to be the case. Screens can provide a low demand way for children to connect with others. Parents and children can sit alongside each other and watch, and children can play with others in an online world. For children who find it hard to connect with others, a game can provide a lower demand way to interact. There is a shared enterprise, and fewer choices than in the outside world. It's easier to take a short break if you need time away than if you have an actual child in your house.

Screens play an important part in the life of many pressure-sensitive children because they provide a safe and familiar portable environment, away from home. A child who is finding a situation stressful can put on their headphones, sink into a game and immerse themselves in another world. This can help them manage the environment for a bit longer, so that (for example) their siblings can stay and play, or their parents can finish a task.

Another role screens play in the life of pressure-sensitive children is that they can reduce demands by providing a distraction. Distractions can be really useful. They give the child something else to focus on apart from the task at hand. This can reduce anxiety and enable children to do things they otherwise find challenging. Many children who struggle to eat at  the table find it easier when food is placed alongside them while they are watching something. Others are able to do things like brush their teeth when they are paying attention to something else at the same time. Parents often worry about using screens in this way, but if something is important – and eating and teeth brushing are – then we need to think of ways to lower barriers so that they are easier to achieve. Screens are one way to do that.

Having said all of that, I think the most important thing is that, for many children, the things they do on their screens bring them joy. When playing on their screen they feel good about themselves, and this is something that is harder for them in the rest of the world. The glee and excitement when a child plays a good video game is wonderful to see.

Our relationship with screens

It sometimes feels like modern parenting is characterised by tension. This is the tension between children who want to spend time on a screen and parents who want to prevent them from doing so. Parents learn when they have very small children that they will be judged by how strictly they control their children's screen time, and how compliant their children are in accepting these controls. Not only are parents told all the terrible things that might happen to their children if they spend too much time on their screens, they are also told that it will make them a terrible parent. Newspaper articles scream about distracted parents using electronic babysitters while they scroll on their phones – and the parents feel guilty. They respond by trying to control their children.

Screen-time controls are so much part of mainstream parenting culture that many parents think nothing of dropping a child off for a playdate with an edict about how much time they are allowed (or not allowed) to spend on their screen, which they expect the other parent to enforce. It's also part of mainstream parenting culture to break up children who are happily playing together in a video game, because 'you've been on that for long enough', even when the same parents would do anything to avoid disturbing children who were playing an imaginary game together.

Good Parenting™ culture doesn't see play on a screen as 'real play', and as such it isn't valued in the same way as other forms of play. This is a shame, because playing on screens is increasingly how children play as they get older and their play gets more sophisticated. For children who are developmentally out of sync with mainstream expectations, it may be that the first time they really get into creative role play is in a video game, at the age of eight or nine. I've met many children whose imagination was first grabbed by a computer game, and who then went on to act it out at the local park, draw pictures of it, make models of it and even write stories inspired by it. As they get older, they start to design their own games.

As children get older, the amount of time they spend in play often decreases, replaced by schoolwork and structured activities. Except on screens, where teenagers play together, setting goals and building worlds for themselves where they are in charge. They research how to do better using YouTube videos and through talking to each other. The world of video games is sometimes the only place that they can be free of the expectations of others and can explore aspects of themselves. But we typically don't value this teenage play, instead seeing it as something to limit so they can get on with the 'more productive' work of school, sports or other organised activities.

How do parents behave around screens?

So we have this tension-filled situation. Children want to play on their screens. Parents are afraid and want to stop them. They are both pulling in opposite directions. What happens next?

Well, usually in my experience what happens is that parents get anxious and bring in strategies in order to limit their children's time on screens. These strategies are fairly consistent across the families I work with. There are three main parenting strategies around screens I hear about: making screens scarce, making screens a reward and talking screens down. Most parents use all three at different times. All of them have the potential to become traps.

Parents implement these strategies with good intentions. They want their children to enjoy doing things other than on screens. They want them to play outside and have fun. However, their strategies have unwanted effects when it comes to both the child's relationship with screens, and their relationship with their parents.

Making screens scarce

The first thing that most parents do is to make screens artificially scarce. They make them less available than they really are, in order to prevent their children from being able to spend so much time on them.

The most obvious way to do this is simply with a time limit of less time than the child would want to spend on their screen. Thirty minutes a day perhaps. This is then enforced by parents who either set timers or limits directly on the devices or the router.

This has the appeal of being straightforward and clear. The idea is that the child will learn this limit, will comply with it and will get on with doing other things in the time they are not allowed to be on a screen. Screens are limited simply by being not available. Another variation of this is when parents deliberately don't buy enough electronic resources for all the children, so that children have to 'learn to share'.

Of course, there is natural scarcity as well. You can't afford everything, there may well not be enough devices to go round, and you might not be able to afford the latest console so you have a second- or third-generation one instead. This can still have an effect, but I think there is a significant difference between scarcity created by someone else, and genuine scarcity. Not least in how the child feels about the person creating the scarcity.

Creating scarcity is a powerful technique. So powerful in fact that advertisers use it all the time. 'Only two left in stock!' they cry, or 'Sale ends in two days!' When humans see that something is scarce, we want it more. It gains value.

This is unfortunate for parents, for it means that when it comes to screens, creating artificial scarcity has the side effect of making them more, not less, attractive. Suddenly children are determined to get every second of their thirty minutes, and if there's a particular restriction (like no screens after 5 p.m.), they will do everything they can to make sure that they are back home in time to get their full allowance.

This changes children's relationships with screens. Because the screen has gained an artificial attractiveness due to scarcity, they will be reluctant to give any of their time up. This means that they won't any longer be asking themselves whether they actually want to continue to be on a screen; instead they will be asking themselves how many more minutes they have. They may spend that time doing less adventurous things, because there is no time to waste.

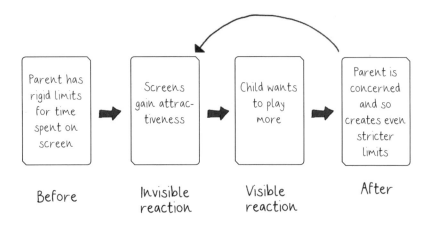

Before	Invisible reaction	Visible reaction	After

Making screens a reward

Once they have made screens artificially scarce, many parents also make them special. They do this by using the screen time as a reward – if a child is well behaved, they get more screen time. If they are badly behaved, they lose their time.

This is a really powerful psychological technique. When an activity is repeatedly used as a reward, it gets associated with positive feelings. This is called associative learning.

Think of the way that young children are given gold stars and stickers as a sign of adult approval. Those stars and stickers are meaningless in themselves, but pair them with adult approval (or chocolate buttons) and they start to be something that makes the child feel good, and then the child wants more of them and can be controlled using them.

The impact of using screens as a reward is that, yet again, screens become more attractive and desirable. Now they aren't just a device, they are a special device associated with reward. This means that the child's attachment to them increases again, and they may become increasingly furious if they are taken away – because it feels like a punishment.

Parent uses screen as a reward	Screens become more attractive to the child	Child wants to play more	Parent sees that as a sign of addiction and puts in rigid limits

Before · Invisible reaction · Visible reaction · After

The combination of making screens scarce and making screens special is that now screens aren't just attractive, they are super-attractive. This is simple associative learning. Pair screens with a sense of being rewarded, and screens will start to feel more rewarding. It's like the way I trained my cats to a whistle. For the cats, the whistle and food are paired together. For children, it's screens and being rewarded. Once screens become super-attractive, the child isn't just making a choice based on how much they enjoy spending time on their screen. Screens now have a special aura because they are a scarce reward.

Talking screens down

When I talk to parents about screens, I sometimes ask if they ever play video games with their children. 'No!' is the usual answer, followed by 'I don't have time for that.' It's an interesting question, because it's clear to me that the Good Parent™ answer is quite different to the answer expected in other areas of life. If I ask a parent whether they ever read with their child, for example, they know that the expected 'good' answer is 'Yes, of course!' If I ask whether they play sports with their child, or board games, then again, participating with your child (or at least showing an interest) is deemed Good Parenting™.

Not so with screens. Here, the rules are reversed. Now the Good Parent™ shows no interest at all. Instead, the good parent limits screen time and often has no idea what their children are actually doing. Lack of interest is the gold standard.

It is very common for parents to denigrate the activities that their children engage in on screens. Particularly video games. 'Why are you wasting your time on that?' they ask, or 'It's such a beautiful day, don't you want to go outside instead?'

Talking it down doesn't just have to involve talking. Parents show that they aren't interested in what their children do on their screens in many ways, mostly by their lack of interest. They don't ask, they don't play with their children and they only reluctantly invest in new games or devices. They say things like 'They just watch crap' when asked what they do.

The impact of this is that children learn that their parents don't value something that they really do value. They learn that this is an area of their life that should be kept away from parents, because they won't be interested and might say it's a waste of time.

Given this triad of approaches, it seems unsurprising that our children quickly develop a complicated relationship with screens. Quite apart from the initial reasons why they enjoy spending time on their screens, screens are now more attractive due to (inadvertent) marketing strategies on the part of their parents – and in addition, their parents are giving them a clear message that this thing they enjoy is (in their eyes) a waste of time. For pressure-sensitive children, the pressure is coming from all angles. They are caught.

Hang on a minute, aren't there problems with screens sometimes?

Yes. I'm not saying that all time spent on a screen is good, nor that all things that children and young people do on screens are good for them. For some children and teenagers, some things that they do on a screen are a problem. What I'm saying is that many of the things parents do to try to limit 'screen time' actually make it more attractive to the child – and that I don't think 'screen time' as a category is very useful. 'Screen time' hides the distinction between a child playing stimulating games online with friends or learning something from an app or YouTube and a child who is miserable and being bullied online. It all comes under the same heading.

Some young people use screens as a way to retreat from the world. For pressure-sensitive children who find life highly stressful, being on a screen might feel like their only option, even if they would prefer to be doing something else.

For others, what they are doing on their screen can be a problem. Online bullying can mean that a young person can never get away from their peers, even when they are not at school. Even good relationships can feel very pressured online, as in Lauren's case.

Lauren was thirteen and had just got a smartphone. She was in a small WhatsApp group with several of her friends. One day her family went swimming. When they came out of the pool, Lauren had forty-three messages on her phone. Her friend had messaged her while she was in the pool, and Lauren had glanced at it briefly when she was getting changed but hadn't responded. Her friend had messaged again and again, and then had got very angry, saying Lauren was ghosting her. When Lauren responded to say she had been swimming, her friend said that she shouldn't have gone dark like that without letting them know and that if she did it again she'd kick her out of the group. Lauren started checking her phone constantly, and worrying about doing anything that might mean that she forgot to check her phone. It got worse when her friend did kick another girl out of the group over a misunderstanding. Lauren was highly anxious, but didn't want to tell her mum what was going on in case her mum took her phone away. She started to jump every time she heard the notification alert.

Teenagers are highly susceptible to social influence, and there is new evidence that this spreads very effectively over social media. Studies in Germany have found that symptoms such as tics (involuntary movements or vocalisations) have been spread to thousands of young people by social media influencers. There are communities of mental health influencers on TikTok and YouTube, monetising symptoms – and the effect on young people is that some of them develop the same problems. There is a lot of misinformation out there, particularly regarding mental health. Young people may become convinced that they have a serious mental health problem because there's an influencer who claims that their (very common) experience is a 'Top symptom of. . .'

This isn't the same as copying – they are not consciously copying the influencers. Social influence is far more complicated than that and it's likely that young people won't be aware of the ways in which what they watch is affecting their brain and their behaviour. The videos are quite compulsive viewing – you might want to go and have a look yourself if this is something that your child is into.

The first thing to do about all of this is to talk to your child about it in a non-judgemental way. Don't make it about them. Talk about yourself and your own relationship with social media – or talk about other people and what they do online. Ask for their opinion. Find out what they are watching and who they are talking to.

In some cases, you may need to step in and keep your child safe even if they object. For example, if your child is being bullied online, and they cannot stop themselves from checking their phone all night and so can't sleep, you need to get that phone out of their room at night or stop the messages coming in. No one can remain mentally healthy under those circumstances. They may disagree about this, and they might be very angry about it. You still need to work out how to stop their sleep being disturbed, regardless of how much they disagree with you. The question needs to be 'This has to happen, so how can we make it easier?'

This isn't the same as blanket 'screen-time bans'. It is a nuanced approach, born out of seeing what your child is actually doing on their screen and how it affects them. The question to ask yourself is, how can we make this easier? With phones at night, for example, it might be easier if the whole family puts their phones somewhere else to charge or if the WiFi is switched off overnight rather than it being about one person. For younger children, it can help to put all the devices 'to bed' at a particular time, and then have a period when you all do something else.

Resetting your relationship with screens

Okay, you're saying. We want to have fewer fights about screen time and to move beyond scarcity and rewards. But how do we do that? What's the magic answer?

The first thing to do is an exercise from the previous chapter – the Reality Gap.

The Reality Gap with screens is often a particularly deep and entrenched one. The gap between where parents think their children should be and where they really are is a big one, and parents spend a lot of their time trying to force their children into compliance while the children resist. Instead of this fight, spend some time thinking about where you and your family really are. Be honest with yourself about your child and your own behaviour around screens. You can use the worksheet at the end of the book or do your own.

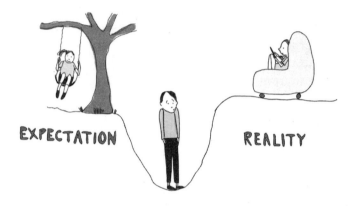

EXPECTATION   REALITY

After acknowledging your Reality Gap, the next step is to try to reset your relationship with your child around screens. You want to avoid the traps – but what do you do instead? I suggest that you go through the process below, joining up with your child to hopefully build a healthier relationship with screens for both of you. This exercise has the acronym JOIN UP.

Join in with what they are doing.
Observe what they enjoy (and don't enjoy).
Improve the quality of what is available.
Notice what is working (and what isn't).

Unblock communication.
Protect them if you need to.

I'll go through those steps to explain how it works.

Join in. How can you increase your connection with your children when they are using their screens? Sit next to them and show an interest in what they are doing, and observe what brings them joy (or makes them furious). If they don't want you to see, show an interest or download the games and try them out for yourself.

Observe. Try to switch off the critical voice that says *screens* and look at what they are really doing. Are they spending their time watching YouTube, or playing games? What do they watch, and what sort of games do they enjoy? Observe with an open and curious mind – what is it that they are getting out of this? What's the pull for them?

Improve the quality. Once you have some idea of what they are doing and what they enjoy, think about how you could improve the quality of what is available to them. Are they playing free games because they have no money for the paid ones? Are they fighting with their siblings because they don't have enough devices between them?

Free games are often really low quality and have very little play-ability, because they want you to pay to advance the game. Do they have access to high-quality things to watch about the things they are interested in? You can search online for 'games like. . .' and put in the game that they are enjoying most at the moment. If you don't have enough devices and you can't afford more, then you might want to think about how to change that in the future – would people give them money towards a device for a birthday or Christmas present, for example? Think about how you can make their device a high-quality curated environment for them.

Notice what is working (and what isn't). Children (and adults) will do lots of things on their screens, some of which are interesting to them and some of which aren't. Without jumping in and trying to change things, spend some time noticing what sort of things really bring your children to life – and think about how they are using their device.

Some children use their devices to unwind and decompress after a tough day at school, and they might be doing things that appear quite limited to you – watching the same video over and over perhaps, or playing 'clicker' games where you have to tap something over a thousand times. Then there are other times when they are immersed in a game because it's really fun and stimulating. Or there might be other times when it's a way to connect with other children. Try to stay non-judgemental as you notice all the different ways in which they use a device.

Unblock communication. If you've had a history of being quite restrictive or negative about screens, you might find that your children don't want to talk to you about what they are doing. They are defensive, worried that you are going to say it's not worthwhile and a waste of their time.

This isn't ideal, because it means that if something does happen that you need to know about, your children may not feel able to tell you. They'll be more worried about getting into trouble than they are about the strange person who is sending them private messages.

This is where you need to use low demand communication, and you need to start by being less reactive or controlling around screens. You could start by learning how to play some of the games that they play, and discussing them with them. You could also talk about your own experience of screens when you were growing up, and what your own parents thought and said about TV and computers in the pre-historic days before tablet devices (maybe they said you'd get square eyes?). If there are things you feel that you need to talk to them about – perhaps online safety – it can help to talk about someone else rather than them. You could use either your own experience or someone else you've heard about. A way to make that even more low demand is to have the conversation with someone else in their hearing so there is no pressure to respond.

Your aim here is to make talking about stuff online or the things they do on their devices as natural as talking about other things. You will have some repair work to do if most of the conversation you've had about screens up to this point has been about how they need to stop now because the time is up. You will need to build up trust that you are really interested in what they are doing, and that you will help them do more of the things that interest them.

Protect them if you need to. Sometimes you need to step in because what they are doing is not safe. They might be talking to adults online whom you do not know and whose motives you do not trust. They might be watching things they should not be seeing at their age. They might be being bullied by others online, yet feel they can't step away from the groups because they need to know what is being said. Or you might be concerned about social influence and what they are learning about the world from TikTok influencers whose main motivation is monetisation. You might see that there is a detrimental effect on their mental health and their relationship with you.

In these cases you need to step into your parental power and say 'No, this isn't good for you and I am going to stop you' – and then you need to make that happen. Safety is a non-negotiable. They might well disagree with you and express this very loudly and clearly, but you still need to protect them. You can appeal to a higher power here – say something like 'Yes, I know you don't like it, but my job as a parent is to keep you safe and I don't have a choice about this.' They will disagree with you about how safe things are – and in this case, your view overrides theirs. You have more life experience and the buck stops with you.

How is this different to blanket screen limits? It's specific. You are stopping them doing a particular thing because it is not safe for them. You could replace it with something else – better-quality video games, for example. Your aim is not to restrict their screen use, no matter what they are doing on it – your aim is to keep them safe.

Also, I don't recommend you jump straight to this step. Go through the other steps first, spend some time observing and noticing what they are doing, as well as joining in and unblocking communication on this issue.

What can we expect?

If you stop using scarcity and give your kids more autonomy over their screen use, you can expect a bounce back. Most children will start using their screens *a lot*. They are working out whether you are going to clamp down again, but they are also working out where their own limits are. Having a strict limit in place prevents children from working this out for themselves. When that limit goes, the child doesn't know when to stop because the answer to 'When do I stop?' before has always been 'When my parent says so'.

That's fine and to be expected. It's better for them to work this stuff out now when they are young than to do it when they are in their twenties and the consequences are more serious. Over time, they will work out their own balance – as long as they have other opportunities, and screens aren't being used in a way that makes them artificially more desirable (scarcity and rewards). This balance will look quite different for different people. One child might discover a passion for coding and want to spend hours on it, while another will decide that they prefer clay and getting their hands into stuff and may not touch a device for days. You can't really tell until you let them work it out for themselves.

Eliza and Naomi:
What do you do with your screen time?

NAOMI: Tell me about your screen time, Eliza. What do you do with your child on screens?

ELIZA: Even though I like computer games myself, I've struggled to get alongside my child because games are so different now. I've been around to just sit there, watch and ask questions. I give a seemingly unlimited amount of time to that.

   We also use devices as a research tool. Using the iPad to look up stuff has been really good. It can also dispel quite a lot of anxiety. If they say something like, 'I want to buy this', and it's really expensive, then I can turn it into research. I'll say, 'Oh, yeah, let's see how much it is and why it is that much.' We can bring in different realms of investigative stuff.

NAOMI: We played a lot of video games when my kids were younger. There was a stage where one of them only wanted to be on iPad the whole time. I used to look up new games late at night. I'd find ones that were very closely adjacent to the ones they were already playing. I would put them on their iPad without comment because if I made a direct suggestion, I'd get a no. Instead I wanted the new games just to appear there. There are a lot of barriers to trying a new game if you have to first find it, then choose it, then go to the App Store to download it – by the time you've done all that, it's already too much to actually play the game because you are overwhelmed by the process of finding it.

I did find some really cool games. We still reminisce now about all the games that we played together. Narrative games like *Machinarium* and *Broken Sword*. One of our longest-standing things was *Minecraft*. I played *Minecraft* with both my children.

We used to play these games where one of them would build a hotel, another one of them would build a shop, and I'd have a farm and we'd move between these three places. It was this amazing imaginary world where they could be in control. Playing together in a video game took away some of what made life hard outside.

ELIZA: Some of the games after *Minecraft* that I played, things like *The Sims* and stuff like that, they're quite advanced, aren't they? They're creating the world with people and families.

NAOMI: They're really advanced. It's funny because there's a lot of imaginative play that goes on in video games, and we tend not to see it as imaginative play. We think if children are playing at having a tea party with dolls that's imaginative but if they're constructing this amazing world in *The Sims* now, that's *just* a video game. We denigrate it.

ELIZA: Sometimes we wouldn't necessarily make a cake, but we'd look up how to on our devices.

NAOMI: You can watch a YouTube video of someone making a cake. My daughter went through a stage where she was really into videos of things like how to make Japanese cheesecake or how to make Japanese pancakes.

ELIZA: Yes. There were nice videos.

NAOMI: There were all kinds of beautiful videos of how to do it, and it was never quite the same when we did it.

We used to have a YouTuber we watched together, and she would release her videos at the same time every week. We would be waiting for that video to come out, and then we'd watch her together. It was a ritual. We had rituals around screens.

Now we play a lot of board games together on screens. I have a really strong preference for board games on screens as opposed to board games on a board. They are much less demanding! You can't lose the pieces. You don't have big boxes to carry around. They're cheaper. And you can just set them up and stop when you have had enough. You get bored, you can just put it down.

ELIZA: You can see if you like it and it doesn't matter.

NAOMI: You don't have to do all the set-up. When my children were younger, the set-up would be enough of a barrier for them not to want to play. By the time I'd got it out and set it up, they'd be like, 'No, I don't want to do this anymore.' It's a big demand, isn't it? Having to get it all ready.

Whereas with board games on the iPad, it's like, okay, start it. Invite. *Bam*. Let's go. We've removed a lot of the demand and we can get to the fun bit faster.

ELIZA: We used to use devices in the evening to start to wind down as well. We'd look up things and there would be this scrolling, which would create sleep.

NAOMI: People say that screens won't help you wind down in the evenings. But I think that's really dependent on the person. For some people it can help them switch off their internal dialogue, which means that they can come into a place where they can start to unwind, which is helpful.

My children always listened to audiobooks to go to sleep.

ELIZA: Yeah, we have the same in our house, listening to stuff at night. Because it was on the iPad, then they could choose themselves and there was some autonomy to that.

Too much to read, too little time?

1. Many parents are scared of screens and the effect that screen time has on their children. It's a sticking point for many low demand parents.
2. They respond to their fear of screens by using three main strategies: scarcity, reward and denigration.
3. All of these can work as traps.
4. There are sometimes problems with children's screen use, but to identify that we need to look closely at what they are doing rather than put blanket bans in place.
5. An alternative to the traps is to JOIN UP with your child. This stands for Join them, Observe what they do, Improve the quality, Notice what works, Unblock communication and Protect them if necessary.

More to read if you are interested

Killing Monsters: Why Children Need Fantasy, Super Heroes and Make-Believe Violence – Gerard Jones

Reality is Broken: Why Games Make Us Better and How They Can Change the World – Jane McGonigal

Taming Gaming: Guide Your Child to Healthy Video Game Habits – Andy Robertson

'The Twitching Generation: Around the world, doctors have noticed teenage patients reporting the sudden onset of tics. Is this the first illness spread by social media?' – Helen Lewis, *The Atlantic*, 27 February 2022 (https://www.theatlantic.com/ideas/archive/2022/02/social-media-illness-teen-girls/622916/)

9

What About Other People?

When I arrived in the bakery queue there was a small boy standing alone in front of me. He was crying. His parents were standing awkwardly nearby.

'Go ahead,' the mother said to me. 'Go home,' she said to the man. 'I'll manage this.' Then she came to stand next to the little boy.

'You threw it on the floor,' she started, 'we can't just buy another one.'

The boy's sobbing redoubled. 'But I wanted it!' he wailed.

His mother sounded resigned. 'I know,' she said, 'but you threw it on the floor.'

The boy wept. They stood together, saying nothing. Then the mother picked up the little boy.

'It's okay,' she said. She nuzzled his hair. He curled into her and started to relax. The sobbing slowed down.

Then she spoke again. 'We can't just buy another one,' she said, 'you need to learn. You don't just throw food on the floor.'

The boy's crying got louder.

'But it had germs!' he cried. 'I gave it to Daddy to hold, not to eat!'

The mother sounded caught.

'He shouldn't have taken a bite without asking you. But you shouldn't have thrown it on the floor.'

The little boy's distress was right back up again now.

'It was dirty already! It had germs! It wasn't good anymore!'

The mother went back to soothing. 'I know,' she said. The little boy relaxed; she understood. They cuddled.

I could almost see the mother's thought processes and emotional responses. She understood why it had happened, and she wanted to soothe her child. But she couldn't (she thought) let the behaviour of throwing the bun on the floor pass. People were watching. She tried to find a way out.

'I'll buy one for me, and you can have some of it,' she said.

'No!' screamed the little boy. 'I want one for me! It had germs!'

'I can't buy you another one,' said the mother, 'you have to learn it's not okay to throw food on the floor.'

I wanted to tell her it's okay. I wanted to tell her that her son will not grow up to throw all his food on the floor if she prioritised soothing him over trying to shape his behaviour in this moment. I wanted to buy a bun for her son – it was only £1.50.

But I didn't. Because I was worried she'd feel judged by me, and I know what it's like to be caught in this place of public parenting. To be caught between your need to soothe your child, and the voice in your head that says, 'Are you going to let them get away with that?'

And I wondered why people feel it's okay to tell parents to be more strict, but not less. For I've been told, in public, to 'Get your child under control.' I've been told, 'I'd never allow a child of mine to speak to me like that.' I've even been told, 'No wonder they behave like that if you give in to them all the time.' I've never been told, 'It's okay to let it go.' Strangely, it feels like saying something like that would come across as more judgemental than telling a parent off.

I felt for that mother, stuck in the queue and trying to find a way out that would allow her to buy her son a bun without feeling like a bad parent. I felt for that boy, whose bun felt dirty once his dad had taken a bite without asking.

They got to the front of the queue. The mother said, 'One bun please.'

The boy shrieked, 'No! Two! I want one for *me!*'

I walked away from the shop. I could feel the distress through my body as the wails continued to reverberate down the road. And I reflected on how every part of my body was telling me to soothe that child, and I'm sure that his mother felt that too – but she had a voice in her head that was telling her that holding boundaries was more important. Maybe she even thought that I was watching her and judging her ability to hold those boundaries. Judging whether she was a Good Parent™ or not.

The gaze of others

I've started with this real-life story because I've found that it res-onates with many parents. They can feel the tension of the mother and the distress of the little boy – and the dilemma they are both in.

There are apparently only two main characters in that story, but really there's a third important character. That 'character' is the other people in the bakery. They are the context and in some ways the driver for this story. We have no way of knowing what this mother is like behind closed doors, but it's likely she's more relaxed. The gaze of others is powerful.

Public parenting is hard. This mother wants to soothe her son, but she thinks that a Good Parent™ sticks to their boundaries and that others are watching her. She needs to play by the rules since she's in public. She can't risk being seen as a Bad Parent by 'giving in' to her son. Parenting in public isn't like doing it at home. When parents tell about me their worst parenting moments, they usually take place in public. Social judgement cuts deep.

For parents whose children's behaviour is unusual, it can feel like judgement is everywhere. Going to the park feels like entering a sniper zone. There are so many ways to get it wrong. From not sharing in the sandpit, to asking for three ice creams, to refusing to let another child touch their ball even when it rolls right past them, to placing their hand over your mouth so that you can't speak – each step of the way it becomes clearer how your child isn't conforming with the expectations of 'good' behaviour. And the gaze of others hurts. Not only are you struggling with your child's behaviour, but you are also being judged for struggling. Judged and found wanting.

I've spoken in earlier chapters about Good Parenting™, the rules with which parents in a particular culture and time are expected to comply. I've talked about how parenting is judged by outcome, and so when a child's behaviour is unusual, the first place most people look is how they are parented.

There is a particular difficulty with low demand parenting when it comes to other people. Low demand parenting is a thoughtful and responsive form of parenting, but to those who haven't seen the long and painful process it took you to get there, it doesn't look that way. It looks like you don't know how to parent properly. You aren't follow-ing the rules of Good Parenting™ and they assume that this is why your child is behaving as they are. Just follow the rules, they think, and then that child will change.

They think that your child is behaving the way they are because of low demand parenting, when in fact your parenting is low demand because of how your child behaves. Parenting isn't just something we do to children; it is something parents do in relationship to children. It is a bidirectional process.

The rituals of parenting

Most parents have a story of their worst moment of parenting – and often that moment is in public. They tell the story of the time that their six-year-old pushed another child off their bike with no provocation at all, and the look of horror on the other parent's face. They describe the time that their eight-year-old started throwing stones in the playground and hit a window – and the look of shock on everyone else's face. Or the time that their thirteen-year-old swore loudly at them when they were taking too long to leave the swimming pool, and how aware they were of the flimsy cubicle walls.

The gaze of other people is ever present when parenting in public. Even if there is no one there, someone could walk past at any moment. And there are very strong expectations – one could even say rituals – around parenting behaviour.

Most parents discover this early on, often at a local playground. Your child wants a go on the swing but another child is already there. They express this to you loudly. Parenting culture kicks in. You're meant to tell them about turn-taking, or sharing or waiting their turn. Even if they are very young and apparently have almost no understanding of what you are saying, you're meant to give them a mini-lecture, distract them and wait politely while the other children have their turn. The child's role is to accept this and to look contrite. If a child does something like refusing to share the roundabout, or taking a bucket and spade off another child (even if that child doesn't seem to mind), people look expectantly for the telling off and the enforced 'Sorry.' It's a ritual. Child transgresses, parent tells child off, child says sorry, justice has been served. Everyone breathes out. The circle is complete.

Except if you have a child who responds really badly to the expected consequences. If you know that your child is likely to go completely ballistic if you tell them off, definitely *not* say sorry and probably then refuse to leave the playground at all for the next few hours, then you're in a really tricky place in that park. Your child has transgressed, all eyes are upon you – and you aren't doing your part. You aren't telling them off, or them giving the lecture. You aren't forcing them to perform the rituals everyone expects, because you know that it will make everything worse. This means that *you* are now the transgressor. You are not fulfilling your part in the ritualistic behaviour of parenting.

Social transgression comes with a high price. You feel the pressure. You feel the eyes upon you, and perhaps you hear the muttering. Parents say things to their children, just audible enough – 'Some mummies don't teach their children to behave', 'That little girl needs a good telling off', perhaps even 'spoilt brat'.

'Bad parent' vibes resonate around you. The playground doesn't feel friendly anymore. Your child's behaviour reflects on you – everyone thinks they know why they did the thing they did. It's because you are a bad parent and you haven't taught them how to behave. You have broken the unspoken rules and you have only yourself to blame.

As children get older, these moments aren't so often taking place in playgrounds, but they still happen. The clash between mainstream expectations and your reality – and the judgement that goes with that. Perhaps it's the playdate where your child really wants to play *Minecraft*, but the other parent tells their child loudly at the beginning that their screen time is used up for the day. Your heart sinks as you wonder how you are going to navigate the next two hours with craft activities while your child asks insistently for *Minecraft* and wants to know why they can't play. Or the birthday party where all the other parents are making the children finish their savoury snacks and cheese sandwiches before they are allowed ice cream and birthday cake ('Only if you say please!'), and your child is going straight for the chocolate cookies – and you aren't stopping them. As they get older, it might be them storming off when they are losing at Monopoly, or not being flexible when it comes to deciding whether a group of friends will play *Mario Kart* or go for a walk outside. The other teenagers look askance and you aren't sure how to smooth this over.

Because that is the crux. This isn't so much about your child's behaviour, it's about what others expect you to do in response, and what they assume about you (or you think that they assume about you) when you don't do it.

We've talked already about the Reality Gap in this book, but it's when you're out in public that the Reality Gap gets brutal. For then the expectations aren't just in your head, they're in everyone else's heads as well – and they don't stay in their heads. You can see them in their expressions and even in what they say.

They don't understand what they are seeing. From the outside, low demand parenting often doesn't make sense to others. They don't see the supportive relationships, the collaboration, humour and all the work you put in. They don't see all the emotion regulation work going on behind the scenes. They don't see the way that you carefully approach new topics, the way that you tread carefully to avoid overloading your sensitive child's nervous system.

What they see is an absence of what they expect. They see parents not setting boundaries, not telling children off, not giving lectures – and often in our society this is equated with neglectful or permissive parenting. It's equated with doing nothing, with not caring. This is seen as an absence of parenting because parenting is thought of as control. *Good Parents™ control their children.*

This leaves many parents feeling constantly stressed in public, particularly those who have spent their lives being well behaved and conforming to expectations, and now suddenly have children who are the absolute opposite. You quickly find out who your real friends are when your child bites theirs and you don't tell your child off. In most cases, there's no going back.

The unspoken rules

Parents tell me that several things about parenting a pressure-sensitive child are very difficult, but one of the things that keeps them up at night is feeling misunderstood. They know that everyone in the playground thinks they are neglectful. They know that they are being talked about behind their backs. They know that their child's behaviour is the talk of the neighbourhood – and the most shocking thing is that they, the parent, are not holding boundaries as expected.

They know that they are breaking the unspoken cultural rules of Good Parenting™ that everyone accepts without thinking about it. If you're living in the culture that you grew up in, then you will probably have learned the unspoken rules, although some people do find these unspoken rules harder to work out than others. If you've felt 'wrong' in particular environments, it may be that you don't know the unspoken rules everyone else is operating by. Being the first person in your family to go to university, or the first to move away from where you grew up, means entering a world with new rules, and generally, no one is going to explain them to you. They don't even realise that they are there because unspoken rules are invisible to those within them. They don't think of them as rules, they think of them as just 'how things are'.

When you do know the unspoken rules but you're not able to keep to them, they can feel like a burden. It's particularly hard if it's your child who is breaking the rules, either because they are someone who finds these rules hard to work out, or because they just don't care. You as their parent will have a good guess at what others think and you will feel bad because you will know that you are getting it wrong, but ultimately you can't control your child and people will judge you for that. There's no time to shout 'We have thought carefully about this, and telling her off will make things worse! It's not because we are bad parents!' as you prevent your child from clobbering another child over the head with a toy spade without telling them off.

Changing other people's minds

When I'm asked what to do about other people, parents often think it's a matter of getting the right information. 'What books can I give my children's grandparents so that they will understand?' they ask. Or 'Is there an audiobook my husband could listen to so he realises why punishments don't work?' It's tempting to reel off a list, but at the same time I know that it's more complicated than that. Really what they are asking is 'How do I change their minds?' and information is often not a satisfactory answer to that.

In all my training as a psychologist, they never gave me the secret of how to change other people's minds. That's because there is no information that is guaranteed to change everyone's mind so that they agree with you – if you think about it, the world would be a very different place if there was. We all see the world in different ways, and the way that we interact with information reflects this. One person's 'a-ha' moment can be a total yawn for someone else. I can't be alone in having had books enthusiastically recommended to me as life changing that have seemed to me utterly banal when I've read them.

Motivation matters, and many other people do not want information about why you are parenting the way that you are. They see no need to change their perspective, even though you would really, really like them to. If people are not interested in changing, then the likelihood is that either they won't read any books you give them, or, if they do read them, they will read them in order to poke holes in the arguments and to show you how wrong you are. It will entrench them further. You can't change other people's perspectives against their will.

That can feel like a rather hopeless message. Does it mean that you have to hide away and only go to the playground after 10 p.m. until your children are twenty-three? Do you need to resign yourself to being a social pariah and hermit? Are you going to fall out with your whole family and have no friends?

Well, I'm not going to lie. You are unlikely to change mainstream parenting culture and you can't force other people to change their minds. The judgement will continue no matter how hard you rail against it – but hopefully over time it will matter less. You will hopefully find people who will start to understand you and your child. You will start to recognise them yourself. You see the hovering parent and the child who is clearly slightly on the edge of managing. You see the noise-cancelling headphones and the tablet ever ready to be pulled out. You notice the parent who can't chat with the others, because they are constantly on the look-out for things to go wrong. If you're lucky, they might recognise you too and give you a terse nod when their child isn't looking. They might even send you a text message apologising for not being able to say hello. You will find others who understand.

Accepting this reality doesn't mean that there's nothing you can do and that the minds of others won't change. It just means that managing other people isn't as straightforward as finding the right information and distributing it to them. It means there is no one size fits all.

The message of this chapter is that since we can't reliably change other people, you need to start with you. You need to be selective about where you put your emotional energy. You only have a limited amount, so don't waste it on people who don't matter. I'll give you some methods for deciding whom to spend your energy on, and how to use that time and energy. There is no point in spending all your emotional energy on people who just aren't going to change. Better save it for yourself and your children.

Influence, importance and openness to change

There are three main areas to consider when thinking about other people:

1. Influence: How much influence do they really have?
2. Importance: How important is this relationship to me and my child?
3. Openness to change: Are they willing to consider change? Do they see the need for change themselves?

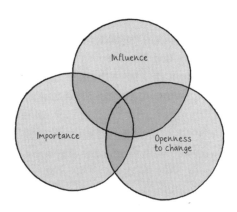

These three things are crucial in deciding whether it is worth investing any emotional energy in this person – and if so, what form that should take.

Some people have no influence, and very little importance. This doesn't mean that it doesn't feel painful if they tut at you, but ultimately, tutting is all that they can do. Onlookers at the park, for example, or commentators on social media. Friends whom you've met in one context and who aren't going to continue to be friends now it has become clear how different your approach to parenting is. For these people, the ongoing relationship is not important and so it's mostly about managing your own emotional responses to them.

Others (for example, relatives) may be important people in your child's life. There are only a relatively small number of people in the world who will care about your child, no matter what. Those people are precious and irreplaceable, even if they disagree with you on parenting. Some of these people may think that they should have influence, but in actual fact they cannot make decisions about your child. For them, it might be about thinking of ways to preserve the relationship between them and your child if that is possible.

Then there are those who are both influential and important. This includes the child's other parents or step-parents, or could involve other relatives if you live with them or if they are directly involved in your child's parenting. The child may live with them part of the time if you are not living with their other parent.

What About Other People?

Some people have high importance and high influence but this is short-lived – for example, if you have involvement with the family courts, or if social services are involved. It can be hard to explain low demand parenting to professionals, but it's really important to do so in a way that makes sense to them.

If you are in a low importance, low influence situation (such as when you're surrounded by strangers on a train or in a shop), then it's not worth investing any time trying to convince them or change their minds. It's about getting through it with minimal harm to you and your child.

With all of these different people, you need to think about how open they are to change. If someone isn't open to change, then no quantity of information is going to help. They won't suddenly read a book and decide that you are right to do what you're doing. They are more likely to dig their heels in and find all the reasons why you are wrong. It isn't worth spending time searching out books and videos for them because they won't watch them, except to ridicule the ideas.

This openness to change may vary over time, however. They may start to see for themselves that there are good reasons for the approach you are taking to parenting, and you can prepare the groundwork for this. However, this change is less likely to happen if you pressure them. Remember the Pressure Paradox trap? The more pressure you put on, the less likely something is to happen? It applies here too.

If someone isn't open to change, you can expend a lot of energy and money doing things that are utterly futile. Buying them books, sending them articles they don't read, even paying for tickets for talks – all of which will make them feel pressured and more likely to double down on their position. Better take that energy and use it elsewhere.

Influence, importance and openness to change

You can use the table below to think about people in your life whose opinions about your parenting are causing you distress. Have a think about those three factors – influence, importance and openness to change – and rate them out of ten on each.

Name	Influence	Importance	Openness to change

When others are not open to change

If people are not open to change, are not important and have no influence then there is just no point in investing any emotional energy. You will never change all the tutters in the supermarket. That means that you need to focus on you and your child instead – on getting through it with minimal emotional stress. It's more complicated when people are not open to change but are important or influential, and I'll talk about them below.

Keeping yourself calm and focused is really where it's at. There's a three-part strategy for these situations, and because you are hardly going to be able to remember anything in the heat of the moment, the acronym is as easy as it could be. A B C.

Accept – Breathe – Connect

ACCEPT   BREATHE

CONNECT

Accept

The first step for dealing with difficult situations is to reduce the fight inside your own head. You have enough to deal with right now – you don't need to also be fighting thoughts like 'This shouldn't be happening' or 'If only I'd prepared better' or 'I should have avoided this whole situation, I knew it would be a nightmare.'

You need to turn towards reality and see it as it is. The other parents watching, your child doing something terrible – the whole situation in its technicolour reality. I know you'd like it to be different, but right now, it isn't.

Sometimes it can be helpful to have a mantra to repeat to yourself like 'This is just how things are in this moment' or 'Right now, we are right here.'

Some people find a metaphor works better for them than a mantra – they imagine themselves in a boat on stormy seas, or wending their way through a forest during a thunderstorm. You're looking for something that allows you to acknowledge that this is tough, but you can't change the storm or the thunderstorm. It's about getting through this, not stopping the weather.

Breathe

This is the point when you take a deep breath and connect with your sense of yourself as being capable and competent. You breathe into your power.

One of the most effective ways to do this is by using imagery of yourself doing something well. Most of us try to talk ourselves out of tricky situations, but when we are overwhelmed by intense feelings, words generally don't cut it. Words don't connect with our emotions or body sensations. Images connect with a different part of our brain, and can allow us to avoid the endless semantic struggles that many of us get caught up in.

The 'I've Got This' imagery exercise in Chapter 5 is really useful for this. If you didn't do it then, you could go back and have a look now.

Connect

In the final stage, you bring together Acceptance and Breath to Connect with your child. This is the point when you remind yourself that your relationship with your child is the most important relationship in this space. I don't say this in a flippant way. When you are surrounded by judgemental adults, their views feel very important – but actually, they are far less important that your relationship with your child.

That relationship with your child is likely to be the longest-standing relationship in your lives. Hopefully, it will still be there when everyone else in this space is just a memory. Certainly if they are acquaintances in the park, or even teachers at school. Your relationship with your child is where you can have the most impact. You will never manage to convince all the others that you are a good parent, but you can genuinely try to be the parent your child needs in that moment.

Connection means seeing your child and connecting with them on an emotional level, rather than a behavioural one. It might mean empathising with them. It might mean seeing that they are hungry and tired, and it's time to leave. It might mean just getting alongside them and doing what you can to soothe them. It means turning towards your child, and away from the other voices and eyes.

It means showing them that you are there for them, even when their behaviour is at its worst and when everyone else seems to be against them. It means being their anchor and showing them that your love for them is unconditional.

This isn't easy, and sometimes this connection might just be managing to stay quiet and not shout or cry while you leave the area (or stay right there because your child refuses to budge).

Not open to change – but influential and/or important

You can use A-B-C with people who are important and influential as well – but then you also need something more. It isn't enough just to keep yourself calm and focused on your child. You need to think about how you are going to present your parenting choices, and how you can gradually introduce information.

The way that you might do this depends on who the other person is, and what their motivations are. Relatives and other parents are usually motivated by love and care for the child. They want to know that they are being well-parented and cared for, and they often think that low demand parenting, as they perceive it from the outside, doesn't fit the bill.

Professionals have different motivations depending on their role. Some may be focused on safeguarding – they want to know that this child is being properly cared for and not neglected. Others are focused on health or wellbeing, or on education. They want to know that you are thinking about your child's wellbeing and that you are making decisions with that in mind.

Asking yourself what the other person's motivation is will help you decide how to approach them. You will need to reassure them that you are taking your child's wellbeing seriously and making intentional and thoughtful choices about parenting. In all cases, it will help if you can stay calm and not take it personally (I know this is practically impossible to carry out, but there are things you can do to practise this).

Relatives

The opinions of relatives can be hard for many parents to deal with. Relatives are often important in your life and your child's life and they may well think that they should have lots of influence, even if you disagree. Their importance is likely to continue for years, and even if they aren't that important in your own life, they might be important for your child. Even if you aren't that close to them now, you might be again in the future.

What About Other People?

It's rare, in my experience, for relatives who don't spend a lot of time with your child to recognise the reasons why you might use a low demand approach.

Grandparents are often genuinely concerned. They care about their grandchildren and they want things to go well for them. They may say things like 'But how will they learn to [say please and thank you, tidy up after themselves, share with other children, stop hitting, etc.] if you don't make them?' or they may be more openly disapproving, saying things like 'We'd have never let you get away with that.'

Whatever grandparents say tends to echo in the ears of parents. Which is understandable because they are, after all, your own parents. You know them better than anyone else, and you know the weight of opinion behind what they say and don't say. When you were a child, what they said mattered, and it's a rare adult who completely breaks free of that.

You may also be in the position of not wanting to upset grandparents because they are the only people who are prepared to help you out with childcare or with whom your children are happy to be left.

All of which is really saying that relationships with grandparents are complicated. One way in which this shows up is that the feelings of judgement may well go both ways. Grandparents see their adult children parenting in a very different way, and to them, that seems like a criticism of their own parenting style. Each of your choices can seem like a judgement of them. They punished you so you would learn how to behave, yet now you aren't punishing your children. They told you off and stopped your pocket money, and now they see your children behaving in ways they disapprove of and you aren't doing the same. They worry that you are 'spoiling' your children. They spent years reminding you to say please and thank you and to tidy your bedroom – and now you just aren't playing your part with your children. It can feel like almost everything that you do is a criticism of them.

Grandparents have less influence on children than they do on parents

Santos was concerned about the impact his parents were having on his children. He was a low demand parent, but his parents were not low demand grandparents by any stretch of the imagination. They reminded the children to say please and told them to share (among other things) and it made Santos bristle with irritation. He wanted to know how to get them to stop – but at the same time, needed his mother Maria to look after the children every week because she was the only person with whom the children were happy. Tensions were rising. Maria could feel that Santos was not happy and she was frustrated because she was putting in a lot of effort to make her time with her grandchildren fun.

The first question I asked Santos was whether there was in fact a problem. Did the children mind that their grandparents reminded them of things and told them to share? Did it result in conflict between them? Santos hadn't thought of it like that. He knew that it caused problems for him when he did the same. But actually, the children didn't seem so bothered when told to do something by their grandparents. The children had a different relationship with their grandparents than Santos did. Maybe the problem wasn't so much how to change the grandparents but more that he needed to let them get on with it and make his peace with things being different with them.

What About Other People?

All demands are not equal. Not all pressure is the same. Relationships are different, and sometimes children can tolerate demands from one person when they can't from another. This is particularly true when it comes to parents. Children know their parents very well. They know their tones of voice, the things they are not saying, and what they are thinking. The relationship between parents and children is often loaded with expectation – just the fact that parents want their children to be happy can feel like a demand. Parents can often get away with very little when it comes to their children. They have no advantages like a novelty factor.

Grandparents are different. The relationship is, while important, usually less significant in the child's life, and the child knows that. They know that being with the grandparent is temporary, and that while their grandparent might do things differently, this doesn't mean that things are always like that. As they get older, they are often able to reflect on that. They might say 'Granny wants us to say thank you, but at home you don't make us' or even 'I feel Grandpa wants me to do lots of things with him. I can't relax for long there.'

This is okay. It's okay for children to have different experiences, as long as it is not putting too much strain on them. Things said by a grandparent often affect (or annoy) the parent more than the child. That's because the relationship between the grandparent and parent is more complicated, has years more history and, of course, was originally a parent–child relationship where the parent (now grandparent) held the power. Children don't have this legacy. They know that they will be going home at some point and this isn't how things are all the time.

All of this is a roundabout way of saying, the problem might not be as great as you think. Grandparents may do things very differently to how you do them. If the child can manage the level of demands and the relationship is good, then I wouldn't mess with it. Relationships with grandparents are precious, so do what you can to give your parents and your children the space to make their own connection. Even if it means biting your tongue.

Important but not open to change

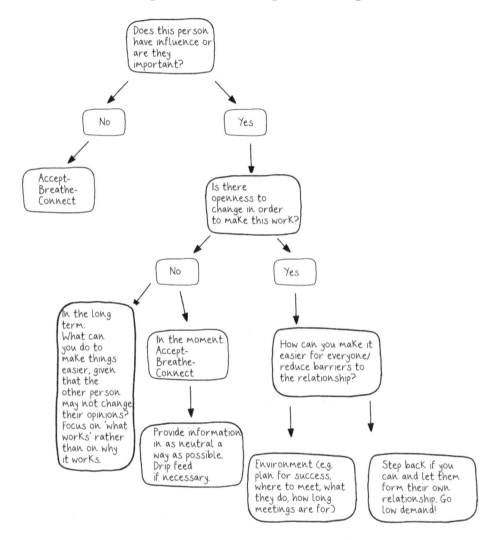

If other people aren't open to change, but the relationship is important and you want to maintain it, then the answer is to focus on the environment and what you can change to make things easier.

Plan for success. Arrange to meet on neutral territory, or make it very clear when a meeting will end. State in advance anything you need and make it easy. Don't make it a discussion or go into why you do things, but instead focus on 'what works'. Eliza knows a family who emailed their grandparents before Christmas to explain that their children wanted pizza for Christmas dinner and that they would bring the pizza. It wasn't a problem. Everyone ate what they wanted.

Over time, relatives may become more open to change, particularly if they can see that your approach is 'working' and everyone is happier.

If they are willing to try to change, there are a few different approaches that have helped some people. One is making a 'crib sheet' for people who interact with your child, explaining briefly how to use low demand communication and giving examples. An example of this is given at the end of this chapter. Don't make the examples too long; just keep to the things that are most important. No one is going to be able to absorb too much information and really, less is more. People are more likely to be able to hold a few changes in mind than a long list.

Professionals

The voices of professionals can feel very powerful for parents. I've talked to many parents who tell me things their doctors have said that they still remember years later – often something that to the doctor probably felt like a throwaway comment or 'just common sense'. Things like:

- 'You'll want to get them out of your bed before they're two or they'll never sleep by themselves.'
- Or 'You mustn't let them get into bad habits.'
- Or 'Don't give into tantrums, they'll get worse.'
- Or even, 'Home educating them will ruin their lives.'

The thing to remember here is that most professionals have very little idea about the reality of your family and your life, and in most cases they are simply expressing mainstream parenting views. Those views have acquired an extra power because they are being expressed by a doctor or psychologist. I can vouch for the training of clinical psychologists: there was very little about day-to-day parenting and what there was focused on behaviourism. Lots about mental health and how to treat mental health problems, but not much about the reality of living with children. Any training we had on parenting was on running parenting courses. I'm guessing that other professionals had similar experiences. The views of professionals gain weight because of their training, but this training might not actually have included much about the things they are telling you about now with such confidence.

These professionals don't need to have any influence if they aren't useful to you. However, I would also guard against making quick decisions about professionals. I have met some families who have sacked professionals after the first meeting because they used deficit-focused language like 'disorder' or 'impairments'. The reality is that most professionals will have been trained using these terms, and they may not be aware of alternatives. It doesn't necessarily reflect any intent on their part to pathologise you or your child – and they may well be open to change.

Influential professionals

If you have professionals involved in your life or your children's whom you have not chosen, then it is possible they will have a lot of influence and, for a period, be really important. You might be being assessed for the family courts, or have social services involved. Your children might be fostered or adopted and there might be related services involved as a result. In this case, professionals want to know that your children are safe and well cared for, and some aspects of low demand parenting may make them nervous because they diverge from mainstream parenting notions.

In this case, it does matter how you explain your parenting, but the aim here is quite different. You aren't really trying to change their minds because, in the long term, this doesn't matter. What does matter is how they perceive you now. You need to show that you are making a conscious and intentional choice about your parenting style and that your children are safe and well cared for. You want to make it clear that it isn't that you simply haven't realised that most other parents do things another way, or you can't be bothered to set boundaries. In other words, you need to make it clear that the reason that (for example) your child's hair is unbrushed, or they wear pyjamas all weekend, isn't because you are neglectful.

For this reason, I'd think carefully about how you talk about your parenting.

Some parents talk about low demand parenting in terms of absence: 'We don't have rules, bedtime, tell them off, make them eat their greens. . .'

I don't advise doing this. This is going to make many professionals nervous, because they don't know what you actually *are* doing. They just hear the absence, and think 'neglect' and 'chaotic'.

Instead, focus on the things you are positively doing – frame it in terms of 'What works for us'. Make it clear that you are intentional, involved parents and that you have thought about the way you parent. Emphasise ways in which your life is structured and how you provide a loving environment for your children. For example:

- 'We've noticed that Katy responds very badly to punishment in the moment so instead we respond calmly and talk with her later when something goes wrong.'
- 'Mikah can feel under pressure if we are enthusiastic so we often play things down a bit.'
- 'We offer them lots of opportunities to. . .' (even if they don't take you up on those opportunities).

- 'We don't put Sally's pictures up on the walls because she doesn't like us doing so. We store them safely instead.'
- 'We provide regular healthy meals and allow them to choose what they eat from the table.'

If professionals are interested and want to know more, you could suggest they read this book or you could show them the explanation at the end of this chapter.

School

Dealing with school is a special type of 'other people' situation. School can be particularly challenging for pressure-sensitive children. There are standardised expectations that can be out of sync with those who are on different developmental trajectories. There are often behavioural systems based on rewards and consequences. As a result, school can feel like a place of many demands and lots of pressure.

Children show that school is challenging for them in a range of different ways. Some are disruptive at school and get into trouble regularly. Others are perfectly behaved at school and then explode when they get home. When this happens, parents often feel blamed

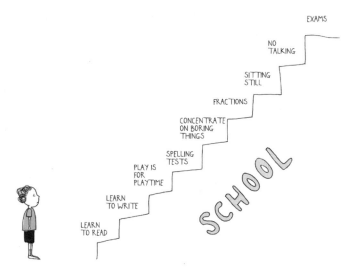

and that the problem is with their parenting. Schools will sometimes say that a child is 'fine at school' and may even suggest that parents adopt similar behavioural strategies at home to those used at school, as they clearly 'work'. Other children become reluctant to attend and beg to stay at home.

The reason that children appear to be fine at school and then explode afterwards is because they feel safe to show you their real feelings at home. They are working hard to keep going all day, and then when it comes to the end they just can't do it anymore.

In Chapter 7, I talked about the Reality Gap – the gap between how you imagined life would be, and how it really is. Many of us spend our lives wishing that things were different, and sometimes accepting how life really is can free you up to start to solve the problems.

The school Reality Gap is a particularly tough one, because almost every parent wants their child to do well and be happy at school. We would love it if they skipped in every day, full of joy, to spend another day learning. The reality can be very different, and parents can spend their days on tenterhooks, waiting for a call from the school. One mother told me that she would often get to work just in time for a phone call saying 'Mrs. Phipps, can you come up to school? Jayden is on the top of the portakabin roof again.' In the end her employer told her she'd have to choose between taking the calls from school and continuing to work. As she said, it wasn't really a choice.

EXPECTATION   REALITY

When it comes to working with school, it's important to realise that they will probably not know the solutions any more than you do. They may not have met another child like yours and they may well be working from the assumption that more pressure is the way to success. If you can help them to understand your child better and work together, then things might go better for everyone.

Start with thinking about what you know about your child, and then think your way through the school day. Some people colour code the timetable with red (really hard), amber (quite hard) and green (relatively easy). Ask yourself what the flashpoints will be, based on what you know of your child. Do they find transitions really hard, or is it the playground that is the toughest part of school? Is it going into a busy classroom first thing, or are they worried about going to the toilet? Then share that information with the school, or make a 'What works for us' crib sheet. Agree to try out different ways of doing things, and to meet again to assess whether it has made a difference. Sometimes minor changes like a key person meeting a child at the start of the school day or a quiet place to go at break to decompress can be enough to make it work. Tell them about low demand language, and how to frame things so as to avoid putting on extra pressure. Parents tell me that when things go well, it's often because there is a teacher who really gets their child.

For some pressure-sensitive children, schools aren't able to be flexible enough and they stop being able to attend, or attending school results in intense distress and behavioural challenges. When this happens, you may need to make the difficult decision to take your child out of school and educate them differently. Just thinking seriously about this option can sometimes reduce the pressure that everyone feels about school – which can then have a positive effect on the child. I do know children who, when they were told that they could leave school to be home educated if they wanted, found it easier to attend school. Knowing that there was another option lifted some of the pressure off.

For parents, this can feel like a terrifying decision. Sometimes parents tell me it feels like they are jumping off a cliff without a safety net. They worry that they will be ruining their child's future.

There are many different ways for children to learn. You do not have to replicate school at home. You need to provide a suitable, full-time education, but that can be done however you choose. Many pressure-sensitive children stop attending school and then come back into formal education when they are sixteen or eighteen. Education at this stage is often less pressured and more flexible, with more autonomy. There are some stories in Chapter 12 of families who have taken this route.

Whatever you choose to do, putting more pressure on your child will not help. Sometimes adults will tell children that there will be dire long-term consequences if they don't attend school, with the hope that this will motivate them to attend. This is likely to backfire with your child, who might believe in the predicted consequences while still unable to attend school, making them despondent about their future.

Other parents and step-parents

Here we get to people who have both high importance and high influence in a child's life. Other parents have a right to a say in how a child is parented, and if you disagree, this can make for constant conflict.

It is very common for the parent who spends the most time with a child to have a different perspective on how they should be parented than the parent who is out of the house most of the day. Parents who aren't primary carers often don't see the most challenging times, or if they do, they may blame laxness, lack of boundaries, permissive parenting – all the things everyone else blames too.

The parent who has put the most legwork into thinking about parenting (very often but not always the mother) sometimes feels that the other parent needs to come on the same journey as them. They recommend books or podcasts, which the other parent doesn't read or listen to, and then feels guilty about. It becomes an area of tension. The more one parent suggests things, the more the other parent doesn't want to read or listen to them (sound familiar? It's the Pressure Paradox!).

Pressure won't help. Think of this like you would with your child. Go low demand. Drip-feed new ideas. Offer suggestions in a tentative way ('I find this works but it might not work for you'). Try to resist the urge to blame them when things go wrong, and remember that they too are motivated by wanting the best for your child. They just disagree with you about what that 'best' means.

Co-parenting

If you are no longer with your child's other parent, and you are co-parenting, this can be a particularly challenging situation. Things can quickly spiral into blame and hostility, with both sides pointing to the failures of the other. The child gets caught in the middle.

These relationships are important. Unless your child's other parent is abusive, the research indicates that having an ongoing relationship with both parents is a predictor of better outcomes in later life. It's also important for the child to experience relationships with different people who care about them, even when they get things wrong and there are conflicts. Learning that we can disagree with people who love us is an important developmental skill.

This means that as the parent who is reading this book, you may need to be planning for the success of your child's interactions with their other parent, when a large part of you wants it all to go horribly wrong so that the other parent can see what it's really like. The reason to do this is that it's about the long-term wellbeing of your child. In the short term it may well feel easier for them to just not see the other parent, but in the long term, they will miss out.

There is no sure-fire way to convince another person of something (or indeed control them – isn't that the whole message of this book?), and I can't teach you any magic spell that will convince a sceptical parent that they should stop using Time Out, for example. What I can do is make some suggestions that have worked for some:

- Go low demand! If your child shares genes with this parent, it's highly possible that they will share characteristics. Use declarative language. Drip-feed new ideas. Ask for their help rather than telling them what to do. Expect change to be slow. Leave useful information around for them to find.
- Don't expect someone else to go on the same journey as you. Don't expect them to love the books you loved or follow the influencers you like – they need to find their own way and it won't be the same as yours.
- Be pragmatic. Focus on what works. Say things like 'One thing that works for me is. . .' and then leave it.
- Let them get on with it. Let them make their own mistakes and find out what doesn't work. It will not harm your child for them to get it wrong sometimes.
- Don't start blaming them for mistakes, particularly in front of your child. Don't lecture. Remember that pressure is likely to make things worse.

The table below summarises the different approaches you might take with different people:

What About Other People?

Influence	Importance	Openness to change	Who this might include	Strategy
No	No	Doesn't really matter	Strangers, onlookers, acquaintances	**ABC** You won't change them (and don't need to do so), so put your energy into yourself and your child.
Short term	Short term	No	Professionals, teachers	ABC. Think carefully about how you present what you are doing. Talk about 'what works'. Show that you are making considered choices. Do not bombard people with unasked-for information. Find other people to talk to about how it makes you feel.
No	Yes	No	Relatives and grandparents	ABC. Ask yourself if the problem is a problem for the child or mostly for you. Environmental changes. Plan for success. Focus on 'what works'.

Influence	Importance	Openness to change	Who this might include	Strategy
Yes	Yes	No	Child's other parent/carers	Recognise that the concern usually comes from a place of love for your child. Recognise that this relationship will be important in the long term. Think of ways to facilitate this relationship and allow them to make mistakes. Show that you are making a considered choice about parenting. Focus on 'what works'.
Yes or No	Yes	Yes	Relatives, grandparents, other parents, professionals	Information! But don't assume that what you find useful will be the same as what they find useful. Drip-feed. Offer but don't insist. Find things that start where they are. Think about what they really need to know and what will be helpful to them when interacting with your child.

How much do they need to know?

Let's say you have grandparents or other relatives or family friends who really want to know how to help, and who also want to understand your child. How can you explain to them what you are doing, and why it works?

Even when information is the answer, not all information is equal. People are going to be in different places, and therefore what is most useful for them will vary. There are some books I'd recommend that are more mainstream than this book, for example. At the end of this chapter there's a list of books I sometimes recommend to those who are just starting to think that perhaps this child needs something a bit different.

Firstly, I'd ask yourself how much they actually need to know. Not everyone needs to know everything, and you don't want their eyes to glaze over. It can help to think of this in three levels. Those with a passing interest get Level 1, those who want more get Level 2, and those who are really interested get Level 3. I'd only suggest books or videos to people on Level 2 or 3. Level 1 is more about your specific child and what works (and doesn't work) for them.

- Level 1: What works for us. Crib sheet.
- Level 2: Why we do it. More explanation.
- Level 3: In-depth explanation of low demand parenting, the Pressure Paradox, the problems with punishments and rewards, etc.

Example of Level 1: What works with Finley

Finley gets very anxious when he feels out of control, and so we interact with him in a way that helps him feel as safe as possible.

This means that we:

- Avoid direct questions like 'Can you put your boots on?' and instead use statements like 'Your boots are here.'
- Avoid frequent reminders (even gentle ones), as these make him feel stressed (e.g. nagging him to put his shoes away).

- Don't insist on 'please' and 'thank you' or sharing.
- Give him choices whenever possible – 'We could go to the park or the museum' for example – and make it clear that he will be able to leave when he has had enough.
- Accept his response if he says that he doesn't want to do something or go somewhere. He is more likely to say yes if he knows that he can say no.

Additionally, don't be overly positive about things – Finley feels pressured if adults are too enthusiastic. We find it's better to show an interest but play it down.

Lastly, telling Finley off is likely to make him very upset and angry, and so if things go wrong, we focus on getting him out of the situation and calming him down. This might involve going on his tablet with headphones. Don't worry about telling him off; you can just tell us and we'll talk with him later about what happened.

Example of Level 2: Why we do what we do

Some children are super sensitive to pressure. There can be lots of reasons for this. When they feel pressured, it makes them feel really anxious. Lots of aspects of life that other children don't seem to mind so much make them feel pressured – things like being asked to sit at the table, or say please and thank you, or even things like getting dressed. For them, all these things can make them feel like they are being continuously poked. They all accumulate, even when we can't necessarily see that they are stressed.

Because they feel under pressure and anxious so much, they react by trying to control the world around them to help them feel safer. This often means saying no to suggestions, or refusing to do things. They may do this very loudly and vehemently. This means that other people sometimes think that they are badly behaved. Unfortunately, this can mean they get told off, which makes them feel more anxious – which makes their behaviour worse.

The way to manage this most effectively is to help them feel as in control as possible, and to lift the pressure off. We do this by taking a low demand approach to parenting. This means that we really pick our battles, and that we make sure that we don't put too much pressure on them.

A few of the ways in which we do this are by limiting the number of questions we ask, not insisting that they say please and thank you, not telling them off if they do something wrong and always making sure that they know that they can say no. This can feel a bit strange because it means saying things like 'We thought we could go to the park but you might have a better idea' rather than 'Let's go to the park.'

Our priority is helping them stay calm so that they can stay in a state where they can learn. We've noticed that if we put pressure on them, they are often too anxious to participate. It seems a bit strange, but the less pressure you put on them, the more likely they are to join in and do something with you. That even goes for trying to persuade them or motivate them with things like buying an ice cream if they come. Pressure can be both positive and negative. Enthusiasm might just be too much for them, so it's often better to be off-hand. That way, they feel less of a demand is being placed on them.

A great way to get started is to show an interest in what they are doing, even if you personally think it's a waste of time. You could watch a YouTube video with them or play a video game, for instance. That is likely to be more successful than suggesting an activity that you have planned.

Eliza and Naomi: Protecting ourselves from the storm of other people

NAOMI: How do you deal with other people, Eliza?

ELIZA: I used to have a stock sentence I started with when talking to professionals, which was 'I'm doing a holistic child-led and non-behaviourist approach.'

Most were very accommodating with that. Mostly, you could see them sit back and relax and think, Okay, I know where we're at. If they don't know where you're at, they will probably come from the perspective that you would like some more behavioural strategies to get your child to school.

Starting from that point meant that they knew where I was at and we could hopefully meet there. I don't think I ever met any that said, 'No, no, no, don't do that.' They knew what I was doing and then we could move towards it.

NAOMI: I think professionals want to know that you've thought about it, that you're doing things thoughtfully. If you can say, 'We have thought about this and this is what we've chosen, we've made these decisions, this is why we're doing it', then that puts you in a place of power and professionals often respond well to that.

I've been on both sides of this, as a parent and a professional. The relationship is hierarchical and professionals aren't always aware of their power until they are on the other side of the table. The relationship can be a bit like the relationship between children and teachers at school. It can feel like as parents we want the professionals to validate us and to tell us we're doing things okay, but they may not be able to do that.

I think parents have more expertise in their child than any professional will. You live with them, you know them, you've been there since birth. There's no way that a professional is going to understand them better. They can offer a perspective, but they won't understand your child in the way that you understand your child.

If we're thinking about those three things – importance, influence and openness to change – then I think with professionals, it's about asking yourself, 'Is this person actually important and do we actually need them to be involved?' Because if someone is less than helpful then you might actually be better off just saying, 'Thanks, but actually we're going to go our own way.' Even if you've waited for years to see them.

ELIZA: I ask myself 'What is the outcome I'm looking for here? What do I hope they can achieve?'

I've got this illustration where I'm a nightclub bouncer stopping people coming into the house saying, 'No can do, mate. Your friend came last week.' That's something else that we have to consider: is this person coming in going to be beneficial for our children? Sometimes it could actually be detrimental.

NAOMI: Because of course, having too many people coming in is stressful and it makes you feel observed as well. You feel that gaze of other people watching and possibly judging.

ELIZA: If your child is perhaps not very well and not in school, you can have three different people come round in a week all asking the same question, 'Don't you like that school?' That's an enormous pressure on your child.

NAOMI: Yes, it is. And all starting from the same point as well. They're all starting from the beginning again, and you're stuck going round and round.

ELIZA: I find that scripting is something that can work really well across the board. It was a good polite shield.

NAOMI: What kind of scripting?

ELIZA: I had different scripts for professionals and family and friends. Even saying things like, 'She's doing really well at the moment' can work to turn it around because sometimes it's all very negative.

The negativity opens up people wanting to help and to fix. Just saying 'She's doing really well' would stop people putting input into how you could do it or what you could be doing.

NAOMI: They think they have to offer solutions. What do you do with people if they're just not open to change at all?

ELIZA: I think it's deciding how much you want to have them in your life. Sometimes you can have these people around you and you just choose not to talk about it with them.

If they're quite fun to talk with about cooking or music or whatever else that you've got in common, just avoid the subject of children. You can have different relationships for different reasons. You don't have to have all these people on board.

NAOMI: You can have people in your life whom you know that you would disagree with about certain things, and you can choose to compartmentalise.

ELIZA: I think as parents, we feel that we are not fulfilling our responsibility if we're not constantly talking about it, but it's okay to have different relationships and not talk about it.

NAOMI: You're right. Also, I think it puts things in perspective because if people don't have children, then to them, it just doesn't feel catastrophic in the same way. It's catastrophic in your life, but in their life, it's just like, 'Oh, okay', and let's talk about something else.

Too much to read, too little time?

1. There are three factors to think about when deciding what to do about other people: influence; importance; and openness to change.
2. Parents often assume that the problem with other people is lack of information, but providing information will only work if the person is open to change.
3. You only have limited emotional energy, so choose where to direct it for maximum impact.
4. If the person isn't open to change (but the relationship is important), focus on the context and environment.
5. Even when you do provide information, think about what that other person is really asking and what they need to know. Start with 'what works' before you get into the 'why'.

Books to suggest to people who are open to change

The Explosive Child and *Lost at School* – Ross Greene

The Family Experience of PDA – Eliza Fricker

How to Talk So Kids Will Listen (and Listen So Kids Will Talk) – Adele Faber and Elaine Mazlish

The Myth of the Spoiled Child: Coddled Kids, Helicopter Parents and Other Phony Crises – Alfie Kohn

And if you are considering home education:

Changing Our Minds – Naomi Fisher

A Different Way to Learn: Neurodiversity and Self-Directed Education – Naomi Fisher

How Children Learn at Home – Alan Thomas and Harriet Pattison

10

Will It Be Like This Forever?

When parents find low demand parenting, there's often a moment of relief. Things are calmer and more harmonious at home. Everyone breathes out. The number of battles is reduced.

This relief is short-lived, because in most cases parents are then flooded with negative thoughts (and often comments from others) about what this will mean for their child's future. If we accept that this child needs less pressure, goes the worry, how will they ever cope with work, paying rent, higher education. . .? Don't we have to spend their childhoods preparing them for these things by getting them used to dealing with pressure? Effectively, by pressuring them?

The catastrophic predictions pour in. How are they ever going to learn how to tidy up after themselves, if I don't make them? Don't they have to learn that other people have needs too? Shouldn't I insist that they do things they don't like, so they can learn that life isn't all fun and games? Am I going to raise a selfish hedonist who never thinks about other people and is incapable of waiting their turn? It can feel like a dam has burst and the worries are like the flood.

Parents imagine their child in the future as they are now, leaving their wet clothes in the bathroom, their dirty plates under their bed and with unbrushed hair. Refusing to do their job the same way they refuse to do homework. Rarely leaving the house. Unable to say yes even to things they would like to do because the anxiety is just too high. It's no wonder that parents feel anxious.

First, breathe out. Panicking about the future is only going to stop you focusing on the child you have right now – and it won't help. Low demand parenting is a developmental approach. This means that it is about providing the environment a child needs in which to develop and grow. Remember the metaphor of the garden from Chapter 3? Low demand parenting is all about nurturing that garden so that the plants can grow. It involves trusting that they don't need to be forced. If you start getting worried that the young plants aren't doing well enough and keep digging them up to check, they will not thrive.

As I've said throughout this book, for some children, mainstream parenting and educational techniques aren't just unhelpful, they are actively harmful. They push children out of their window of tolerance and both children and parents get stuck in traps. This means that children are consistently in a state of high psychological stress. Being in a state of psychological stress is not a good way to grow. The child's resources will be focused on surviving day-to-day rather than on learning.

Reducing demands aims to keep the children in a psychological space where they can learn and thrive. This means that they acquire skills they might otherwise not have acquired, and that they learn to know themselves. Parents are helping children to gradually expand their window of tolerance at the same time as helping them stay within it.

Doing this takes a lot of courage, because society tells us that Good Parents™ should be controlling their children's behaviour and learning. We're told that it's important to get children 'under control' from early on, to ensure that they grow up into functional adults. Even when it's really clear that this isn't working, it's hard to let go of the voices that whisper 'It's all very well now, but what about in ten years' time?'

In this chapter, I'm going to encourage you to think about some of the messages you might have picked up without realising from mainstream parenting culture about how you should be parenting your child (and the effect of parenting on your child's learning).

It can be hard to visualise what child development looks like when you take a low demand approach and aren't pushing your child onto each new stage. For that reason, I'm going to start this chapter outlining how low demand parenting changes over time, and what you can expect to see as your child grows up. These stages are based on the experience of the many families I have worked with and heard from through the course of my work.

Stages of low demand parenting

When you're in the thick of it, each phase of parenting feels like it will go on forever. You are immersed in *Peppa Pig* and you know every word from every episode. Then you blink, *Peppa Pig* is out and it's *Paw Patrol* all the way. Peppa is last year's news and all the toys gather dust. You forget that she was ever so popular until you find the box of toys in the loft. Low demand parenting is no exception to this. Things change, but it's hard to see that when you're in it. Not every family will go through every stage, and you may go backwards and forwards between stages.

Low demand parenting often starts from a place of crisis. That's because it's not mainstream, and it often takes quite a lot for families to realise their child really does require something quite different to what they are being offered in parenting programmes and books. Families often believe (and are told) that the reason their child isn't responding to Time Out or sticker charts is because they aren't firm or consistent enough, and so there can be years of trying before something cracks. Many families will have a story of the time that they realised something had to change. The following table outlines the stages that most families go through.

Stage	What's happening	What it looks like
1. Crisis	Things are going wrong. The ability of the child to cope with demands has been exceeded and the 'wheels are coming off'. It becomes clear that mainstream parenting isn't working and/or school isn't working. A breaking point is reached, and parents decide that they have to try something else.	Parents often initially respond to crisis by becoming stricter and more controlling; They may attend parenting courses that recommend behavioural methods. There are lots of conflicts. Life isn't fun for anyone. The child may be violent or make threats to hurt themselves or others.
2. Recovery	Start of low demand parenting. Child's window of tolerance is very narrow. Life feels like a minefield. Parents (and relatives) may feel they have given up trying or they have no influence. Relationships between parents and children are often highly conflictual and full of anger. Life may change dramatically – parents may give up work, children may stop going to school. Levels of pressure will be reduced significantly.	It feels like the child is 'on a knife edge' and cannot cope with any demands at all. Child may refuse to leave the house or say no to everything. Child may be doing nothing but playing video games. Child may be refusing to get dressed. Child may have extreme sensory sensitivities, more so than before. It can appear that there is a 'regression'. Children stop doing things they could do before. Life is likely to be extremely low demand and organised around what the child can cope with.

Stage	What's happening	What it looks like
3. New normal	Everyone is getting used to the new way that things work.	Child is calmer and happier but still can't tolerate any challenge.
	Parent is putting work into curating the environment for the child.	Things may seem very different to the rest of the world regarding behaviour, video games, sleep, food and education.
	Relationships are becoming less hierarchical and recalibrating based on low demand principles.	Child may still be refusing to leave the house.
	Child is experimenting with being able to say no without parents pushing back.	Any suggestion likely to be met with 'No'.
	Child is pushing the limits to see if parents will go back to how things were before.	Emotions may be getting less extreme but only when the environment is very low demand.
	This may seem like a plateau, that nothing is changing.	Parents may feel trapped and be asking themselves if this is going to be how things are forever.
4. Green shoots	Child feels confident that they can say no and that this will be respected.	Child asks to do something different – even if they then change their mind.
	Child is starting to trust the parent to have their back, no matter what.	Child is starting to experiment with what they can manage.
	Child is starting to believe that things will not go back to how they were before.	Child tries things that are too much, becomes overwhelmed and then retreats again.
	Child is starting to show an interest in the world again.	Things can go wrong more often in this stage because more risks are being taken.
	Child's window of tolerance is gradually expanding.	One step forward and two steps back is the norm.
	This can be a very bumpy time of highs and lows.	

Stage	What's happening	What it looks like
5. New challenges	Child now expects parent to be low demand and unconditional.	Child may choose to tolerate some stress in pursuit of a goal that is important to them. Sometimes this will go well and sometimes it won't.
	They don't expect to be punished or rewarded for behaviour.	Their independence is increasing.
	They know they can quit if they want to.	At this stage children are usually able to tolerate some demands, while knowing that they can say no.
	Child expects non-hierarchical relationships.	Children may find loopholes for themselves so they can reduce demands.
	As a result, their window of tolerance is wider.	The role of parents is to support them while they experiment with what they can manage.
	Children are starting to be aware of their limits and manage them for themselves.	Becoming more independent can be a time of vulnerability and there may be increased distress as they go out of their comfort zone.
6. Finding their own way (usually only from adolescence onwards)	As the young person goes through adolescence, they develop an awareness of their own motivation and how they move through the world.	Young people start to think about the future and what they want.
	They learn to manage their own limitations through experimenting with them.	They take on more of this for themselves, meaning that their parents are less involved with every aspect of their life.
	Their window of tolerance will vary depending on the situation but this is something they will be increasingly aware of for themselves.	Young people start to plan their days and their time, based on their priorities and goals.
	They are developing an awareness of what they can manage and what they can't.	They may be extremely motivated to do the things they want to achieve (which may not be what their parents want them to achieve).
		The role of parents is to help them to do things that are important to them and to support them in acquiring the skills they need.

You can think of these stages as a gradual handing over of responsibility from the parent to the child – low demand parenting aims to create the space for children to come to know themselves and their limits, and so as they become more mature, they are able to create environments that work for them. In the early stages, parents are working extremely hard but, over time, the child becomes more able to do some of this for themselves. Children start to create their own environments and to manage their own demands.

This process is not linear. In fact, it's more like a game of Snakes and Ladders. Just as you think you're doing really well, you land on a snake and it seems like you're going right back to the start.

These stages are going to look different depending on how old your child is and when you started low demand parenting. If they are already a teenager by the time you start, then the recovery time is going to take longer. There will have been more difficult experiences and relationships will be harder to repair. This is tricky because it's common for parents to think that their teenagers must recover more quickly than younger children so they can do exams. They want fast results, but actually it can take years before young people start to recover and you can't really rush it. Pressure to do things like exams 'on time' will make things worse. Low demand parenting is a long-term approach; you won't see the effects overnight.

'They have to learn'

When I meet parents, they often tell me guiltily of the ways in which they are responding to their child's needs. New parents feel bad about things like rocking their baby to sleep (bad habit!), feeding their baby to sleep (terrible habit!) or pushing their baby to sleep in the buggy (how will they ever learn to sleep in a cot?). Or (even worse), they tell me that they co-sleep. Actually, the parents who tell me about co-sleeping aren't just those of babies. Parents of eleven- and twelve-year-olds tell me that their children still prefer to sleep in the same room as them, or come through to them in the night.

Parents who talk to me feel bad about having found ways to care for their child while soothing their distress. They think that as a psychologist I'm going to start saying things about how important it is for their child to learn to sleep in their own bed. They think that a Good Parent™ would ignore their child's distress in favour of creating healthy habits.

I remember feeling like this myself. With my first baby, I believed the books. I thought that he had to learn to sleep alone. We tried swaddling him, we tried a baby hammock, we tried white noise machines. He had different ideas. We bought a side-along cot and fixed it to the side of our bed. He refused to go anywhere near it. He wanted to be right next to me, all night. If I tried to sneak away, he woke up. At first I worried, and then I thought about how ridiculous I was being. He would grow up and things would change, and he would not be in my bed forever. I had every confidence in that. Turns out I was right – he moved out of his own accord when he was ready.

I spent a lot of wasted time worrying about what bad habits I was establishing when I would have done better to focus on what was needed in the situation right then. My fears for the future stopped me from simply seeing him as a baby who was telling me quite clearly what he needed. This focus on habits morphs into a core mainstream parenting assumption as they get older: We must make children do things, otherwise they won't learn how to behave and won't become functioning adults.

We must make them sit still, for fear that they will run around in circles forever. We must not let them quit their swimming lessons, otherwise they'll never stick at anything. We must make them do things they don't enjoy, otherwise they might grow up without realising that life can't all be about having fun. We must make them share, in case they grow up selfish and self-centred. We must make children wear white shirts and grey trousers or skirts so that they learn to dress smartly for work as adults.

Parenting through this lens is almost like programming: make the child do now what you want them to do in the future. Set the path right from the start and they won't deviate. Keep them on the straight and narrow.

This belief is used to justify making children do things they clearly don't want to do, because the projected future consequence of not doing so is thought to be so terrible. It sees the process of developing from a child into an adult as one that has to be imposed from the outside, often against the child's will.

This isn't a developmentally informed way of thinking about children. What I mean by that is that children need and do different things at different stages of their development, and we don't gain anything by trying to treat them as if they were in a later stage. A baby has needs an older child does not have, just because they are a baby. A developmentally informed approach says that we can meet those needs (by rocking or feeding the baby to sleep, for example) without fear that this will mean that they will never develop into a child who can go to sleep by themselves.

Essentially, a developmentally informed approach says:

We don't have to make our children do things now out of fear that they will never be able to do those things in the future.

We focus on meeting the child's needs now, whatever they are, rather than worrying about some future feared outcome. This is important for all children, but it's particularly important for those whose development is slightly unusual.

Pressure-sensitive children are often developmentally out of sync in at least a few areas of their life. This means they are more likely to end up being told off or punished as adults try to make them comply with expectations. Adults just can't understand how they can be so capable when doing something that interests them, but still struggle to keep their cool when they are given the wrong flavour of juice to drink.

Low demand parenting is like preparing the way in front of our children. Clearing their developmental path of unnecessary debris so they can move forwards and focus on the things that really matter.

The developmental needs of childhood

Brains change as children grow. We all know that a four-year-old is smaller than a fourteen-year-old or a twenty-four-year-old, but in addition, their brains work differently. No matter how intelligent the four-year-old is, they will not think in the same way as an adult. This is not just about experience or knowledge – as people grow, their brains change. Young children have different strengths and weaknesses to adults, and the way that they choose to spend their time is quite different.

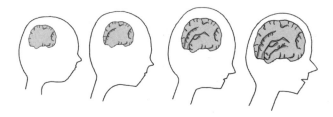

Young children learn through exploration and discovery. Their priorities tend to be in-the-moment – they learn as a side-product of what they do. They are often unpredictable and enthusiastic. They are curious and passionate. They interrogate the world and their parents. They are usually full of energy and are in touch with their interests and what is important to them.

They have weaknesses. They aren't great at thinking realistically about the future or working towards a goal. They aren't usually very good at sticking to things or thinking strategically. Most of them are not at all good at sitting still or keeping quiet on demand. Impulse control and abstract thinking are not usually their gifts. These are higher-level skills that really develop around adolescence, in the period of intense developmental change neuroscientists now know happens between the ages of ten and twenty-five.

Young children learn very effectively through play. They learn in ways adults no longer can, and in ways adults do not always value. Their learning is hard to quantify and unpredictable, and adults like to measure and test. They like to set 'learning objectives' and give children grades. This does not fit with the way that young children learn. They do not plan things in advance and they don't set long-term goals (or if they do, they don't work towards them effectively). This isn't because they are deficient adults and need to be made to do so, it's because they have different strengths and a different way of approaching the world.

We aren't good at recognising that this phase of human development has value in itself.

Many parents and schools spend a lot of time trying to persuade young children to do things they aren't yet neurologically capable of. We make them practise things, telling ourselves that they need to learn how to do so. We make them sit still and listen, telling them and ourselves that this is an important future skill. We worry that if we don't make our six-year-olds sit still, they'll never be able to do so as adults. There is no evidence for this. Adults who have never been to school are still adults. They do not behave like young children, and if they are illiterate and they learn to read as adults, they will learn in a different way to children.

As children grow beyond early childhood into middle childhood, their thinking becomes more sophisticated. They start to be able to think about the future more, and to consider the thoughts and feelings of others. They acquire skills like reading, which give them access to the wider world. And they become more capable of managing their emotions for longer periods without an adult's support.

These changes happen at different rates for different children and do not need to be forced. They do, however, opportunities and support – development doesn't happen in a vacuum.

The (dramatic) changes of adolescence

Puberty is a big deal. Not only do children's bodies start to change as a result of the hormonal changes that take place, but their brains change too. This change is really important in the process of becoming an adult. When I studied neuropsychology as an undergraduate in the late 1990s, we were taught that most significant brain development happened before puberty. I now know that this is wrong. Neuroscientists now see adolescence as a crucial period of brain development that lasts much longer than the period we usually think of as 'adolescence'. It starts around age ten and continues until at least age twenty-five. This is a period of intense change and high vulnerability, but also great opportunity.

During this time, young people start to look outwards towards their peers, and the approval of their peers becomes more important to them (leading in some cases to risky behaviour). This is due to changes in their brains that make spending time with their peers more rewarding. There are other changes too. The system in our brains that enables us to think about our thinking and to control what we do matures during adolescence. This is the part of our brain that enables us to think about the future. Young people become able to hold a future goal in mind and work towards it. Adolescents become more capable of controlling their impulses. They start to be able to problem-solve. They become able to make choices with the future in mind – for example, a young person might choose to practise the piano because they want to get better and play in a concert, even if, right now, they'd rather watch TV.

This change is gradual and dependent on experience. Young people become better at making choices by making choices – not by being told what to do. They get better at working towards goals by doing just that, not by being made to work towards a goal set by someone else for them.

Adolescence is a time of vulnerability, but because our adolescents look so grown up we often underestimate just how much development they still have ahead of them. This is particularly the case for young people whose development is very different to the average. They may show no interest in planning for the future at age sixteen, but by their early twenties be in quite a different place. The task of parents is to continue to keep options open for them.

The following table summarises some of the changes that take place as children grow.

	Ages	Developmental changes and expectations
Early childhood	0–8	Children acquire skills of mobility and communication. They learn to feed themselves, use the toilet and dress themselves.
		Children move from total dependence in babyhood to relative independence.
		They go from no emotion regulation skills at all to being expected to manage their emotions in group environments for the majority of their waking day at school.
		Parents are the most important people in their children's lives.
Middle to late childhood	6–12	Children's social understanding becomes more sophisticated.
		Children's ability to think about the future and to plan starts to develop.
		At the end of this stage, they are often expected to go from an educational environment where they usually have one teacher who knows them to moving from lesson to lesson with teachers who may not know them at all.
		Emotion regulation – outbursts are tolerated less and less, with children expected to be compliant and not to show frustration.
		Parents are still important but peers often become important too.
Early adolescence	11–16	Bodies start to mature.
		Adolescence is a time of vulnerability to mental distress.
		Brain development means that young people become more focused on their peers and less on their families.

		Young people may start to take more risks, particularly when with groups of their peers.
		Social approval becomes more important than before.
		They often have a particular drive for autonomy at this time, even if they did not as younger children.
		They need experiences of making mean-ingful decisions and of feeling in control of their lives.
		A lot of pressure is put on this age group by the school system. Young people are often told that the exams they take at sixteen will influence their entire lives.
		Their ability to think things through is still developing and the drive to be accepted by their peers can mean that this age group makes decisions adults see as irrational.
		They start to be aware that their parents cannot make everything okay, and that there are non-negotiables in the environ-ment. This can make them very angry.
Mid to late adolescence	16–25	By this point they may look like adults and be treated as such by others.
		Brain development continues and some young people may not really start to be able to plan for the future until they are in their early twenties.
		They are still developing the skills of self-management and organisation.
		Setting goals and thinking about the future is still in development.
		Social judgement by peers is still a strong motivator.
		The balance between the need to be accepted by peers and the ability to think things through is still developing throughout this period, meaning that risky behaviour can continue.
		This is a time when second and third chances are essential.

Different ways of developing

Okay, you're thinking, but my child isn't developing in a typical way. Do the same things apply to them? Don't I need to make them do things, in case they never catch up? Doesn't their diagnosis mean that I must force them to learn? I've met parents who have been told that their autistic child must have a strict routine from an early age, or their child with ADHD won't be able to self-regulate and so must be incentivised with rewards and punishments.

I think this is misguided, particularly if it is (as it often is) based on assumptions about every child with that diagnosis, rather than on an understanding of the individual child and their needs. Those needs can be very different from child to child.

When I was a psychology graduate student I did a lot of testing of children. I'd check out the big black suitcase from the Test Library, and set up all the various tests. The way that tests like that work is that we do lots of different mini-tests – called 'subtests' – which are all meant to assess different things. I'd get children to do tasks like putting pictures in order and telling me the story. I'd ask them questions like 'If you found a stamped addressed envelope in the road, what would you do with it?' I'd ask them to make trails connecting up circles in alphabetical order. I'd give them lists of numbers to memorise and repeat back to me.

I would then grade the results. At the back of each test manual were tables of data. Each test was given to thousands of children of the same age, and the averages were calculated. I would compare each child's score to the average for other children their age. Sometimes I would plot their scores onto a circular grid.

Many of the children I tested had what is sometimes called a 'spiky cognitive profile', which essentially means that they differed from the average for their age in ways that were not consistent across the board. So they might have a really good working memory, performing at levels way beyond what would be expected for a child their age, but then find verbal comprehension extremely difficult, and be significantly below the average.

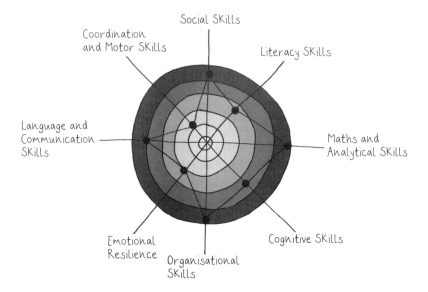

If a child is performing at approximately the same level in all the different domains, their scores form a circle or near-circle. If they perform really well in some areas while performing badly on other tests, their scores form a spiky star-like pattern.

Essentially a 'spiky profile' means that we can't easily predict a child's skills in one area by knowing how they do in other areas. It means that it will be harder to fit this child into a standardised system, because they might have the needs of a much younger child in some areas, but have the ability of an older child in others. It means that people may assume that this child should be able to do more than they can, because (for example) they may have excellent language production skills but really struggle to understand what is being said to them.

Psychologists use the idea of the 'spiky cognitive profile' in relation to cognitive tests. I think it's a useful idea to apply more widely to help us think about what unhelpful expectations we might have of children without even thinking about it. If a child is using a lot of complicated words, for example, it's easy to assume they should also be able to tell us how they feel with words rather than exploding – but actually the skill this requires is emotion regulation, which may be at a very different level to their verbal skills.

The following table outlines some of the different dimensions of child development. It's not meant to be comprehensive, and the examples are definitely not comprehensive. It's just meant to help you think about the different dimensions and whether your child's 'spiky profile' might mean that you have unrealistic expectations of them in some areas.

Dimensions of development	Examples
Social skills	Being with other people Relating to other people Playing Keeping calm around other people Managing relationships Coping with difficult or unpredictable behaviour from others
Academic skills	Reading Writing Numeracy Essay writing Test taking

Emotion regulation skills	Managing disappointment Managing frustration Calming themselves down Coping with being without a parent or carer Looking to an adult to help them calm themselves
Self-management skills	Setting goals and working towards them Problem-solving Impulse control Flexibility Working out what order to do things in Working memory Time management
Practical skills	Using tools Using machines (like the washing machine or lawn mower) Fixing things
Communication skills	Making themselves heard Expressing their needs Understanding what is said to them
Life skills	Feeding themselves Toileting Dressing themselves Sleeping Shopping Cooking
Motor skills	Big movements (climbing, bouncing) Small movements (writing, picking up small things)

As you read this list, you might be reflecting on your own profile – and realising that there are things you yourself have always found hard. Maybe you have always found getting to places on time hard, and have been told that you were rude as a result. Or you might have always struggled to follow verbal instructions, and assumed it was because you 'weren't listening properly'.

It's really common for people to reach adulthood feeling bad about all the ways in which they struggle. Rather than being able to think, *This is something that I find hard*, we think, *I shouldn't find this so hard*, and then we give it a self-critical spin – like, *I'm lazy*, or *There's something wrong with me*, or *Everyone else does this with no problem*. Our self-critical thoughts make all of the things we find hard even more difficult – and they stop us from feeling good when we do achieve something, because we tend to think, That shouldn't have been so hard or I should have done that ages ago.

I think one of the aims of low demand parenting is to avoid our children reaching adulthood with a large burden of self-critical thoughts about the things that they find hard. We do that by not responding to them with criticism, but also by modelling. It isn't enough to tell our children not to be critical of themselves; we have to show them that we are not critical of *our*selves when we find things hard. We have to show ourselves empathy, just as we show it to our children.

We want our children to grow up surrounded by the message that they are okay just as they are – even if their behaviour is extremely difficult for us to manage sometimes. Pressure-sensitive children are at risk of hearing a lot of negative messages about themselves because their behaviour is often so extreme and so challenging for the adults around them – as low demand parents we are consciously turning that around.

Reflective exercise

If you want to, spend some time thinking about all these different aspects of your child's development and which areas are strengths or weaknesses for them. Ask yourself whether some of your frustrations with your child could be due to expecting them to be at a similar level on everything. What are the areas in which they are behind what you might be expecting, and what support might they need there, over and above what you might have expected for a child of their age?

Variability leads to a lot of frustration for parents, particularly for children who have good language abilities. They seem to be 'so bright' or 'so articulate' and yet when it comes to their emotions or practical skills, they are acting like a child who is much younger. They may have a great vocabulary but limited problem-solving skills and a poor working memory. There's a tendency for adults to assume this must be intentional, and to treat it like 'behaviour'.

This is particularly a problem when it's their capacity to regulate their emotions that lags behind other children their age. I meet children who are academically capable and who are capable of highly sophisticated discussions but who find it impossible to soothe themselves when they are distressed. They still need intensive support from adults to do so, just like toddlers do – but because they are now ten or twelve, their parents and other adults don't understand why they can't just 'behave'. 'They are so intelligent,' these parents tell me, 'but when they get upset, it's like they're three again.' They are distraught, violent, unable to communicate – and their parents are desperately worried.

What's the low demand approach? Meet children where they are, and provide the support that they seem to need right now, rather than the support that you assumed a child of their age would need. If they find it really hard to manage their emotions, they need the co-regulation and support that you might expect to give a younger child. What that does is open up the space for them to learn. What they don't need (and what won't help) is punishment or blame for being developmentally different to what is expected.

Managing your own fears about the future

Even when things are going well, we can get stuck worrying about the future. Parents often get stuck between what they can see is working in the here and now, and what everyone else is telling them they should be doing. They are in a sort of reverse Reality Gap. Reality is actually fine, but parents feel that the expectations are that they should be being less pleasant to their child, in order that the children learn the things they have to learn.

Parents see the expectations, start to worry about the future – and before you know it, they're back to controlling parenting techniques. They think that maybe they got it wrong after all, and it was all just because they weren't firm enough. They start to panic about screens, or food or sleep, they put in place a ban or lay down the law – and very quickly, everything has deteriorated again. It's another trap.

Here is an alternative to try when you are tempted to become more controlling – or 'having a wobble', as people sometimes say.

Sending your thoughts down the river

This exercise is going to feel strange. We're used to trying not to think about our fears, and when we bring them up with other people they will often reassure us or tell us not to think about the worst case scenario. This can often be helpful, but there's a downside. Sometimes we get stuck in the 'what if's but never actually answer the question of what exactly would be so terrible. Our minds are stuck in perpetual anticipation of something awful happening, but we aren't quite sure what that awful thing would be, because we don't allow ourselves to think about it.

Do this exercise at a time when you are not with your children and when you know you will be uninterrupted.

Take a few deep breaths and just let yourself feel the breath going through your body. Notice any areas of discomfort or tension, and imagine the breath going to that place.

Imagine yourself by a river. You are standing on the bank, watching the water go past. There is a strong current. Debris and leaves are going down the river.

Let yourself think about the future, and just notice the thoughts and predictions that come into your head.

Some common thoughts are:

- They will be unhappy and it will be my fault.
- They will think that I have let them down by not making them do things.
- They won't have any skills.
- I am trapped.
- I am not good enough.

As each thought comes to mind, don't try to answer it or fight it. Instead, put it on a leaf or log, and put it into the river. Watch it go down the river. You don't need to do anything to intervene to make that happen. The only way that you can interfere with the process is if you start wading into the river and trying to get those thoughts out – and you don't need to do that. You just need to watch them go.

You can try this exercise every time that you find yourself being taken over with negative thoughts. Another variation is to imagine yourself on a train, watching your thoughts pass by in the countryside. You don't have to do anything, you just have to stay on the train, and the thoughts will go past.

Eliza and Naomi: Our spiky cognitive profiles

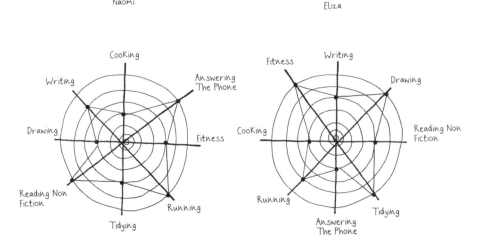

NAOMI: We were talking about 'spiky cognitive profiles': essentially when a person is much better at some things than other things. If you have test scores that are very different, so if you have a really high score for working memory, but a low score for problem-solving, then your profile looks spiky when we draw it on the graph – just like these profiles you've drawn for us, Eliza.

Sometimes we talk as if spiky cognitive profiles are a problem because there's this assumption that children should be the same level for different things, and it's weird. Because as adults, it makes no sense to say that we should be at the same level for everything.

ELIZA: You can't draw.

NAOMI: No. Imagine if we were to say, 'Oh, Naomi has to work on her drawing.' You could write me a report saying that my drawing is well below what would be expected for my age, and I need to be encouraged to draw every day.

You'd say that I can't be allowed just to do the writing even if that's the bit I like.

That's made me think about the strange idea that each person has to be good at everything for themselves and that we can't collaborate and work together. Between us, you're really good at drawing and I know a lot about psychology and that's great because it means we can work together.

It would be bizarre if we were told, 'Naomi, you have to work more on drawing. Eliza has to spend more time on psychology.'

Everybody would be bland, wouldn't they? It would be like, I could work really, really hard on my drawing and I'd probably get to a mediocre standard. Hooray. I've levelled up.

ELIZA: There's this one period in life (childhood) where you're told you have to be a well-rounded person in all subjects and it's quite strange because the rest of our life isn't like that.

I think it built up a lot of resentment in my school experience because I knew very early on what I was interested in and what I wasn't. It felt like an enormous waste of time that I was asked to sit and do science because I had no interest in it.

NAOMI: Also, in school, some things are valued much less. Generally, art is valued less than science.

ELIZA: It made me think that I was lesser because the one thing I was really good at was the thing we were taught the least amount of.

NAOMI: The thing you really wanted to do wasn't valued. It's an odd way of educating young people when you think about it. It's like we are ironing everything out. You've got to do everything. You mustn't have choices about what you do between the age of five and sixteen. You have a little bit of choice at fourteen, but still not much. You couldn't choose to just concentrate on art until you were an adult.

ELIZA: No.

NAOMI: When children are young and things are hard it's often difficult for parents to imagine a future when it isn't like that anymore. They can't imagine a time when they're not lurching from crisis to crisis anymore and life is quite stable. But things change. You're still a low-demand parent. But it's so much part of how you live and how things work that you're not firefighting anymore at the time.

ELIZA: I was thinking about this the other day. When you're in the system and you're doing those reports then everything is around looking at progression. It's all about where they're at and what they need to attain, how to get them to the next stage.

When you're not doing that stuff because you've pulled out of that system, then you realise that it doesn't really work like that. When you are doing these forms and assessments, you're planning out the next term and saying, 'They should be able to do that', but then you realise that in life, we don't really work like that.

We get there much more effectively with positive experiences. Often we're doing these things when children are really struggling in an environment and we're trying to get them to the next stage, but actually, when we change that environment, stop trying to push them and they're in a much more positive place, they get there organically at their own pace.

NAOMI: We don't have to push them.

ELIZA: I thought about it around things like food or cooking and the idea of thinking, I must learn to cook a meal for myself. That might be a goal on a report. It's going to happen at some point. I don't know when that will be for many children or young adults, but they will get there when they get there. That incentive might be a TikTok video.

NAOMI: Might be just being hungry and needing a meal!

ELIZA: It can't be orchestrated or made to happen. I've seen these developments happen as we've pulled back. They've happened very much at their own pace. They are doing all the things that they want to do and are independent, but it happened when they were ready.

NAOMI: Yes. It's letting go of that control. It's tempting to say things like, 'This term, they will learn how to cook scrambled eggs.' It's a measurable goal, which makes adults feel that they are doing something.

With low demand parenting we instead say that we're going to work on getting the atmosphere in our home right and we are going to work on the relationships. We will try to help this child feel okay and then trust that they will develop, they will grow and they will learn.

ELIZA: That cooking for themselves wasn't going to come from a cooking class starting with how to make a cheese sandwich. It comes because they want to do it for themselves, whether that's been through seeing peers or watching videos. That comes when they're ready to do that.

NAOMI: For pressure-sensitive kids, that is even more important, because the pressure of 'You're going to learn how to do this now' can actually kill the desire to do it.

ELIZA: It makes it less likely. When you're in this low demand world, your child will probably start cooking by making a Thai green curry. Whereas in a class you might have to start with a boiled egg.

NAOMI: It's a bit like learning languages. I remember I always used to get so put off by the first chapter in the text book, which was usually the alphabet or how you pronounce letters. I would think, I don't want to know how to pronounce letters. I want to talk to people.

When you break things down to their building blocks, they can lose their purpose. They lose any meaning because you might be thinking, Well, I don't like boiled eggs. I want to cook Thai green curry or chocolate cake.

It's the same with reading. Lots of children I know have learned how to read because they want to read an instruction manual, or they want to learn how to read the text of a video game.

They don't want to 'learn how to read' in the abstract, but they want to learn how to read for meaning because it is useful to them. That's the way of living a low demand life, really. We're living life, we do things because they're meaningful.

ELIZA: When you're doing that other way – when you are doing all these assessments, it can't help but focus you on what they're not doing and what we should be forcing them to do.

NAOMI: I was talking to a parent just the other day whose daughter had just finished Reception class at school. They got a report and she said, 'It's so demoralising. It's basically a list of all the things she can't do.'

I was thinking, What a bad start to someone's school career to send them home with a bit of paper that says all the things they can't do yet, like writing their name and reading and all this stuff. It's this strange idea we have that pointing out to children and their parents all the things they can't do is going to help them do it.

ELIZA: I had a similar conversation recently because when we get school reports now (from an alternative setting), they're positive. Now that could be seen as. . . what's the term? Toxic positivity? All you're saying is the good things.

I think young people often know the things they can't do. I think they're probably more aware of the things they can't do than the things that they can do, so I think you don't need to point it out.

Too much to read, too little time?

1. Low demand parenting goes through stages and often starts in a time of crisis. At first parents need to be extremely low demand and then as children recover, their window of tolerance widens.
2. Over time, children become aware of their own needs and can take on some of the responsibility for creating an environment that works for them.
3. Good Parenting™ is often about establishing habits or doing things for the future. Low demand parenting is about meeting the developmental needs of the child right now.
4. When children have a 'spiky cognitive profile' it means that some areas of their development are significantly different to the average for their age group. This can lead to frustration for parents, particularly if children are very capable in one area and much less so in another.
5. Low demand parenting takes time and change is gradual, but a key part is that it allows children to develop at their own pace, even when that is very different to what society expects.

More to read if you are interested

The Gardener and the Carpenter: What the New Science of Child Development Tells Us about the Relationship Between Parents and Children – Alison Gopnik

Inventing Ourselves: The Secret Life of the Teenage Brain – Sarah-Jayne Blakemore

The Science of Parenting: How Today's Brain Research Can Help You Raise Happy, Emotionally Balanced Children – Margot Sunderland

11

What About Me?

Claire contacted me for help with her children, but when we first met I only asked one question, 'What has brought you here?' before she started crying. She cried through most of the session. She told me how hard it had been since the first of her three children had been born ten years before. She loved her children, wanted to do everything that she could for them, but she felt like she had lost herself in the process.

Her whole life, from dawn to dusk, was consumed with children's needs. She was often woken before 6 a.m. by her youngest child, who would come through to their bed in the early hours and would sleep vertically across the pillows and kick her in the ear. She made breakfast for them, she cleared up for them, she tolerated being shouted at while they got ready for school. Once they were at school and nursery, she had a few short hours, which she used at the supermarket and cleaning and tidying the mess from the morning, before picking up the youngest child from nursery, spending a couple of hours at the park with them and then picking up the other two from school.

Her eldest child, ten-year-old Denny, was having a hard time with friends at school and she was always on tenterhooks picking him up in case something had gone wrong. He would often come out of school furious and would refuse to talk to her, or would kick his sister on the way home, resulting in screams and tears all round.

She would take them home, feed them, break up the fights between the older two and then it would be the long haul until bedtime. None of them liked to be alone and all of them wanted time alone with her before they went to sleep. This left her with an impossible conundrum. She would often get to 10 p.m. shattered, and then would realise that she hadn't eaten anything except for a leftover fish finger for supper. Her husband worked long hours, and when he did come back he would make suggestions about how they needed firmer boundaries and how when he was ten, he'd made breakfast for himself and his younger siblings and cleared up afterwards. He'd say this in front of Denny, who would become furious and would then refuse to eat or go to bed. Claire would end up trying to calm down both Denny and her husband while almost crying with exhaustion.

Claire used to think that she had good local friends whom she had met when Denny was a baby. They had met up in local playgrounds and had a WhatsApp group for meet-ups. Then, as Denny got older, his behaviour had become harder to manage. She hovered nearby all the time but sometimes she wasn't fast enough. One terrible time he had bitten a younger child and left a bruise. She had been right there, had apologised profusely, but it was clear it wasn't enough. 'Why can't you control your child better?' hung in the air. The WhatsApp group had gone silent and she suspected that an alternative group had been set up, without her. Everyone was suddenly too busy to meet up. Then she saw on Facebook that the parents had met up for a meal without children in a local restaurant, and she hadn't been included. She was devastated. She tried to talk to her closest friend about it, but Emma said she didn't know what Claire meant and said everyone was just busier these days. This was several years ago but Claire had never felt welcome with those parents again, and she hadn't found new local friends.

As Claire told me about it, she talked about how isolated she felt. 'I can't tell anyone how hard it is,' she said, 'because they will tell me that it's my parenting that's at fault. They'll say I must lay down the law. But when I try to do that, it goes so badly wrong so quickly.'

It is hard to have a child who doesn't play by the parenting rules, and it's hard to choose to parent them in a different way. Most parents come to low demand parenting because their children need it as they respond so badly to conventional parenting, but to the outside world, it looks like the lack of conventional parenting has caused the child's behaviour.

In addition, low demand parenting is hard work. It might be low demand for the children, but for adults it can be anything but. It can feel relentless. You never stop picking up after children, making food, cleaning up abandoned art projects and calming distressed children. You are constantly on high alert, waiting for the next cry or crash. You are co-regulating your children for years longer than other parents seem to be, you are not using power over them, you are giving them space to develop – and all of that can mean that there is more for you to manage, for longer. You are trying to create an environment within which your children can flourish, rather than putting the onus on them to behave. You aren't using behavioural approaches because they don't work, but in the short term those behavioural approaches get results for many families. They get parents a bit of 'peace and quiet' – and you don't get that with low demand parenting.

Alongside this is the issue of lack of recognition of how hard parenting pressure-sensitive children is. It's the case across the board that parenting isn't respected as the work it is. If someone is paid to do the work of a parent then it becomes a job, but if you're unpaid then it's like the work aspect vanishes and it is perceived as a life-style choice, or even a 'luxury'. People will talk about full-time parents as 'doing nothing' or 'having a few years off', as if working outside the home is the only work that really counts. If you do work outside the home, very little recognition is given to the fact that you are doing a second and third shift at home. Parenting is talked about as 'rewarding', and you're assumed to enjoy it. It's rare for anyone to say, 'Well done', particularly if your children aren't getting plaudits and winning awards.

Parenting is typically judged by outcome, and the outcome is the child. Compliant children are considered to have good parents, and when children struggle, the first place that people look is their parenting. There are all sorts of ironies attached to this, but one is that it means that the parents who have the most straightforward parenting journey will often assume that this is because they are doing it better than anyone else. They assume that the reason their child is easy to manage is because of their exceptional parenting, rather than due to a lucky combination of that child's individual temperament, experiences and the local environment suiting that child.

Those parents who have the hardest time typically do not think of themselves as exceptional or even adequate parents, because (they think) the evidence is right there in front of them. They are the one who is being pulled into school because their child isn't cooperating, and the one who receives emails from friends saying that they won't be seeing them again because of their child's behaviour – or are simply ghosted.

It's hard to feel good about your parenting when your children are not meeting the milestones other parents are announcing on social media. You see the proud photos of children playing the clarinet, winning dance competitions or football matches, and you compare them to your own child, who won't do any after-school activities and who wouldn't pose for photos even if they did.

You, on the other hand, are everyone's worst prediction come true – you aren't controlling screen time, and look, the children are on their screens for hours! You let them choose what they eat and they never eat vegetables! You don't tell your children off or punish them, and look, they won't share and don't say please and thank you!

It can be particularly difficult for parents if you felt like you had few choices in your own childhood. It feels like your turn never came. You grew up thinking that adults got to do the choosing and that when you were an adult, you'd finally be able to do what you wanted – and now you're the parent but you rarely get to do what you want.

I'm not going to pretend that this book will make those feelings and thoughts go away. It's hard to be on a path that others don't understand, and it will never be the case that everyone else understands. We can't change everyone else.

You can, however, think about how you react to the world, and whether there are ways in which your life is harder than it has to be. You can look for the places where small changes might add up to a significant difference. And you can help yourself remember the good moments as well as the bad.

This chapter is a practical one. It contains several different exercises for you to try. The first few are all about your internal world, identifying and managing critical

thoughts. The last one is about thinking about what changes you might be able to make to your life to make it more sustainable. Because sustainability is essential. Without that, you will burn out and the whole thing will fall apart. You have to make it work for you as well as for your children and the rest of your family.

This first exercise is about acknowledging how much work you put into your family, and how hard and unrecognised that can be.

The Reality Gap

EXPECTATION   REALITY

I've talked a lot in this book about the Reality Gap, and how parents can get stuck in it when thinking about their children's behaviour.

Now I'd like to apply it to you and your life. Give yourself some time alone (even if that is really hard to find) to think about what you expected for yourself at this time in your life when you were younger.

What did you think life would be like when you were a parent? When I ask parents about this, some of them tell me that they imagined being part of a large supportive community, with children running in and out of each other's houses – but actually there is no way their child could tolerate an unexpected ring at the door and they dislike all the other children in the neighbourhood. Others say they imagined living in a house with enough rooms for every child to have a bedroom, but actually they are renting a small flat and everyone has to share. Still others say they wanted to have a career and have money to spare but in fact it made no economic sense for them to continue to work and they couldn't find childcare due to the needs of their children, and so they gave up work but now feel that they are not really contributing financially and miss having colleagues.

Let yourself sit with those expectations for a while, and let whatever feelings there are come. There's no need to judge the feelings, or try to suppress them. They aren't disloyal to anyone, and it doesn't mean that you don't realise how lucky you are to have your children and your current life. It doesn't mean that you are lacking in gratitude. You don't have to remind yourself that other people have it worse than you and you are very lucky to have a roof over your head and enough food to eat. Just let yourself sit with the gap between how you imagined your life, and how it is right now. If you want to, you could draw it, or write a little sketch, or do something else that symbolically commemorates those expectations.

When you've done that for a while, I'd like you to visualise yourself turning towards the reality of how things are. Take some deep breaths and allow yourself to see how things really are. The good and the bad. You don't have to put a shine on it. Your family, in all their messy reality. Just let the feelings come and notice where you feel it in your body. If you want, you can draw this, or write something about it – or you can just imagine it.

Now I'd like you to acknowledge to yourself just how hard you have worked and continue to work. No one else is going to see this unvarnished reality, so you need to do it for yourself. Choose a phrase to repeat that validates just how hard this journey has been and how much it has taken from you.

Some parents have chosen phrases like:

- I am doing the best I can in difficult circumstances.
- I am working really hard.
- I am developing exceptional parenting skills.
- I am good enough.
- I keep showing up every day.
- I am trying so hard to get this right for my children.
- I see myself.
- I completely accept myself.

Sometimes a phrase that fits this model can help:

- Even though [something hard in your life], I completely and utterly accept myself.

For example:

- Even though I find parenting very hard, I completely and utterly accept myself.

- Even though today was a disaster, I completely and utterly accept myself.

Read these phrases to yourself and see if any of them resonate. If they don't, write one of your own.

If you can't find a phrase, ask yourself what you would like an all-knowing, all-forgiving friend to say to you. Say the phrase to yourself and let yourself notice any resistance you have to accepting it.

Depending on your cultural background, you may feel differently about different phrases. I have found that British people do not like saying things, even to themselves, that are overtly positive. They think it's over the top. For that reason, I don't suggest things like 'I am fabulous' or 'I am awesome', but if that works for you, go for it!

The next exercise is about helping you to refocus your mind on the good things as well as the difficult things in your life. It's easy to feel overwhelmed by all the problems, but there are always moments of hope or of joy. This exercise is to help you hold on to some of those.

Redressing the balance

Our brains selectively attend to threatening information. This makes perfect sense, because they are focused on keeping us alive. If something feels threatening, we will look in that direction, we will pay more attention and we will remember it for the future.

Many things happen when parenting that feel threatening: children's behaviour, fights between children, difficult moments at school or out of the house. When we feel highly stressed, our brain is more likely to interpret events as threatening – and the more threatening experiences we have, the more stressed we feel.

This is all useful when it comes to keeping us alive – and rather less useful when it comes to living a contented life. It means that all the difficult things that happen loom much larger than the good moments.

One thing we can do about this is deliberately refocus our attention on the good moments, even if they are just tiny glimmers. For this, first we have to notice that the good moments are happening, then we have to allow ourselves to pay attention to them.

For this, I'd recommend starting some sort of record. This could be a journal, but doesn't need to be. You could just use the notes app on your phone or a piece of scrap paper or a recording app if you prefer to speak rather than write.

Whenever something good happens, jot it down. Don't ask yourself whether it's really good enough to bother recording, just jot it down. Give yourself enough detail to remember later. These can be really tiny things; no one is going to judge you on them.

Here are some examples of the things parents notice:

- Child doing something independently they hadn't done before.
- Child tolerating something they had found hard before.
- Child enjoying something.
- Managing to get through something challenging (even if there is a meltdown afterwards).
- Child trying something new.
- You enjoy a moment with the children.
- Child says or makes something.
- A developmental leap – maybe they can use a fork, or hold a pencil, or say a word they couldn't say before.

Here's Claire's list:

- *Denny was really sweet to Karina when she didn't want to go into school.*
- *Nathan said 'I love you mummy' when he woke me up this morning.*
- *Hannah drew a picture of all of us swimming and smiling.*
- *Denny and Hannah played Minecraft together for ten minutes before arguing.*
- *Denny lost at Snap and didn't storm off or hit me.*
- *Hannah tried a carrot (didn't like it, but she tried it).*
- *I managed to not shout when Hannah hit Nathan.*
- *We got to school before the bell!*

- *I got all the children in the car after school before Denny had a meltdown.*

Once you have your positive list, keep adding to it. And read it back to yourself when things have been tough. Remind yourself that there are moments of hope, and choose to focus on those sometimes.

The next exercise is thinking about change and what changes you might need to make in order to make your life sustainable.

Emotional batteries

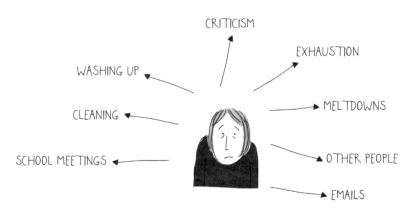

It is an unfortunate and ironic truth that low demand parenting demands a lot from parents. There are many things low demand parents do for longer than other parents, and many ways in which they are more involved, even when that is invisible. You are providing a constant flow of emotional regulation for your children, even when they are at their worst. You are doing what is probably the hardest job you have ever done, 24/7, with no holidays. In fact, usually holidays are the hardest part. It is also the case that there are generally fewer immediate 'pay-offs' with low demand parenting. Other people are unlikely to praise you for your child's exceptional behaviour or comment on how smartly turned out they are.

One way to think about this is through the metaphor of batteries. We all have emotional batteries we draw on when times are hard – but we also need to keep on recharging those batteries in order to keep going. If we don't, they run dry and we risk burn out. This is particularly the case if our emotional batteries are being drained by criticism, either self-criticism or the criticism of others (either implicit or explicit).

The first thing to do here is to identify what drains and recharges your emotional batteries. Be honest. Something that drains a lot of parents' batteries is the expectation that they should enjoy time with their children. They hear people say things like 'spending the weekend relaxing with the kids' and feel terrible because it's never relaxing to be with their kids.

EXTERNAL CRITICISM
SELF CRITICISM

Drains emotional batteries	Recharges emotional batteries
What are the things you do that leave you feeling exhausted?	What do you do that helps you feel better?
What are the things you say to yourself that leave you feeling drained?	What do you say to yourself that helps you feel good?
Are there other people who leave you feeling drained after you spend time with them?	Are there people you spend time with who help you feel good?
Are there things you feel obliged to do that leave you feeling drained?	What sort of day leaves you feeling energised?

Here's an example from Claire:

Drains emotional batteries	Recharges emotional batteries
Poor sleep.	Time alone.
Lack of good food.	Time to chat to a friend about something other than children.
Never being able to choose what we do.	Watching a film or TV programme.
Arguments between children.	Time to chat to my husband.
Self-critical thoughts: 'Everyone else is doing this better than me.' 'My children would be better off with another mummy.' 'This would not be so hard if I were a better parent.' 'I am not contributing enough to this family.' 'At the very least I should be cooking fresh meals for us all and not feeding the children fish fingers again.'	Times when I feel proud of the children – yesterday Denny was so lovely with his friend before school when she didn't want to go in.
Scrolling on Facebook and comparing myself with all the successful parents.	Listening to podcasts or audio-books that aren't about parenting.
Not being able to finish a thought without being interrupted.	Exercise classes.
Talking to family members who criticise my parenting.	Uninterrupted sleep.
Talking to other parents who can't stop telling me how well their kids are doing.	Talking to other parents who get it.

The next stage is to see if there is any way you can reduce how much time you spend in the 'Draining' column, and increase the amount of time you spend in the 'Recharging' column. Be realistic and look for tiny changes you might be able to make. Lots of tiny changes can add up to something bigger, even if on their own they feel insignificant.

Making changes

Making changes is hard. Changes fall into two main categories: small changes that can be made right now to the current situation, and bigger changes that need more time and negotiation with others.

Small changes could be things like ordering food online rather than going to the supermarket, or joining an exercise class. They could involve being selective about who you spend time with, and being more intentional about how you spend your few minutes off.

When it comes to making small changes, there are various tricks you can use to make it more likely that the changes will stick (you could think about these as addressing barriers for yourself, just as you thought about addressing barriers for your children).

Make it small, make it easy

One trick is to start small, and to make it as easy as possible for yourself to make the change. If, for example, you want to start attending an exercise class after dropping your children at school, put your sports clothes on first thing and go straight to the class from the school, to reduce the number of transitions for yourself. If you want to listen to more interesting podcasts or audiobooks, find them and download them onto your phone so they are there already. If you want to reduce the amount of time you spend on social media, then make it hard for yourself to check it – log out of your accounts or delete the app from your phone.

In Claire's case, she realised that because she felt guilty about not financially contributing to the family, she wasn't taking any time off at all. She was using the few short hours she had alone to go to the supermarket and clean the house so she felt less guilty about not earning money. She would finish just in time to pick up the children but that meant that her day was completely relentless, from before 6 a.m. to after 10 p.m.

She decided to make a few changes. She started ordering food online and stopped going to the supermarket. She set it up as a regular weekly order so that she didn't even have to think about it. She ordered some healthy ready-meals she could eat when the children were eating. She removed the Facebook app from her phone and stopped other notifications.

And she decided that those few hours every morning were for her, not for the housework. She joined a gym and started going to a kickboxing class. There, she met new people who had nothing to do with the children. She got a subscription to an audiobook service and found a new audiobook to listen to in the car when she was driving back from dropping off the children.

Bigger changes might be important as well, but don't let the big changes you want to make stop you from making small changes right now. Big changes can take years to implement. If you put the rest of your life on pause while pinning all your hopes on a big, transformative change, things will be more difficult and frustrating than they need to be for years.

Bigger changes could include realising that you really want to move house to somewhere where the children could walk to school, for example, or wanting to return to studying or to work. They might include redressing the balance of childcare in your house so that there is a more equal split, or they might involve leaving a job that isn't working for you. These changes will have consequences and will need to be thought through. You could try breaking those bigger changes down into smaller steps – for example, if you want to move house, you could start researching likely areas.

The next, and final, exercise is about making sense of your past. This is the most intense exercise in the chapter and has the potential to be upsetting. I would not do it when you are exhausted and feeling like you're at the end of your tether. Do the other exercises first and try to get yourself on a more even keel before trying this one.

This exercise is about thinking about things from the past that might be making your present life more difficult than it needs to be.

Telling your story

Most parents I meet have had multiple difficult experiences as parents and have also supported their children through difficult experiences. These often start with pregnancy and birth, which frequently do not go to plan.

For some mothers (in particular) this can be a moment when it feels like their life starts to fall apart. They had believed up to that point that they could take control of things, and that if they worked hard, it would pay off. Then they came to give birth, and despite all their hard work beforehand and the carefully written birth plan, none of it went as they imagined. Many mothers are left with a feeling of having failed that they take forward into motherhood. There's never any time to think about it, because once the baby has arrived, their needs are all-consuming. Everyone says how lucky they are to have a 'healthy baby' and it's time to move on. The same can happen for fathers.

Then as the child grows up, their needs are often so intense that there is no time to think. Many parents continue to feel like failures because their children are not meeting the expectations of society, and they feel to blame for this.

One way to help yourself move beyond this is to tell your story. By doing so, you can take control of the narrative, but you can also retell it with different slants. There is never only one story. There is never only one way to think about the events of your life.

There are many ways to do this. The most straightforward way is just to start writing things down, as and when they occur to you. There's no need to start at the beginning. If you notice yourself think-ing about something that happened a lot, write a story. There's just one rule to these stories: give them a beginning, a middle and an end. And the end has to be hopeful. Even just a tiny bit (it doesn't have to be true yet). Don't write stories that end with everything being terrible.

If you don't like writing, you could try recording your story, or drawing it – Eliza started drawing cartoons to help her process what was happening in her life. Later she turned this practice into several illustrated books, one (*Can't Not Won't*) about her daughter's difficulties with school, and another (*Thumbsucker*) about her own childhood. She drew her story and, in doing so, took control of a narrative in which she had often felt powerless. You could write music about your story. It doesn't have to be any good and no one else ever has to hear it if you don't want them to.

The only thing that is important is to get it out. Don't just keep it in your head. When we tell our story in our head, it can sometimes get stuck. We go round and round. Getting it down on paper or on record helps us to reflect on it, and to decide whether we want to tell it differently.

If you find this really difficult or upsetting, find someone who will do it with you. This could be a friend, family member or a counsellor. The important thing is that they are able to sit with you, listen and be supportive. You could even tell your story to someone and ask them to write it down for you.

What About Me?

When you've written your story once, go back and write it again from a different perspective. Tell it in different styles. Focus on different elements. If your story seems too long and complicated, just focus on part of it and then write something like 'many other things happened' and write yourself an end that you'd like. You can make your story a fantasy if you like – it doesn't have to stick to reality. You could make the characters dragons or animals. It's often easier to write a story if you do it in the third person rather than using 'I', which can feel too close. Writing as if it was about someone else creates distance. Writing it as a fantasy is another way to do this.

Here's a story that Claire wrote about her experience with the other local parents. She called herself Corinne in the story and Denny, Dan.

Corinne was happy in her local area. She thought she'd made friends for life. They'd hang out together in the park and chat and drink coffee. She'd tell other people how lucky she was to have found such a great community. Their babies would play alongside each other and they'd joke about how they'd use the photos at their weddings and they'd all be there, proudly watching their kids walk down the aisle.

Then her little boy started to grow up. His behaviour was different to the other children's. Corinne didn't notice at first because she thought that all toddlers were like that, but then she started to see that he was pushing and hitting other children. The other children weren't doing that. Corinne kept a close eye and would intervene. She soon realised that if she told Dan off, he'd be furious and his behaviour would get much worse, so she stopped telling him off. Instead, she'd get between him and the other child and try to distract him.

Soon, the gatherings in the park didn't feel relaxing or happy. Corinne was on edge the whole time. One time Dan pushed another child over; luckily, they weren't hurt. Corinne was pregnant now and really tired.

Then one day Dan bit a younger child – really, the child wasn't much more than a baby. The baby took his spade at the sandpit. It was terrible. Dan sank his teeth right into his arm. You could see the toothmarks and the younger child screamed. Corinne felt dreadful. She apologised and apologised but the other mother wouldn't look at her. She took Dan and left the playground crying.

It was never the same after that. Corinne felt like an outsider. She felt ashamed of Dan's behaviour and like she had been branded a BAD MOTHER. She wasn't invited to the park when the others went and she started to avoid the times that she knew they'd be there. She would see their photos on Facebook and feel like they'd put them up just to show her how happy they were without her. Corinne felt like she'd failed at parenting already and everyone knew.

For a long time, Corinne felt isolated and lonely. She felt that no one wanted to know her or her children.

Then, her children started to grow up a bit. Dan was able to talk more about how he felt. Corinne realised that Dan was very sensitive to other people, and that he had found those groups stressful. Hitting and biting had been the only way he could express that at the time. She realised that she wasn't to blame for this, and it didn't mean that she was a bad mother.

What About Me?

Corinne started to look for new friends with whom she shared interests other than children. She decided that she would never let what had happened to her happen to another mother, and when they were out she started to look out for mothers whose children were similar to Dan. She'd go and make friends with them deliberately. She imagined herself as a mama bear, protecting her children and feeling proud of them. She started to find hope in the future.

Claire wept as she wrote this story. It was still painful for her to think about what had happened and how rejected she had felt. But it also felt cathartic, because she realised that she did now have more information about Denny and what he found challenging, and when he was young she was just working all of that out for the first time. She forgave herself for not knowing how to help him best.

She wrote another version later, and this time it was less painful. She was better able to see the hope and the change in the story. She wrote it two more times before she felt that actually this story could be laid to rest now. It made sense to her and she felt like it was finished. She used the image of herself as a bear at times when she felt the old feelings of shame and failure creeping back.

Writing your story is hard, and I would encourage you to rewrite it several times and allow yourself space to reflect in between.

Eliza and Naomi:
Time for a cup of tea

NAOMI: What about you, Eliza? What about parents? Where are we in all of this?

ELIZA: I think it's very difficult because we do know that words like self-care get bandied around and people feel disillusioned about it. It's like being given a scented candle, as if that's self-care.

I think that what is important is finding and keeping relationships with other people who really do get you. They don't even have to be people who understand what you are doing right now.

It could be that you're just hanging out with a friend and you don't even talk about this stuff. Something that makes you feel good is having time for yourself and reconnecting to yourself because there can be a massive loss of that sense of self within this.

NAOMI: Yes, because it's such hard work.

ELIZA: It's such hard work, but it's you yourself who will bring the things that your child needs. That's the bit you don't want to lose. The energy, the fun, the humour, the enthusiasm, those are the things that your child needs. That means that keeping the energy around yourself up and thinking about what will do that and what will maintain your own wellbeing is really important.

NAOMI: It's absolutely critical, isn't it? Basically, low demand parenting can't really work if you're not looking after yourself because you will burn out. But it's really hard to find time to do that. Parents often put their own needs last because it feels like everything else is so important that they can't make that space for them.

ELIZA: I think that probably one of the more difficult things to talk about is that it's still important that the child sees that we have our own sense of being ourselves when we're not being their parent. It's important that they see that we do have more going on in our lives.

Sometimes I talk to parents and they say, 'I've not been able to leave the house in three years.' Those things are really important to do. If your child is with their other parent or with someone that they love and feel safe with, it is important that you have that time away, even if your child would prefer you to be there always.

NAOMI: They need to be able to see you as a separate person. You are modelling being an adult. You are showing them that there's a hopeful future. If their needs mean that no one else in the family does anything, everybody's experience can get really narrow. Even if the child is not ready for anything more, you have to make sure that there are other things there when they're ready for it.

ELIZA: When I was at home full time, I still needed to be doing something. I didn't have much time at all to myself. That time was very early in the morning, so I'd get up when it was deathly quiet and it was just me. I would draw then and that was a way to expel quite a lot of anger. A lot of the things we experienced were nonsense, and it was really nice to actually be able to say, 'This is utter nonsense' in a drawing.

NAOMI: There's catharsis in being able to express your own story and either laugh or cry.

Too much to read, too little time?

1. It's really hard being a (low demand) parent.
2. The work can feel relentless and you can feel like you are at the bottom of the heap.
3. Prioritising yourself sometimes is essential if your life is to be sustainable.
4. In order to be compassionate and accepting with your child, you need to start with compassion and acceptance towards yourself. This chapter suggests several different exercises to help you do that.

More to read if you are interested

Can't Not Won't: A Story About a Child Who Couldn't Go to School – Eliza Fricker

Raising Good Humans: A Mindful Guide to Breaking the Cycle of Reactive Parenting and Raising Kind, Confident Kids – Hunter Clarke-Fields

Superhero Therapy: A Hero's Journey Through Acceptance and Commitment Therapy – Janina Scarlet

Thumbsucker: An Illustrated Journey Through an Undiagnosed Autistic Childhood – Eliza Fricker

What Mothers Do (Especially When It Looks Like Nothing) – Naomi Stadlen

Writing to Heal: A Guided Journal for Recovering from Trauma and Emotional Upheaval – James Pennebaker

12

Low Demand Parenting in Action

It's all very well reading this book, and us telling you that it can work. But it's very hard to visualise what might actually change and how your life might be if you choose to embrace low demand parenting. You are probably surrounded by people saying that you've got to 'get a handle' on your child's behaviour and be firmer and stricter. It might be particularly challenging to visualise how your child might change as they grow up if you don't know any other families who have taken this route. Right now you might be in a very difficult place with your child, and you might be finding it hard to imagine that things will ever be different.

For that reason, we've gathered some real-life stories. We asked these parents to be honest about the highs and the lows, the things they regret and the things that they have struggled with. Some of them have come quite recently to low demand parenting, while others have older teenagers and have been doing it for years. They all told me about the process and the change that they've seen. I asked them about the challenges as well as the best parts. They are all real people but identifying details have been changed in order to protect the anonymity of the young people.

The dire warnings didn't come true

For Amy, finding low demand parenting was a big change from how she had expected to parent. It required her to really see her son and to stop seeing him through the lens of wilful misbehaviour.

I didn't start off as a low demand parent, in fact, quite the opposite. My own mum was a 'tough love' parent and I didn't question the need to parent any differently. I wanted to be no nonsense: do as I say, if I say, 'Jump,' the kids would say, 'How high?'

And then my eldest was born. From the outset they had their own unique challenges, but I was determined to hold the line and do what 'good parents' do, i.e. take charge, get and maintain control.

But the more I tried the worse it got. TV parenting gurus and family friends' advice was ringing in my ears: 'Just keep returning them to the Naughty Step', 'Don't indulge the behaviour', 'Don't give an inch, they'll take a mile', 'Don't give them control', 'If you don't get on top of this now, you never will'.

It became a pitched battle between them and me, and I felt like I was losing. But not only was I losing the 'battle', I felt like I was losing my child. I felt like I was walking on eggshells around them. Getting the simplest thing done like getting dressed for school, eating, getting shoes on, leaving the house, following any kind of instruction or complying with much of what was expected, was difficult. Resistance ranged from misdirection, distraction and procrastination at one end to extremely challenging and violent at the other.

It was not unusual for the house to be trashed, objects thrown and chairs overturned off the back of expected compliance. I was being regularly hit, thumped, kicked, bitten and head-butted. School was just as difficult as home.

Over time, my experience, research and observations resulted in me realising that my child wasn't wilfully misbehaving and wasn't out of control because I wasn't strict enough. It was that they simply couldn't manage with what was expected of them. They were actually doing the best they could within the environment and expectations in which they found themselves.

Changing the way I looked at, and interpreted, their behaviour was a game changer. I started asking myself 'What does my child need?' rather than 'What do I want my child to do?' I started experimenting with doing things differently and gradually, slowly, almost imperceptibly at times, things were starting to change; life was getting less volatile.

By the time they were about seven years old I was starting to get a clearer view of what my child needed. They had a string of diagnoses and frustratingly an EHCP (education, health and care plan) that was useless. School was increasingly problematic and it was becoming more apparent to me that it was entirely unsustainable and completely at odds with what I knew they actually needed. It became crunch time; we really couldn't carry on as we were; there was a better way. I took the decision to make two huge changes. Firstly, I took the decision to home educate and remove the increasingly obvious unmanageable demands from school out of our lives. Secondly, I decided that I needed to totally change my parenting and fully embrace a low demand way of parenting. I needed to banish the doom mongers and rewrite the rule book from the first page; it was time to move out of the conventional parenting box.

I instinctively knew that this was going to be a gradual evolution of easing demands into low demand parenting. I knew that this was primarily a process of me changing and that this was going to be gradual. I also sensed that jumping to an extreme of throwing my hands up into a totally permissive 'do whatever you want' was also not going to serve any of us. As I now had a full view of our lives and with no external demands that I had no control over, I could start to see where the most serious triggers and issues were and start with those areas. It was a case of deeply questioning what was really important, what was really needed, asking whether there was a different way and being more creative with solutions.

For example, getting dressed was a huge flashpoint, so I questioned whether it was really necessary to get dressed first thing and every single day. On days where we weren't leaving the house, pyjamas were the clothes of choice. This led to a lot of PJ days for a long while. However, when we were leaving the house, getting out of PJs was the aim. On these days finding the least demanding way to enable it to happen was key. Rather than insisting they stop what they were doing and head upstairs to get dressed, I would bring the clothes to wherever they were and get them dressed while they were distracted. We found clothes that were comfortable even if that meant wearing a football kit to everywhere on every occasion.

I took the same tack with teeth cleaning, eating, hair brushing, hair cutting, nail cutting, showering, constantly asking questions such as: Do they have to sit at the table to eat? Is it more important that they sit at the table or more important that they eat? Do they have to shower every day? Do they have to have short, neat hair? Do we have to brush hair every day? If we are showering, brushing, cutting and so on, how can we make it as low demand and easy as possible? Sometimes we would come across a problem and we would need to find a solution, for example if they didn't want to get their hair cut and also didn't want to have their hair brushed. Despite trying different brushes and infrequent brushing it got to a point where we needed a solution. It took several weeks to get to a solution, but in the end they chose to go to a barber, chose which barber, the barber was primed, the Nintendo Switch was used and I stayed right by them.

Today my eldest is mid-teens. They voluntarily get dressed every day, not always first thing, but every day. They voluntarily clean their teeth twice a day, in the bathroom. They voluntarily shower every day. They voluntarily brush their hair every day. They voluntarily make their bed every day. The list goes on. None of this happened overnight; in fact, it all took a very long time, often involving small changes constantly moving towards a goal when the time was right and always in a low demand and collaborative way. Occasionally they have undertaken a big shift when some intrinsic motivation has propelled them. Patience has been of prime importance. It has been about flexibility, partnership, discussion, problem-solving, patience, connection, respect and trust. Low demand parenting is not a trick or hack you can use to gain compliance. It has to be a genuine shift in your relationship. And this takes trust, courage, faith and patience on our behalf.

Even today there is much still ongoing. To this day they do not eat at the main dinner table for the family meal, though recently sometimes I have noted that they do voluntarily join. Over years we have worked on exposure and experiences in cafés and restaurants and other places in general society and today they do act entirely appropriately when in them (though we always take entertainment to help with any waiting). We are constantly gently responding to them, being sensitive to when boundaries can be flexed, creating exposure to new circumstances while being supportive and low demand.

Today it feels like a different lifetime when I think of those early years. The dire warnings of 'If you don't make them do it as children, they will never learn and will be wild and chaotic when older' simply haven't borne out. We continue to tackle life's events, expectations and challenges in the same supportive, flexible, low demand way.

Her wants are coming back

Nicola told me about her family's journey into low demand parenting. It has been one of change in response to her daughter's needs. She told me how she has had to embrace things that make her slightly uncomfortable in order to support her daughter's interests.

My fourteen-year-old daughter Ella is super good at detecting pressure. She can detect any agenda, any inauthenticity, any level of hypocrisy. She is on it. She's got you.

I can't get away with any level of inauthenticity or not giving her the full honest picture about things. I have to weigh up all the time whether I am right to give her this information and allow her this space. She knows when something's being kept from her. I am as open and honest with my kids as I can possibly be without giving them information that's going to terrify them.

In our house pretty much everything is up for negotiation. At first I tried to insist on a few things. We would shower every few days, we would brush our hair. I quickly realised that the more I did that, the less likely she was to get in the shower or brush her hair or go out of the house.

Ella makes choices that I'm not a hundred percent comfortable with. For instance, she's really into watching horror movies. She's really attracted to anything dark and scary and grisly. Things that she knows would worry me.

She said, 'I really like watching this kind of stuff.' I said, 'Well, what's your criteria for choosing what you watch? What do you like about it?'

It turned out she was researching every film before she watched it. She was reading all the criteria. I said, 'Look, no gendered violence and I would prefer that you didn't watch 18s' (knowing that she probably would). I was trying to find reasonable ways to satisfy her interest without going too far.

She was open to this conversation as long as I talked to her like she's an equal. I listen to what she's got to say, and I respect that she has done the research. She has her own boundaries that she's established around it.

I said, 'Well, if you're encountering anything that you need to talk about, you come and talk to me. We are always a safe place. I'm not going to be angry with you ever.'

Their dad was resistant to the idea of low demand parenting at first. I had to say to him, 'Are you going to read the stuff? Do you have the capacity to do that?' And he was like, 'No. I just can't.' And I said, 'Well, then you're going to have to trust me.'

I have always had a sense of the bigger picture. I'm bringing up future adults. Children become adults and I want them to have a sense of autonomy and be fully actualising adults.

At a certain point I decided that actually if I can say yes, I will say yes and see how it works. It always seemed to me that adults say no for no reason a lot.

I held on to other behavioural stuff for longer because families have got to function somehow. Sleep and things like that. But in the end. I've had to just trust the process.

One of our children is out of school and one is in school. We are low demand parents for both. You can't have one being low demand and the other one not; it wouldn't be fair. Amelia likes a bit more structure. She's also extremely clear sighted, but she's happier to be part of the crowd and she likes rules. We've had the conversation about school. We've been through the pros and cons and I said to her, 'Well, I can't very well insist that you stay at school or go into school.' If she needs a duvet day, she has a duvet day.

The difficulty is giving her enough attention. One way we did that was that Amelia and I went to Corfu for a week in the summer. We went on holiday together because Ella and

Dave can't deal with the heat. We lay by the pool and spent some time together, which was really nice. That kind of thing seems to help.

When Ella first came out of school she didn't want anything. She had lost all her wants. She was so flat, uninspired by life in general and unable to articulate anything that excited her or motivated her. She had no reason to get out of bed. She was craving nothing. I've been waiting for those wants to come back because that seems to me a really important part of being human.

Now there are things she wants to do and things she wants to have and work for. They don't look how I would like them to look.

She started to say things like, 'I want vampire clothes. Can you go to the charity shops and find me vampire clothes?'

I said, 'What do vampire clothes look like? What am I looking for?' And then I headed out to the charity shops. I thought, I can't just wait for her to want to come to the charity shop with me (even though I would love that).

I look for the wants and I try to pick up on those. It looks to others like I'm legitimately crazy. It looks like I'm really enabling her to stay indoors. I do it because this way she has things coming into the house and new things to be excited about.

It might sound like I'm relaxed about taking this route and have it all sorted. In reality, it feels very scary and I doubt myself a lot of the time. I often feel like I'm winging it.

One thing that helps is that I can see things changing over time. Last night, she started to say that she's clever again. She said, 'Oh, I'm really smart. I'm really clever.' And I was like, 'Yes you are.' She had stopped saying positive things about herself.

She said, 'I love studying and I love learning things.' Then she started talking about the physics of gunshot wounds, how bullets ricochet in the body, and what we've learned about the best and worst places to get shot. We had a laugh about it. I reacted in shock horror, saying, 'This is not going to go down well with the local authority, how the hell am I going to write this up as a report?'

Those are the best bits. Sharing a laugh about what's going on. Listening to her be passionate about anything, even if it's something that I find abhorrent and difficult. When she is interested and excited about something, whatever it is, that's my happy moment.

She's doing art at home again

Charlotte and her family had found low demand parenting after their daughter became increasingly pressure sensitive when she started secondary school. She told me about how she had had to change her approach when it became clear that even gentle pressure wasn't helping.

Matilda went into the secondary school on top of things. Academically thriving. Nobody at school saw anything. They were all very delighted with her. She's not a troublemaker.

She's quiet. She smiles. She does the work. And that's all they saw.

At home, I saw so much distress. From that first September, I was emailing to say she's in tears about the homework. Some of the things were misunderstandings. She thought she had to do twenty minutes of mathematics a day and actually it was only once a week.

In that first year at secondary school, everything was going wrong. Swimming was distressing her like anything. Sometimes I didn't even send her in to school or I dropped her in late to miss swimming and school didn't like this.

She's been learning the piano since she was about six. I read a book about practice, and how much it matters. Now I think what a shame it is that I read that book. When she was little I taught her songs, and we'd sing them in rounds together, and I thought, she's musical. After reading that book, I thought, we need to practise more.

I pushed the piano and I ruined it. I made her practise.

I'd make sure we did practise each week. Just before we went riding I'd say things like 'Before we go, why don't we do ten minutes of piano?'

There would be tears and I didn't really understand the tears. I was annoyed. I never did it for very long but I made her practise and it was against resistance. She didn't want to, but she's compliant. She internalises. It's easy not to really realise the degree of distress that something is causing her.

Then at the spring concert, her piano teacher wanted her to play a piece and play in a group of them doing different instruments.

She got them together sometimes to do pieces. In that group the teacher was saying, 'Oh, it'd be so nice if you'd play this in the concert.'

Then the teacher unfortunately said, 'I'll give you a whole bag of cookies each if you do it.' Her friend was like, 'Go on!' She agreed to do it. At half term, I got her friend around for a play and I said to the mum, 'Why don't you bring his flute and they can have fun practising together?'

I got real resistance. 'I don't want to.' I was saying 'Go on, just this once, go on.' She did it. It was so easy. I think she had to play two notes in time with him.

But it definitely wasn't something she was enjoying. She was very poker faced and unhappy about it. I said, 'Just do it once.' Then I said, 'Oh, do you want to have a go on the other piece as well?' She just burst into tears. I said, 'Okay, let's stop there.'

It was a tiny request to play something that was very easy that would have taken one minute. Matilda is this kid who doesn't cry, really; neither of my kids cry. When they cry, you really know something's up.

We had a meeting with the piano teacher and we agreed to back off all pressure and just make it fun. We agreed that she wouldn't do the concert. Even then, if we were waiting to go to school in the mornings I'd say, 'Oh, should we just do two minutes of piano?'

I think it was just after Easter that we decided to stop piano. It wasn't working. Even two minutes brought her to tears. Music is something I have had to completely let go.

I started reading and learning about demand avoidance and low demand parenting, and I realised that demands have always upset her. I realised that the more demands, the more stressed she is.

There was increasing distress over the whole of that first year of secondary school. We were getting increasingly worried about her. I started to think that she would harm herself.

I started saying to her, 'Matilda, if you want to come out of school and home ed, you can.' Luckily, another friend of hers, who is autistic ADHD, was struggling and they decided to home school, which normalised it. She came out of school a couple of weeks into the second year.

We spoke to Eliza and she said not to put pressure on her or us right now. I came away thinking if I see something I really want her to do then I'm not going to put the pressure on because I'll ruin it, but I think maybe I'd already signed up for King's InterHigh (an online school) with Matilda's agreement.

The first week she did an online English lesson and burst into tears. So I said, 'Okay, let's stop English.'

It became clear that the online mathematics lessons didn't work either. Instead we found an amazing teacher and she has lessons twice a week. Even then, we have to be careful. The teacher messaged me to say she is doing amazingly. She said, 'Should we harness this and do more?'

We tried it. We tried having three lessons a week. Matilda burst into tears and she said, 'It feels like school again.' So I cancelled it. We went back to two lessons a week.

I put as few demands on her as possible. Gradually we're seeing all these things coming back that she enjoyed before. I ordered a book another mum said her daughter really liked. I just put it in her room. Normally she just reads magazines in bed and hasn't read a book at home for three or four years.

But then one night she was really excited to be getting into bed and she grabbed the book, all happy. And I said, 'Oh, you're liking the book?'

She said, 'Yeah, it's really good.'

I do a lot of legwork to find opportunities for her and I don't tell her about that. When I find something I think she would like, I encourage her to go, but I will let her say no. If she doesn't want to stay, I let her go home. So I encourage some demand, but I let her say that she doesn't like it.

Sometimes that's hard for me. I signed up for something and then I thought I'd feel bad for the organisers if we left because they'd think that we didn't like it. I emailed them in advance to explain and I said that if we leave after ten minutes it's not you but I have to just let her lead.

We are definitely seeing changes. She had stopped doing art at home. She did one picture in the last three years. And then she made me a birthday card in September, and in the Christmas holidays she made us Christmas cards.

She's starting to say 'I love you' all the time, which she wasn't before. As she leaves the room, before she leaves, she looks at me and comes up and gives me a hug and says, 'I love you.'

Our priorities completely changed

Beth told me about how she had to go extremely low demand when one of her sons developed a rare and serious neurological illness. Her sons are both now older teenagers, have finished school and are finding their way in life.

Growing up in the seventies, if I questioned why I had to do things I was often on the receiving end of comments like, 'Because I said so!' or 'Just do what you are told!' Life often felt quite unfair, and this resulted in me feeling frustrated, angry and upset at times.

When I had my own children, I made a very conscious decision that I was going to parent them differently to the way that I had been parented. I didn't want them to experience those feelings of unfairness, frustration and anger that I had so often experienced.

I allowed my children to have a very 'experimental' childhood with lots of autonomy. I wanted them to learn from natural consequences, both good and bad. If they didn't want to put their coat on to go to the park, then so be it. When they were cold and had to cut their park trip short then they would learn themselves that wearing a coat in the winter was probably a good idea!

I know that my parenting style was considered 'too soft' by others. My ex-mother-in-law actually sat me down once and told me, 'One of you needs to get a grip on those boys!' I stopped seeing 'friends' who were critical of my parenting, or worse still stepped in and tried to parent my children for me. There were not many things that would evoke more rage in me than someone else telling my kids off!

I had made a choice to use a low demand approach, but when my son was diagnosed with a rare, serious neurological illness just before his eleventh birthday, low demand parenting stopped being a choice and became a necessity. Our lives were turned upside down overnight.

As my son's illness progressed, his anxiety started to soar. The demands being placed on him became more unpleasant and uncomfortable for him but more important for him to comply with as his health literally depended on it.

Being faced with something so serious meant that my priorities completely changed. We had to focus on what mattered now, not what mattered in the future.

My son needed love, empathy and compassion. I knew he needed rest, but not bed times. If he was too unwell and tired to go to school, he stayed in bed. If he didn't want to get dressed, or shower, or come out of his room then he didn't have to.

When demands (like hospital appointments) were a necessity I offered him as much autonomy as possible around these. 'We can go for hot chocolate before or after your hospital appointment.' 'You can have your numbing cream on your left arm, your right arm or both before your blood tests?'

All that mattered was that he felt safe and loved.

I know some people worry that a low demand approach means that children won't be equipped for 'real life'. That they will grow up to be adults who 'don't want to do anything', or who will always want to get their own way, will take the easy route in life or who won't get any qualifications.

A low demand approach allowed both my children to take their own paths in life. They have both now finished school. They are hardworking, polite, caring and funny. I have an amazing relationship with both of them and I am incredibly proud of both of them.

My seventeen-year-old

Eleanor said that writing this had been quite emotional, as she remembered the hardest times with her son, who is now seventeen.

Last week, I went to watch my son perform in a play with a local drama group that he's been with for a year or so. He'd been a bit nervous about remembering his lines, and I'd been helping him run through them every day for the past month or so. And, now here I was, sitting in the audience, waiting for him to come onstage, a slight knot in my stomach, silently willing him to remember all his lines. Finally, he made his first appearance of the evening. He strode on to the stage (he was playing an army officer), tall and confident, delivered his lines perfectly, got a big laugh from everyone with some brilliant comic timing, then strode off again. Sitting there in the darkness, I felt in total awe. I was struck by how, some years ago, if you had told me that this would be in our future, I would have looked at you incredulously. Yet here we were.

A few other things about my seventeen-year-old. He loves sports, and in particular martial arts. In the evenings, he is rarely home as he has so many commitments with his clubs. Some of these are local and a couple require him taking the train and getting back quite late at night. He enjoys the camaraderie of these groups, which, aside from a couple of other teenagers, are made up mostly of supportive adults. If my son feels stressed, he often takes himself off to perform some martial arts movements, as they soothe his nervous system.

My son is also an extremely caring person. He seems to have a particular antenna for me, and can sense if I am ever out of sorts, in which case he'll give me a big old bear hug, or suggest we go for a walk together, as he knows that that is how I like to rebalance.

He loves to read, in particular about politics and history. He is a natural linguist, and generally has around five languages on the go at any one time. He is also taking a course at the local college where he's making new friends. I went to a parents' evening there a couple of weeks ago, and every teacher gushed about my polite, highly engaged and thoughtful son. If someone else wrote all this, I might assume that they had just lucked out. That they got one of those children who just seem to turn their hand to anything. Who sail through life without much effort. Well, I did luck out, but it hasn't been an easy road.

By the age of two, we could already see that my son's wiring seemed different from other children's. He was highly sensitive to his environment, and found being with other children quite stressful. I finally gave up on toddler groups as I would spend my time either dealing with meltdowns or apologising for his hitting. I was driven slightly mad by other mothers who would suggest things like smiling benignly at him while repeating 'Hands aren't for hitting.' No, no one really got it.

I spent a few years quite mystified by him. I felt like I was doing everything 'right', from co-sleeping to baby-wearing and extended breastfeeding. So, I couldn't understand why our lives were so much more difficult than my friends' with their children. He was volatile, easily dysregulated and frequently aggressive. Everything had to be meticulously planned in case there was a meltdown or a refusal of something. So many things would set off a strong reaction in him: too many people, too much light, too much noise, an odd tone of voice or facial expression. Our family got used to a much smaller life than we had hoped for and I often found myself pining for something else.

As he got older and stronger, the meltdowns and aggression got worse, until we were having several meltdowns a week. During these meltdowns, his siblings would hide away, terrified, while we tried to limit the damage. By the time he was about nine, any personal items that held any sentimental value for me had been smashed into pieces. The violence was mostly directed toward his father and myself. We both struggled to maintain calm and this massively exacerbated the situation, yet we didn't know how to change it all.

Within the following couple of years, I was punched many times, had my head kicked, and narrowly missed a broken nose. I found myself constantly on edge, and my son only had to tense his shoulders or frown, and my whole body would go into a stress response, as my mind raced to assess the danger. On top of this was the significant worry of what our other children were witnessing and the effect that this was having on them.

I had no idea where to find help. While our situation was quite desperate, I also felt significant shame around it, and I knew that any way forward that included punishment or discipline would be disastrous, so we soldiered on alone.

When my son was not dysregulated, he was bright and inquisitive. He has always been an avid learner in the things he enjoys, and he became fascinated by the Romans and history in general. Although he wanted to have friends, he found social interactions with other children extremely difficult. We had family friends with children that he got along with, so he wasn't entirely isolated, but he would freeze and go into overwhelm in any social situation where there were more than a handful of people.

By the age of twelve, he had begun to game, and for a couple of years this is where he immersed himself. I had never gamed and knew nothing about it. I had read all the knee-jerk articles about the devastating effects of gaming on our young people and had some significant fear around it. Fortunately, I was able to look beyond that and to learn about what it meant to him. I look back on it now and see that it was his safe space. He mostly played sophisticated strategy games that required huge concentration and dedication. He loved that he could become a superhero, that he could solve things and master new levels. It was a safe environment that he could control and within which he could excel and relax.

By this time I had also come across PDA, and although we didn't yet have a diagnosis, I started to read all I could and to put more low-demand strategies into place. During this period, the meltdowns were still happening, but now I was beginning to understand why, and to see why something that felt innocuous and unimportant to us was extremely important to him. I began to try to see life from his perspective, and to validate his experience. This wasn't easy and he would happily tell you how I messed up on many occasions.

Most importantly though, I stopped only seeing what was 'wrong'. I stopped worrying about his gaming and instead brought him cups of tea and got interested in it. I stopped worrying about him not having lots of friends and focused on the small circle of lovely people that we did have. I stopped assuming that he needed to be something different and started assuming instead that he was exactly who he needed to be. I put our relationship above absolutely everything else. Nothing mattered more than him feeling safe with me, and I knew that we had some profound healing to do after so many difficult years. I realised that every time I tensed up, it gave the message to him that he was bad and violent. I started to practise unconditional trust and used breathwork to undo the reactive patterns that had set into my body. We were extremely fortunate to be in a place where we had almost no one around us to criticise us, give us advice or pressure us into anything else. By this time, we had long since left the education system.

Slowly, and on his own terms, my son began to move out into the world. At first, he could only attend groups if he knew there were no more than six children in them. From there, he started to attend martial arts groups and all sorts of classes and workshops. On his own terms, he is a voracious learner and enjoys learning in small groups, and by going at his own pace he has been able to build up his skills and confidence in social settings. I have trodden that thin line between facilitating and encouraging, and unwittingly putting pressure on. If he feels that there is pressure that is not coming from him, he may well retreat. But this is something he understands well now. He knows that there are some things that are harder for him, but he has strategies to deal with them, and he will do all sorts of courageous things now that I wouldn't have dreamt of at his age. He still gets overwhelmed at times, but he asks for help and he knows that he has a lot of people on his side. He has a strong sense of his own values and is ambitious about his own life and what he can achieve.

I feel enormous relief that I stopped focusing on what was wrong and on all the difficulties and that, instead, I started to trust him. Seeing him stride onto the stage that evening, the thing that most struck me, besides what a wonderful person he is, was that this was not a possibility that I had ever thought existed. And, that this is a self-fulfilling prophecy. The more we trust them, the more space they have to grow into all their unique possibilities. Just because we don't see the possibility, it doesn't mean it isn't there.

Eliza and Naomi: The end

NAOMI: So we've come to the end. It seems a long way from the start. We've covered a lot, heard from lots of families and tried out lots of things.

One of the things I reflected on when writing this book was that really every parent has to face their Reality Gap. It's not just parents of pressure-sensitive children. If you're going to have a healthy adult relationship with your children, then you have to go through this process of really accepting at a gut level that your child is a completely separate person to you. You cannot control them. They're going to go off and live their own lives and make choices you might disagree with. You have to make your peace with that. This happens to everyone at different stages.

I feel like if it happens early, you get a head start. You very quickly realise that you're in a different world to the one you were expecting and you have to adapt to that. Your child makes it clear that a conventional approach isn't working.

Of course, some parents respond to that moment of realisation by becoming more controlling because they think that's what they should do. What we've talked about in this book is finding another way.

ELIZA: I hope what we are doing in this book is bringing the autonomy back to the parent again. I think what gets lost can be the confidence in our own knowing, because most of the parents I speak to will say, 'I do know instinctively' when I explain to them how low demand parenting works. They think that it's the wrong thing to do because they've been told that by other people.

NAOMI: They learn to doubt their instincts. When people are saying things like 'They should be sleeping by themselves', 'You should be putting them down', 'You should be making them eat vegetables and insisting that they say please and thank you', and you just can't, then many parents have this awful feeling that what they are doing is wrong. They think that they shouldn't be doing what they are doing because it's the wrong way to do it. Almost like they are cheating.

One of the things I've noticed from the comments that we get from our webinars is that quite often people say, 'I feel really reassured that what we are doing is okay; that we're not screwing them up forever.' I think many parents fear that what they're doing is so terrible that it's going to result in their child being unable to function in the long term.

ELIZA: Because there isn't anyone saying from the other side of it, it's going to be okay. I think that reassurance is not something that parents of pressure-sensitive children get for anything. There is so little reassurance that is given to parents who are doing things differently.

I think it can be a very different trajectory and so it's hard to see when you're in it. I spoke to a family this week, and the mother was saying, 'Oh, we haven't got that far with things.'

Then, when we spoke about it, it turns out that her son is going to a youth club every week. He even had a falling out with someone and had a couple of weeks off and then returned.

NAOMI: That's amazing.

ELIZA: He was having a sleepover. His friend was coming to stay.

NAOMI: It's so easy to not notice things like that but those are huge. It is exciting when changes like that happen, but also really easy to dismiss them, to say things like 'Well, they still aren't going to school without protesting.'

I talk to many parents who tell me about things that their children have started doing suddenly, having not been doing anything like it before. I talked to someone recently who was saying their child, who is now sixteen, had never spent a night without them, and now they want to go to America for a week with their college. That's going to be the first time they ever go anywhere. I hear a lot of stories like that. Stories of young people who decide that they want to do something, and then they do it, despite not having had much build-up. They decide they want to learn a language, or play the piano, or get a part-time job – and they do it. Without any pressure, because they want to. The desire is what drives them on.

I think that change can be really hard to imagine if you have no role models to base it on. If your kids are younger, it's hard to envisage what they're going to be like and what they're going to be capable of in the future.

ELIZA: It's really hard when you see your child on a screen all day, not getting dressed and not washing. You can't imagine that it will ever change.

You worry about the future. It's always the future.

NAOMI: You're thinking, And what if they're like this forever? What if they're fifty-three, and they're still on the sofa in their pants playing *Minecraft*? What if I'm failing them and what if it's all my fault?

That fear makes everything much, much harder.

ELIZA: It's not an easy approach to parenting, this. There's no road ahead of you. You are beating your own path and you have to learn to trust your instincts.

NAOMI: At one point we talked about calling this book *Not Doing Nothing*, didn't we?

ELIZA: Yes, because people often say that if you aren't controlling your kids, you're doing nothing.

NAOMI: That's always been an important thing for me. Generally, whenever you talk about parenting differently or educating differently, people always say, 'Oh, so you just leave them to it then?' We wanted to say, 'No, this is actually really active, really involved, really connected parenting, but not controlling.'

ELIZA: I just like the idea that you're creating a space, an environment for all of you that is more contented and happy. A more harmonious way to live. I hope that's what people have found in this book.

Appendix:
Blank worksheets and resources

Also available to download/print from https://overcoming.co.uk/715/ resources-to-download

BIVA code breaker

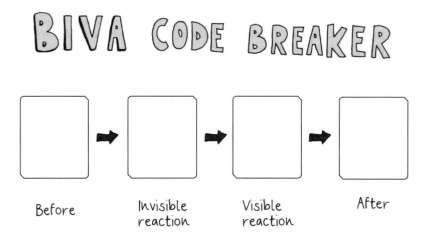

Before   Invisible reaction   Visible reaction   After

The Reality Gap worksheet

Expectations

What were your expectations about this area before you had children? Be honest!

Reality

What is the reality in your home right now?

The Reality Gap

What's the Reality Gap? What's the difference between how you would have imagined things and how they really are?

Have you set up your life for expectations or for reality?

We need to turn towards reality in order to start improving the situation.

PLEASE worksheet

Prioritise

What is the real priority here? State it in simple terms.

Long term

What will matter in the long term? In five or ten years, what will still be important?

Essentials

What is absolutely essential and cannot be let go?

Address barriers

Once you have decided what the real priorities are, how can you address any barriers to this happening? How can you make it easier for this to happen?

Step back

Remember that pressure will make things less likely to happen.

How can you step back and reduce the pressure around this area?

How will you implement low demand principles?

If there's a new idea, drip-feed it.

Encore!

Don't give up if it doesn't happen immediately.

Keep in mind what your priorities are and remember that change is hard and takes time.

JOIN UP worksheet

	What does it mean?	How could you do this?
Join in	Showing an interest in what the child does on their screen. Joining them in their games if they will let you. Asking about what they do. Learning about the games for yourself.	
Observe	Watch what they love to do and how they use their device.	
Improve the quality	Think in terms of making their device a high-quality learning environment. How could you improve the quality of what is available to them? This goes for both hardware and software.	

Notice what's working	Without judgement, notice over time what they really enjoy doing and what they get out of that. Children use screens for many different reasons – ask yourself what different needs are being met.	
Unblock communication	Use low demand communication around screens to establish a non-reactive, non-punitive way of talking about what happens on their screens. Talk about your own relationship with screens. Be around to listen to a lot of talk about their games.	
Protect them if you need to	Sometimes you need to step in and it won't always be popular. They may disagree with you about this but if you feel that they are not safe or if their mental health is suffering, you need to step in and be ready to weather the storm.	

Index

Index

Index

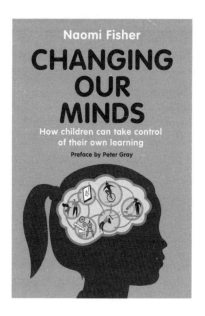

ISBN: 9781472145512

Available Now

Children are born full of curiosity, eager to participate in the world. They learn as they live, with enthusiasm and joy. Then we send them to school. We stop them from playing and actively exploring their interests, telling them it's more important to sit still and listen. The result is that for many children, their motivation to learn drops dramatically. The joy of the early years is replaced with apathy and anxiety.

This is an essential guide, informed by educational theory and personal experience, which presents accessibly the evidence and argument for self-directed learning, getting the child to lead where their curiosity and interests should be developed.